**HARROW COLLEGE
EFL CENTRE**

CAE

Gold PLUS

Coursebook

Nick Kenny

Jacky Newbrook

Richard Acklam

PEARSON

Longman

Contents

Writing reference p.199   See CDRom for extra practice and iTest.

Exam information

The Cambridge Certificate in Advanced English consists of five papers. Each paper tests a different area of ability in English and is worth 20% of the final result. A candidate's overall CAE grade is based on the total score gained in all five papers and it is not possible to pass or fail individual papers. A, B and C are pass grades. D and E are fail grades.

Paper 1 Reading

The Reading paper lasts 1 hour 15 minutes and contains four parts with a total of 34 questions. It contains texts of varying lengths taken from a variety of real-world sources with a range of text type and style of writing. For example, there may be extracts from newspapers, magazines, websites, novels and non-fiction books, as well as material taken from brochures, leaflets and other short texts. Candidates have to answer all the questions.

Part 1 Multiple choice

Part 1 consists of three short texts on a theme. The texts are taken from different sources and represent a range of style and genre. There are two four-option multiple-choice questions on each text which test a range of reading and language skills. ▶ **Exam focus** p.20

Part 2 Gapped text

Part 2 consists of one long text from which six paragraphs have been removed and placed in jumbled order after the text. Candidates use their knowledge of vocabulary, referencing and text structure to reconstruct the text. ▶ **Exam focus** p.94

Part 3 Multiple choice

Part 3 consists of one long text. There are seven four-option multiple-choice questions which follow the order of the text and test a range of reading and language skills. ▶ **Exam focus** p.132

Part 4 Multiple matching

Part 4 consists of one long text which is divided into several sections. The text is preceded by 15 prompts which report information and ideas from the text. Candidates must match each prompt to the correct section of text. ▶ **Exam focus** p.56

Paper 2 Writing

The Writing paper lasts 1 hour 30 minutes and is made up of two tasks. In Part 1 all candidates do the same task which is based on input information provided on the question paper. In Part 2, candidates have a choice of task.

Part 1

In Part 1, candidates read around 150 words of input information, which may come from various real-world texts, and use this information to complete a structured writing task of 180–220 words. Marks are awarded for both the inclusion of the target information, language ability and for writing in an appropriate style for the given task (e.g. letter, report, proposal or article).
▶ Unit 1 p.15, Unit 8 p.101 (proposal), Unit 10 p.125 (report)

Part 2

In Part 2, candidates select one situationally based task from a choice of five which may include: article, competition entry, essay, letter, proposal, report, review, information sheet or a contribution to a longer piece (e.g. book, research document, etc.). Marks are awarded for content, organisation, cohesion, range of language and task achievement. Candidates write 220–260 words.
▶ Unit 2 p.28 (informal letter), Unit 3 p.39 (information sheet), Unit 4 p.52 (article), Unit 5 p.64 (reference), Unit 6 p.78 (competition entry), Unit 7 p.90 (review), Unit 9 p.113 (competition entry), Unit 11 p.138 (article), Unit 12 p.151 (essay), Unit 13 p.163 (proposal)

NB Question 5 relates to the set text which some candidates may have studied.
▶ Unit 14 p.172

Paper 3 Use of English

This paper lasts for one hour and contains five parts with a total of 50 questions. Candidates answer all the questions.

The five different parts are as follows:

Part 1 Multiple-choice cloze

This task features a text from which 12 words or phrases have been removed, which is followed by 12 four-option multiple-choice questions. The focus is on knowledge of vocabulary and the relationships between words (e.g. collocation, complementation, etc.). ▶ **Exam focus** p.158

Part 2 Open cloze

This task features a text from which 15 words have been removed. Candidates use their knowledge of grammar, sentence structure and text structure to complete the gaps. ▶ **Exam focus** p.112

Part 3 Word formation

This task features a text from which ten words have been removed. The base form of each missing word is given as a prompt. Candidates must use their knowledge of grammar and word building to insert the correct form of the given word. ▶ **Exam focus** p.146

Part 4 Gapped sentences

This is a gapped-sentences task with five questions. Each question features a set of three independent sentences. The same word has been removed from each of the three sentences. Candidates use their knowledge of vocabulary to find the common missing word.
▶ **Exam focus** p.51

Part 5 Key word transformations

This is a key-word transformation task with eight questions. Each question features two sentences which express the same meaning in different ways, plus a key word. Three to six words have been removed from the second sentence. Candidates use their knowledge of grammar, vocabulary and sentence structure to complete the gap using the given key word. ▶ **Exam focus** p.76

Paper 4 Listening

The Listening paper lasts for approximately 40 minutes and contains four parts with a total of 30 questions. There are listening texts of varying lengths taken from a variety of real-world sources with a range of text type, contexts and speakers. For example, there may be extracts from media broadcasts, announcements, talks and interviews, as well as material taken from everyday situations. All the listening texts are heard twice and candidates have to answer all the questions.

Part 1 Multiple choice

Part 1 consists of three short independent listening texts. The texts are taken from different sources and feature a range of voices and styles of delivery. There are two three-option multiple-choice questions on each text which test a range of listening skills. ▶ **Exam focus** p.45

Part 2 Sentence completion

Part 2 consists of a monologue lasting approximately three minutes. A set of eight sentences reports the main points from the text. A word or short phrase has been removed from each sentence. Candidates listen and complete the missing information. The main focus is on locating and recording specific information from the text.
▶ **Exam focus** p.80

Part 3 Multiple choice

Part 3 consists of an interview or discussion lasting three or four minutes. There are six four-option multiple-choice questions which follow the order of the text and test a range of listening skills. The main focus is on understanding the attitudes and opinions of speakers.
▶ **Exam focus** p.120

Part 4 Multiple matching

Part 4 consists of five short monologues on a theme of around 30 seconds each. The set of extracts is heard once and is then repeated. Candidates have to complete two tasks as they listen. Each task features a set of eight short prompts. As candidates listen, they match each speaker to one of the eight prompts in each task. The focus is on understanding the gist of what the speakers are saying. ▶ **Exam focus** p.33

Paper 5 Speaking

The Speaking paper lasts for 15 minutes and is taken by candidates in pairs. The standard format involves an interview between two candidates and two examiners. One of the examiners is an interlocutor who speaks to the candidates; the other examiner only assesses the candidates and does not speak. The different parts are as follows:

Part 1 Conversation

The interlocutor asks the candidates questions about themselves, their lives and interests, in turn. The focus is on general interactional and social language. This part lasts approximately 3 minutes. ▶ **Exam focus** p.13

Part 2 Individual long turn

In this part each candidate has a long turn lasting approximately one minute. Each candidate has a different set of photographs to talk about. The second candidate will make a short response after his/her partner has spoken. This whole part lasts approximately three or four minutes and the focus is on language organisation. ▶ **Exam focus** p.170

Part 3 Two-way conversation

In this part the candidates talk to each other. They are given a sheet of visual prompts and a situation or issue to discuss for around four minutes. This part focuses on the language of interaction: exchanging ideas, expressing and justifying opinions, agreement, etc.
▶ **Exam focus** p.70

Part 4 Discussion

In this part there is a general discussion related to the topic of the Part 3 task. The interlocutor asks questions which broaden out the discussion from the specific task in Part 3. This part lasts around four minutes.
▶ **Exam focus** p.70

UNIT

1 Tuning in

Listening: multiple choice (Part 1)

1 Discuss these questions.

1 Should music just be something we listen to, or should we also make music? Why?

2 Which would you rather listen to: live music or recorded music? Why?

3 Do you like hearing background music in shops and restaurants? Why?/Why not?

2 You will hear three different extracts. Choose the answer (A, B or C) which fits best according to what you hear.

Extract One

On a local radio station, you hear some information about a musical event.

1 What type of event are they talking about?

  A a concert

  B an exhibition

  C a music festival

2 What type of people is Terry encouraging to attend this event?

  A people who are capable of contributing to the music

  B people who have a professional interest in the music

  C people who would like to learn how to play the music

Extract Two

You hear part of a radio discussion about music.

3 What is the man's attitude towards background music?

  A He finds it irritating.

  B He's grown accustomed to it.

  C He no longer listens to it properly.

4 Why does the woman sometimes like to play music when she's working?

  A It stops her feeling lonely.

  B It helps her to concentrate.

  C It's a source of inspiration.

Extract Three

You hear two friends discussing a concert they have just been to.

5 What do they agree about?

  A how closely the band managed to reproduce the sound on their CD

  B how dull the band's CD sounds compared to the live performance

  C how disappointing the special effects were at the concert

6 What did the girl enjoy most about the concert?

  A the reaction of the audience

  B the band's choice of material

  C the performance of one band member

3

1 Discuss with other students what kind of music:

- you find inspiring
- helps you concentrate
- annoys you
- is good to listen to when you're happy or sad.

2 Would you be happy to live without music? Why?/Why not?

3 Should musicians be paid more than people doing other types of work? Why?/Why not?

Grammar 1: overview

1   The email below contains ten different basic grammatical mistakes. Find the mistakes and correct them. Then check your answers with a partner. The first one has been done for you.

Hi Carlos

Just touching base to tell (0) ~~to~~ you about the film I went to see last night as you asked. My advice to you are – don't bother with it at all! It was complete rubbish, and a waste of time and money. I really wish I had not gone myself, and if I'd have read the reviews, I'd have given it a miss. I've been going to the cinema regularly since at least six years, and that was by far the worst film I had seen up to now – it's a such terrible film I can't understand how or why they decided to make it. Apart of everything else, I was so bored! So in case you might consider to go, you know my opinion now!

Anyway – enough of my complaints – and in spite of my disappointment with this particular film I haven't actually gone off films in general! So on a different topic – I know that you are interested for live music gigs, and I wondered whether might you like to come with me to the open-air concert in the park next Saturday? It'll be great, and all the others are going. Let me know it what you think – but unless I hear from you by Friday I'll assume you can't make it. I'm attaching some information about the concert with this email so that you can see who is playing, and we can get the tickets on the night.

So that's all for now – speak to you soon.

All the best,

Jose

2

1 Choose two mistakes that you found difficult to spot.
2 Identify the area of grammar in each case.
3 Look up those areas in a grammar reference book. Make notes on what you learn, and explain it to another student.

3 Discuss:

• the best ways of remembering areas of grammar that you make mistakes with
• the best ways of eliminating grammar mistakes from your writing and speaking.

Keeping a grammar checklist

Always keep your written work, and make a note of any areas of grammar that you made mistakes with more than once, like this:

Grammar Checklist	Example
present perfect + for/since	I've been going to the cinema for at least six years.
third conditional	If I'd read the reviews, I'd have given it a miss.

Add to this checklist as you do more written work and become aware of any other typical mistakes that you make, and refer to it before you start a new piece of writing. This may help you to avoid making the same mistake again.

Reading: multiple matching
(Part 4)

1   Discuss these questions.

1   Would you ever go to see a concert by a tribute band – where a group of musicians impersonates a famous group? Why?/Why not?
2   Why do you think tribute bands are popular?
3   Who do you think goes to see them?
4   How do you think they are regarded a) in the music business b) by the original band members?

2   Read the article quickly to see if you were right. In which section was each of your questions answered?

3   You are going to read an article about live music. For questions 1–15, choose from the sections of the article (A–E). The sections may be chosen more than once.

In which section is each of the following mentioned?

The preparation that one tribute band had to do	**1** ☐
A tribute band that now has imitators itself	**2** ☐
How one tribute band dealt with a potential shortage of material	**3** ☐
The good value for money offered by some tribute bands	**4** ☐
The origins of the idea of tribute bands	**5** ☐
The negative attitude of some people in the music business towards tribute bands	**6** ☐
The difficulties that unknown bands have in finding work at live venues	**7** ☐
The widespread popularity of concerts by tribute bands in Britain	**8** ☐
The reaction to a tribute band by a member of the original band	**9** ☐
The enthusiastic response of members of the audience	**10** ☐ **11** ☐
The similarity of the tribute band's music to the original	**12** ☐ **13** ☐
How concerts by tribute bands are unlike those by the original bands	**14** ☐ **15** ☐

SEND IN THE CLONES

A   It's a hot evening in a small town in the English Midlands. And as the live band plays the first bars of the song *I Bet You Look Good on the Dance Floor* at a local club, things are getting very warm indeed. Out on the dance floor, in the middle of a steaming crowd, a couple of dozen young men are hurling themselves around in time to the music, sending glasses and Coke bottles flying. As the song finishes, the club owner takes to the stage and appeals for calm. 'It's a great set by a great band, lads, but let's chill out a bit, eh?' It is, in short, what you might expect from a live performance featuring the music of one of Britain's most explosive rock outfits. Except the musicians on stage are not the Arctic Monkeys, the Internet phenomenon. They are a tribute band called the Antarctic Monkeys, four young men giving a musical impression of the real thing. 'We have a band of our own called Ryde,' says the Antarctic's Ian Fletcher. 'But we couldn't get gigs. And when we did, they always said: "Do you do covers?" We were sitting around thinking about how we could get out there and play, and someone said: "Why don't we do a Monkeys tribute?". We all love their music, so we did.'

B   After two weeks' close study of the Arctic Monkeys' debut album – *Whatever People Say I Am, That's What I'm Not* – Fletcher and his friends had perfected the sound to the point where only the most highly trained ears could spot the difference. 'Venues like us to play for an hour,' he says. 'But the original album only lasts 43 minutes, so we play a couple of songs twice.' And it goes down a storm. Arctic's fans, some so young they are accompanied by their parents, sing along to every word. 'That's the thing about tributes,' says club-owner Julian Harkins, whose stage echoes to soundalikes every night of the week. 'In the audience, there's no holding back waiting to see what happens. These are diehard fans. From the first bar to the last, they're really into it.'

C The spread of the pop faker is by no means restricted to the English Midlands. Check out the live music listings of any UK local paper and you'll find them stuffed with groups like Alike Cooper,
45 and Cheap Purple. All offer not just splendid names, but pitch-perfect facsimiles of the genuine article. Such is the growth of the musical copycat business, there's even an annual festival. Here you can watch an ersatz Freddie Mercury, Marc Bolan and Jimi Hendrix twang away for not much more than the cost of a couple of coffees.
50 Not a bad deal, given that you'll never have a chance to see the originals.

D In a documentary, *Send in the Clones*, to be broadcast later this month, the journalist Andrew Collins traces tribute bands to a failed Beatles musical in the late 1970s. Out of the ashes emerged
55 the Bootleg Beatles, who have now made a 25-year career out of impersonating the most famous band of the 1960s. 'It's like time travel. It's a snapshot of the band as they were at their peak. You can walk into a small unpretentious live music venue and see someone pretending to be the Rolling Stones as they were in the
60 1960s. Go along to the genuine Rolling Stones gig and you'll see the real thing in their sixties. It's a big difference.'

E In a sense, even the Antarctic Monkeys are hailing back to a lost time, the days when the Arctic Monkeys themselves emerged in a small venue in Sheffield in the north of England, rather than
65 playing domes in America. It may have been only a few years ago, but it's still a time that will never come again. Collins continues: 'There's an old rock journalists' idea of authenticity which can veer towards snobbery,' he says. 'The thing about tribute bands is they take the snobbery out of it. These are cabaret acts.' Indeed, such is
70 the surreal spin of the genre, the world's most successful tribute band is no longer a singular item. Bjorn Again, the Australian impersonators of the 1970s Swedish group Abba, have five or six versions of themselves touring the globe at any one time. They have become a franchise. So what do the originals think about it all?
75 The Bootleg Beatles played at the 50th birthday party of Pink Floyd's David Gilmour, and among the guests was George Harrison. The real Beatle was introduced to his imitators after the show and was very complimentary.

4 Tribute bands essentially pretend to be the original artists. Look back through the article and highlight all the words that are used to suggest the idea of copying.

5 Look these words up in a dictionary such as the *Longman Exams Dictionary*. In what context would you normally expect to find them?

hurling (A)	holding back (B)
stuffed (C)	diehard (B)
twang (C)	chill out (A)
covers (A)	venues (B)

1 Decide what part of speech they are.
2 Look at the rest of the sentence, and write down possible meanings for each word.
3 Compare your ideas with other students.

6 Check your answers by looking at the dictionary extracts on page 188, which come from the *Longman Exams Dictionary*. How close were your answers?

7 Discuss these questions.
1 What do you expect to find in a good dictionary? Does the dictionary you currently use give you everything you need?
2 Were the dictionary extracts you looked at on page 188 useful? Were the meanings and examples clear? Did you get all the information you wanted about the words? What other information about the word did you find?
3 When do you try not to use a dictionary? Why? When do you find it useful to use a dictionary?

Vocabulary: word formation (suffixes)

1 Look at this example. What part of speech are the underlined words? How do you know?

Before going on stage, all I can remember is a feeling not so much of fear or <u>nervousness</u>, but of wonderful <u>excitement</u>.

2 Work with a partner. Look at the words in the box. Do the suffixes in bold generally indicate that the word is a noun, an adjective, a verb or an adverb?

weak**ness**   count**able**   alternat**ive**
frighten**ing**   rapid**ly**   opt**ion**
success**ful**   perform**ance**   leg**al**
responsibil**ity**   modern**ise**   politic**al**
enjoy**ment**   delic**ious**   decorat**ive**
confus**ed**   pleas**ant**   combin**ation**

3 Which suffixes from Exercise 2 make

- nouns from adjectives?
- nouns from verbs?
- verbs from adjectives?
- adjectives from nouns/verbs?
- adverbs from adjectives?

4 Make a note of two more words you know with each of the suffixes in Exercise 2. Make sure that you also write down what part of speech it is.

5

1 Read the title of the article. Do you think the article will be about unusual musicians, disk jockeys or music fans?

2 Read the whole article. Were you right?

3 Decide what form the word in brackets should be, then choose one of the suffixes from Exercise 2 to complete the article.

> **TIP!** Make sure that you read the whole sentence, and look out for any plural nouns.

Making music – their way

A recent, rather unusual music documentary showcased not (1) .... (*profession*) musicians, but London buskers who were taking part in a (2) .... (*sponsor*) licensed busking scheme which now boasts 602 performers (3) .... (*regular*) playing at 31 station pitches in the capital. This was a (4) .... (*determine*) departure from the standard approach to musical documentaries, but it was the positive (5) .... (*impress*) made by the quality of the street musicians, and their (6) .... (*intrigue*) personal backgrounds, that led to the (7) .... (*product*) of the show. They are all fantastic musicians in their own right, but what they had to go through to perform is (8) .... (*inspire*).

The mother
As a mother of two daughters and a full-time history degree student, Jordene Roberts has her hands full. But despite having had no (9) .... (*form*) training, she helps to pay her bills with her clear and (10) .... (*power*) soprano voice outside the Royal Opera House. She has no agent and struggles at auditions because she is unable to read music (11) .... (*fluent*).

6 Do you have buskers in your city? How do people feel about them?

7 Complete the second sentence so that it has a similar meaning to the first sentence, using the word given. Do not change the word given. You must use between three and six words, including the word given. There is an example (0) at the beginning.

> **TIP!** Remember that when you say things in different ways, you often have to change the form of a word, as in the example below.

Example:

0 Lena was hugely **disappointed** when she lost the recording contract.
   A
   It came as *a huge disappointment to* Lena when she lost the recording contract.

1 I'm very worried about David's forgetfulness – it's getting worse. **MUCH**
   David's becoming .... and it worries me a lot.

2 People should take more responsibility for their actions. **BE**
   People should .... for their actions.

3 The singer performed brilliantly and received a standing ovation. **BRILLIANT**
   The singer gave .... and received a standing ovation.

4 The young woman took an active part in street busking. **ENGAGED**
   The young woman .... in street busking.

8 Discuss these questions.

1 Do you find street busking acceptable? Why?/ Why not?
2 Which person from Exercise 5 do you find most admirable? Why?
3 Would you like to busk? Why?/Why not? What kind of busking would you do?
4 Can you play a musical instrument? If not, which one would you like to play? Why?
5 What do you think is the most productive way to follow a career in music?

The city worker
For 14 years, Peter Murphy had a (12) .... (*respect*) career as an accountant before one day deciding he wanted to busk for a living. He walked out of his office, made an (13) .... (*appear*) on the streets the next day with a penny whistle and never went back to his desk. Now he plays a Celtic harp. He always wanted to be a musician, and being single and having no (14) .... (*responsible*) for others, has been able to follow his dream. He has his own website and last year released his first CD.

The innovator
One of the first to have any (15) .... (*involve*) with the licensed busker scheme, Hadar Manor is now in (16) .... (*negotiate*) for a recording contract. Her (17) .... (*determine*) to make her way in the music world led her to singing in London stations. She earned enough to pay basic bills, but was happy just to be able to give (18) .... (*perform*). She was eventually spotted singing one of her own songs outside a tube station.

Use of English: open cloze

(Part 2)

1 Discuss these questions.

1 What type of music do you like?
2 What do you think is the best way to find out about new bands, singers or music? Why?

- listening to the radio
- reading the music press
- word of mouth
- going to live concerts
- surfing the Internet

2

1 Make a list of the advantages and disadvantages of downloading music from the Internet for a) fans b) musicians.

2 Read the title, and then read the article below quickly, without trying to fill in any missing words. How does your list compare with the writer's ideas? Does the writer have any different ideas?

3

1 Read the article again and write one word in pencil in each of the gaps. Most of the words are grammatical words (e.g. prepositions, adverbs, etc.) rather than vocabulary linked to the topic. If you are not sure of an answer, put as many possibilities as you think might fit. If you have no idea, then put a question mark.

2 Compare your ideas with another student. Explain which answers you're sure about and why. Rub out any alternatives.

3 Look together at any remaining gaps. Work out what type of word is missing. If you're not sure of the exact word, have a guess.

4 Finally, read the whole article again to make sure it makes complete sense with your answers in place.

4 Discuss these questions.

1 Does the writer think the Internet is a good thing for music generally?
2 How do you think the music business has changed since this article was written?
3 How do you like to get music yourself? Why?

THE POWER OF FILE SHARING

The big music story of 2005 turned **(0)** *out* to be the success of the Arctic Monkeys, a British group **(1)** .... debut single went straight to the top of the charts. But theirs was **(2)** .... ordinary success story in the music business. Far **(3)** .... being discovered and promoted by one of the big record labels, the group had made it **(4)** .... their own; recording their own material and freely distributing it via the Internet. Music fans had downloaded the songs, realised **(5)** .... good they were and then forwarded the files to their friends by means of **(6)** .... became known as 'file sharing'. In **(7)** .... words, the group's reputation had been established via word-of-mouth.

The previous decade had seen a real revolution **(8)** .... home recording. It had become possible for anyone with musical talent, and a modest amount to invest in the latest digital equipment, to achieve home recordings of comparable quality **(9)** .... those produced in professional studios.

To people in the music business, **(10)** ...., the idea of allowing free downloading was unthinkable. Surely, they reasoned, if you **(11)** .... your music away on the Internet, **(12)** .... would buy a hard copy. But the success of the Arctic Monkeys demonstrated that the loss of potential income when people downloaded songs **(13)** .... than buying them, could be offset by the increased exposure the music got **(14)** .... a result. In effect, it was worth making some songs freely available as a way of generating interest in others for **(15)** ...., of course, people had to pay.

Exam focus

Paper 5 Speaking: conversation (Part 1)

About the exam: You take the Speaking test with a partner. There are two examiners, one who speaks to you (called the Interlocutor) and one who just listens (the Assessor).

In the first part of the interview you and your partner will be asked questions in turn by the interlocutor. These questions will be about you, and what you think about certain things. Some typical topics are:

- where you come from
- your home and family
- your hobbies and interests
- what you do
- your future plans
- holidays and travel.

You should try to give as much detail as possible, but remember that your partner also has to speak! Try to relax, and enjoy the interview.

1 Listen to part of an interview. Do you think both candidates:

- said enough? What else could they have said?
- gave interesting answers? How could they have made them more interesting?

2

1 Work in a group of three. Student A is the interlocutor. Ask Students B and C the questions below in turn. After you have asked and answered all the questions, discuss whether Students B and C:

- gave enough detail
- gave interesting answers
- could improve the answers they gave.

1 Do you enjoy listening to the radio? Why?/ Why not?
2 Do you think that the quality of films nowadays is improving or getting worse?
3 Which day of the week do you enjoy most? Why?
4 What do you like doing when you relax?
5 What kind of job would you like to do in the future?
6 Which country would you most like to visit?

2 Think of six other questions you could ask each other, and write them down. Change roles and ask and answer your questions.

Grammar 2: verb tenses (perfect aspect)

1 Look at this sentence from the text about file sharing on page 12. Which event happened first? How do you know?

Music fans had downloaded the songs, realised how good they were and then forwarded the files ...

2

1 Complete the sentences using contracted forms (e.g. *He's* not *He has*).

1 He .... (*be*) crazy about jazz ever since he was five years old.
2 They .... (*finish*) making the film in about six months' time.
3 By the time *Lord of the Rings* came out on DVD, I .... (*see*) it three times.
4 I think I .... (*go*) to that exhibition, but I can't remember when.

2 Name the tense you have used in each gap, and match them to the correct description.

a) a state beginning in the past and leading up to the present
b) an event at some time in past – not exactly specified
c) something that happened before a given time/date/event in the past
d) something that will or should be completed by a specified time in the future

3 Each of these sentences has a mistake with verbs. Find the mistakes and correct them. Use contracted forms.

1 After I was there for two years, I decided to leave the music school.
2 By the time she's nineteen, she'll be away from home for two years.
3 I think that Jose goes to the football game every week last month.
4 He always enjoys music from a very early age.
5 By the end of December, I finish my course.
6 She visits New York every summer since her friend moved there.

┌─ **Watch Out!** *Contractions* ◄─

- *'s* (*has*) – we use this after pronouns and also after proper names. *He's/Tom's*
- *'ve* (*have*), *'d* (*had*) and *'ll* (*will*) – we usually only use these after pronouns, not proper names.

Simple v continuous form

3

1 Highlight the perfect continuous verbs in the sets of sentences below. Then complete the last sentence in each set, using a perfect continuous verb in the correct tense – past, present or future. Use contracted forms.

Example:

A _Repeated habit_

1 I've been buying CDs off the Internet for years now.
2 She'll have been going out with Chris for three years soon.
3 I'd been going (go) to the gym regularly all that year.

B ....

1 I've been working as a waitress recently to earn enough money to live on.
2 Before she moved into the house, she .... (stay) in a small motel.

C ....

1 We'd been trying to sort out the casting of the film for some time by then.
2 We've been looking for the right person to play the part for ages now.
3 We .... (work) on location for six months by the time we finish the film.

D ....

1 Julio will have been training for the whole season, so he'll be looking fit.
2 She'd been studying all night, and she had big circles under her eyes.
3 Zoe .... (practise) really hard, and it shows.

E ....

1 Tom had been dreaming of working in the movies for years when he got the role.
2 She's been hoping to get an interview with the director for the last six months.
3 I .... (wait) here for an hour soon.

> You will usually not be wrong if you use a simple form instead of a continuous form, but the continuous form often helps you to communicate your meaning more effectively.

2 Each set of sentences above demonstrates one use of the form of the verb. Match each set to the use below, and then write the use in the space above the correct set.

Repeated habit _A_
Results apparent later ....
Temporary activity or state ....
Duration emphasised ....
Incomplete action ....

4 What difference (if any) does the change from simple to continuous make to the following pairs of sentences?

1 a) I've bought some new clothes.
  b) I've been buying some new clothes.
2 a) Colin's living in London.
  b) Colin's been living in London.
3 a) They'd been watching television before they went out.
  b) They watched television before they went out.
4 a) I haven't felt very well lately.
  b) I haven't been feeling very well lately.
5 a) I'll have finished by six o'clock.
  b) I'll finish by six o'clock.
6 a) I've been to Paris three times.
  b) I went to Paris three times.

5 Read the comments from a music website about recent concerts. Complete them using the correct tense of the verbs in brackets.

present perfect simple, present perfect continuous
past perfect simple, past perfect continuous
future perfect simple, future perfect continuous
past simple, past continuous

I (1) .... (listen) to rock music for many years – I (2) .... (go) to some fantastic concerts in the eighties and nineties, but (3) .... (go) to one for several years until last week. I was glad I did – the concert was amazing!

I'm afraid that in my opinion the quality of music has declined recently, and I hope it won't take long before bands (4) .... (learn) the lessons of the 'here today, gone tomorrow' pop that I think (5) .... (ruin) music. By 2020 I want to hear cutting edge bands that by then (6) .... (play) good music for at least ten years!

The queue to buy tickets was ridiculous – when I arrived people (7) .... (*stand*) in the rain and one man told me that he (8) .... (*wait*) for over six hours. If the band want people to come to their concerts, then they've got to improve their organisation.

6 Work with a partner. Find an example of something that:

- you've both been doing a lot lately
- you'll both have done by ten o'clock tonight
- you'd both done by the time you were twelve
- you've both enjoyed today
- you've been hoping to do for ages, but have not done yet
- you both hope you'll have achieved in the next ten years.

Use perfect tenses (simple and continuous) as appropriate.

▶ Grammar reference p.197 (16)

Writing: drafting and organising (Part 1)

About the exam: Paper 2, Part 1 is a compulsory task, and you may have to write a letter, an article, a proposal or a report. Think carefully about what kind of text you have to write so that you choose the right style of language to use. You will be given information to base your writing on; this will be in the form of one or more short texts which may be annotated. You should read the texts carefully, and use the information and notes appropriately to complete the task.

1 What do you find most difficult to do when you write? Read these statements and decide how important you think they are when you write in English. Then discuss your answers with a partner, giving your reasons.

1 I must remember who I am writing to, and what overall impression my writing will have on them.
2 I should make a plan before writing, and try to connect my ideas clearly.
3 I don't need to worry about spelling and grammar mistakes when I write.

4 I should try to use lots of different grammatical structures and words.
5 I have to get paragraphing and layout right, and make sure the language is always suitable for what I am writing.

2 In Paper 2 your writing may be assessed on the following criteria:

a) organisation, coherence and use of linking words
b) accuracy, including grammar, spelling and punctuation
c) range of vocabulary and grammar
d) consistency and appropriacy of style and register
e) effect on target reader.

Match the statements from Exercise 1 to the assessment criteria above.

3

1 You are going to write a letter of complaint about a film. First, discuss these questions with a partner.

1 What kind of film do you think is suitable for a family audience?
2 What would you normally expect to find in a film aimed at younger children?
3 Whose responsibility do you think it is to monitor the films young children see?

2 Read the following writing task, and underline the three things that you have to do in your letter.

Your school is raising funds by showing family films at weekends. You took your young cousin to see a film there last weekend, but were disappointed. Read the advertisement, the review and your notes. Write a letter to the school outlining the reasons why you were disappointed, your cousin's reaction to the film, and suggesting what should be done.

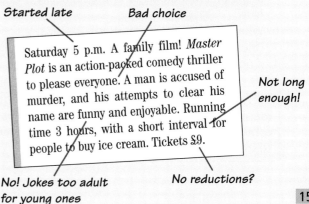

Started late   *Bad choice*

Saturday 5 p.m. A family film! *Master Plot* is an action-packed comedy thriller to please everyone. A man is accused of murder, and his attempts to clear his name are funny and enjoyable. Running time 3 hours, with a short interval for people to buy ice cream. Tickets £9.

Not long enough!

No! Jokes too adult for young ones   *No reductions?*

Suitable or not?

The acting is excellent throughout. Although the plot is complex, and sometimes confusing, it is clever, and adult. However, the humour is black, and not to everyone's taste. The special effects are intense with images that could be hard to forget. These might give children nightmares.

They did!

Write your **letter** in 180–220 words.

4

1 Formal letters should usually follow a similar pattern. Put the sections below into an appropriate order for a formal letter. Each section should usually have a separate paragraph.

☐   any requests for action, or further information
☐   explanation/clarification of the situation
☐   further supporting details
☐   reason for writing

2 Read the letter on page 191 which was written in answer to the task, and answer the questions.

1 Has the writer followed the order you chose?
2 Has the writer included all the information in the notes?
3 What order has the writer chosen to use the information?
4 Has the writer used a variety of linking words?
5 How has the writer expanded the points about a) the practical problems b) the suitability of the film?
6 What style has the writer used?
7 Does the answer deal with all the points equally? If not, why not?

TIP! It is not necessary to include every point mentioned in the notes as long as the task is achieved. You should decide what is important to include and how to use it.

5   To help you think about the organisation of the letter, complete the plan of the content below, adding useful linking words and phrases from the answer.

Opening paragraph: Reason for writing
Information included: ....
Linking phrases: *I am writing to ...*

Second paragraph: .... problems
Information included: ....
Linking phrases: *Firstly, ...*; ....;
.............................; *On top of that ...*

Third paragraph: more ....
problems
Information included: ....
Linking phrases: *However, ...*; ....;
....

Final paragraph: ....
Information included: ....
Linking phrases: *I suggest that ...*;
....

6   Look at the writing task on page 188.

7   Using the model in Exercise 4, and the plan in Exercise 5 to guide your planning and drafting, write your own answer to the task.

8   Exchange your letter with a partner. Evaluate each other's work, using the checklist below.

Have you:

☐   included all the points necessary for the target reader to be informed?
☐   expanded the notes appropriately to achieve the task?
☐   organised your answers into logical paragraphs?
☐   used appropriate linking words or phrases?
☐   avoided copying long phrases or sentences from the input texts?
☐   written approximately the right number of words?
☐   used an appropriate style (in this case, formal)?
☐   used your grammar checklist to avoid mistakes?

▶ Writing reference p.199

1 Choose the correct connector to complete the letter of complaint.

(1) *In the first place / At once*, when I arrived there was no record of my reservation (2) *despite / even though* I had phoned to confirm that very morning.

(3) *Secondly / However*, the table I had asked for was already taken, and I had to sit at a table near the door (4) *even / in spite of* the fact that I specifically asked to be near the fire. (5) *Furthermore / Since*, the menu was restricted, and I was unable to have my first choice of meal.

(6) *To sum up / Finally*, when I was given the bill the cover charge of $5 was excessive for what had been very poor treatment.

I suggest that you think about the way you treat regular customers, (7) *as / consequently* they may well vote with their feet and go elsewhere!

2 Each of these sentences has a different basic grammatical mistake. Find the mistakes and correct them. Then check your answers with a partner.

1 We go never out to the theatre any more – it's too expensive.
2 Where are tickets? I put them in my wallet, but they're not there now.
3 Could you tell me whether is there another cinema in this town?
4 The new arts centre are very nice – I really like it.
5 That's the boy who brother I played football with as a child.
6 The tourist board gave us lots of informations about the city.
7 Unless you don't work harder, you'll fail your exam.
8 We considered to go to the concert, but we felt too tired.

9 I really wish I would have more time to study!
10 She apologised for been late.
11 I am knowing she enjoys going to rock concerts.
12 I can't get used to start work early in the morning!
13 She managed to get to the top of the tower despite of her fear of heights.
14 My teacher won't let me to get out of doing homework.
15 If I'd have known she was in town, I'd have arranged to meet her.
16 They've been living in this town since at least 25 years.
17 He's a such hard worker that he's sure to do well.
18 Computer games are a lot more cheaper now than they used to be.
19 I found the film absolutely terrified.
20 He might decided to become a jazz musician.

3 Complete these sentences using the correct form of the word in capitals.

1 The show was extremely .... for all the family. **ENJOY**
2 The company needed to .... its procedures, as there was no consistency in its approach. **STANDARD**
3 The winner of the lottery made a big .... to charity. **DONATE**
4 I feel very .... that I will do well in the next interview. **HOPE**
5 Many celebrities have benefited .... from sponsorship deals. **FINANCE**
6 There was a very .... discussion about the issues, which led to a possible long-term solution. **PRODUCE**
7 The fact that he never won a gold medal was a great .... to the athlete. **DISAPPOINT**
8 It's important not to show any sign of .... when taking part in competitive activities. **WEAK**
9 The idea that the company would cut salaries was seen as .... by the workforce. **OUTRAGE**
10 It seems to be quite .... nowadays for TV presenters to receive enormous salaries. **ACCEPT**
11 Many young children found the film .... even though it was only a cartoon. **FRIGHT**
12 She found the positive ending to the film incredibly .... **UPLIFT**

UNIT
2 Spend it or save it

Listening 1

1

1 Imagine that you won the following amounts of money. What would you do in each case?

€50   €500   €5,000

2 Imagine that you wanted to save the same amounts of money. How would you do it? What might you save the money for? Why?

a flashy new car   designer clothes
a personal development course
the latest mp3 player   your retirement
an exotic holiday   a donation to charity
a rainy day   anything else?

3 Discuss these questions.

1 Are you a spender or a saver by nature?
2 How easy do you find it to save money?
3 What kind of things are worth saving up for?

2 Listen to part of a radio programme about spending and saving money. Answer the questions.

1 What point does the example of the coffee illustrate?
2 What broader point is the speaker making?
3 Who do you agree with, the self-help experts or the writer?

3

1 Now listen to a psychologist on the programme. She divides people who are spenders into three groups:

1 sleepwalkers   2 status seekers   3 scrimpers

Listen and decide which type of spender would make each of the comments (A–F).

A I couldn't tell you how much I spent today.
B I know that jewellery keeps its value, but it's hard to spend so much at once.
C Basically, I just buy whatever I want. I never look at the price tag.

D There are certain things which everybody has, so you have to buy them.

E I'd hate anyone to think that I couldn't afford the latest fashions.

F I'm good at saving, but I do like to go on the occasional shopping spree.

2 Which of the comments do you agree with? Do you know any sleepwalkers, status seekers or scrimpers?

4

1 Now listen to a continuation of the same programme. What advice does the speaker give for people in each of the three groups in Exercise 3?

2 Compare your answers. Which advice do you think was the most helpful? What advice would you give?

5 Look at the words and phrases in the box that come from the recordings. Which are associated with a) saving or b) spending? Listen again to check.

interest   conspicuous consumption
go on a spree   set a budget   run out of cash
a sound investment   a nest egg   a treat
to economise   in the red   shopaholic
get through money like water   on impulse
put it away for a rainy day   a 'must-have' item

Speaking: giving opinions

About the exam: In Paper 5, Part 3, the interlocutor asks candidates to complete a problem solving task. This involves looking at several pictures which provide ideas for the task.

1 Listen to an interlocutor setting a task, and look at the pictures on these pages. What two things do the candidates have to do?

2

1 Listen to two students beginning the task. Do they describe the pictures? Why?/Why not?

2 Listen again, and make a note of any phrases they use to:

- give their own opinion
- ask for their partner's opinion
- agree with their partner
- disagree with their partner.

3 Now work with a partner and complete the task. Discuss each picture before reaching a decision.

4 Is there anything else that you think is more important than the things in the pictures?

Exam focus

Paper 1 Reading: multiple choice (Part 1)

About the exam: Paper 1 is the part of the exam where your reading is tested. There are four parts to the whole test, and it lasts one hour and fifteen minutes. You must decide how long you spend on each part, and you must transfer all your answers to the answer sheet within the time limit.

In Part 1 of the Reading paper you will have to read three short passages. The passages will all be on a theme, and will include different types of text. You have to answer two multiple-choice questions on each text – and these will focus on different things in the text, for example; the writer's purpose or opinion, the style of writing, the meaning of certain words and phrases, etc.

Suggested procedure

1 Read the first text to get an idea of what it is about and how it is organised.
2 Read both of the questions, highlighting key words and phrases.
3 Find the place in the text where you think the answer is located.
4 Read that part of the text very carefully and choose the correct answer.
5 Read the whole text again to make sure your answer fits the sense of the passage.
6 Go on to the next text.

> **TIP!** Some questions give line numbers to help you find the place – but you still need to read the whole text.

1 You are going to read three extracts which are all concerned in some way with money. For questions **1–6**, choose the answer (**A**, **B**, **C** or **D**) which you think fits best according to the text.

EXTRACT FROM A SELF-HELP BOOK

A CASE STUDY: **MELISSA**

Melissa earns £27,000 per year as the PA to a Sales Director at a large international company in London. She lives nearby in a flat she rents with her best friend, Sarah. The flat costs them £450 per month each. Melissa is a likeable, bubbly person who is also known to be very good at her job.
5 Although she has a slight problem with punctuality and is sometimes forgetful, she is generally forgiven for her shortcomings because of her stylish dress sense and personality.

Melissa will be the first to admit, however, that her personal life is a complete disaster, especially on the financial front. She absolutely loves
10 shopping and has accumulated, and used, a lot of credit cards. Everyone seemed to want to lend her money and she bought a car, went on holidays, furnished her flat and shopped till she dropped – all on borrowed money. On the shopping front, she reluctantly admits that being scatty and disorganised, she constantly buys things that she doesn't
15 really need and never really thinks about what she spends her money on. She spends lots on cosmetics, shoes and clothes, but she has nothing to show for it because a lot of it is cheap junk. Massively in debt, Melissa avoids opening her bank or credit-card statements because the sight of them gets her down. She has no savings at all and frequently borrows
20 money from her mum that she has no hope of paying back.

1 In the first paragraph, we are told that Melissa has problems

   A gaining the respect of her colleagues.
   B dealing with a fairly demanding workload.
   C keeping on top of some detailed aspects of her work.
   D maintaining the professional appearance demanded by her job.

2 In the second paragraph, we learn that Melissa

   A makes some attempt to plan her spending.
   B is unconcerned about her financial position.
   C has been trying to economise in her shopping.
   D is aware that she may not always spend wisely.

DESIGNER BRANDS ARE FOR MONKEYS

EVEN THOUGH I FOLLOW FASHION (in a far from slavish way), there is no phrase that makes me recoil more than 'must-have'. If I read that X boots or the latest Y shades have been
5 decreed to be the latest 'must-haves', my immediate reaction is mutiny. Why must I have them? Why should I humiliate myself to go on a waiting list for this supposedly desirable item? Most of all, why should I fall for the designer's manipulative tactics,
10 which are intended only to swell his or her bank balance at the expense of mine? Far more satisfying is to pop into the clothes shops in my local mall and buy a copy of said designer's gear for a tenth of the price. Waiting lists? Huh! They're for mugs.

15 Actually, designer brands in general are for mugs. They are for people too insecure to trust their own taste. These people calculate that everything with a certain label must be cool, so shopping there is a safe bet. If you shop in the mall by contrast, you have to
20 use your discernment to find the one garment out of three that looks great. If you go to a really cheap shop, the ratio is more like one in 20. But boy is it worth it. Like spotting a little gold nugget in a muddy riverbed, the find gives rise to immense satisfaction. Which is
25 why, according to a survey published this week, the young rich are deserting designer shops for second-hand stores and flea-markets. They prefer to rummage for one-off bargains than to waste their money in some posh department store.

Clicking_through_a_Mag

For me, shopping is a social thing. It means time to gossip, drink coffee and keep up with friends and trends (and trends in friends). My consuming compatriots and I browse, select, try out for size and discuss – and only if the item is perfect
5 do we buy. All of which is by way of explaining why I have never really understood the fascination with online shopping. Who wants to go it alone, sipping a mug of home-made coffee, buying items that you have never even touched, let alone tried on?
10 But **it** doesn't end there. Sitting alone, buying a ridiculously expensive item becomes strangely easier – you end up doing the kind of thing you'd never do in front of a friend who has shared your fears on the state of your credit card bill. True, online shopping avoids the pain of crowds, parking and sore
15 feet, but you miss out on the atmosphere and social stage, and you are, potentially at least, more vulnerable.

3 In this article, the writer is

   A questioning the quality of designer clothes.
   B explaining the consequences of following fashion.
   C encouraging people to develop their own taste in clothes.
   D reporting on ways to obtain designer clothes at good prices.

4 Which phrase in the second paragraph reinforces the idea that there is 'immense satisfaction' to be gained from some types of shopping?

   A shopping there is a safe bet (line 18)
   B use your discernment (line 20)
   C boy is it worth it (line 22)
   D rummage for one-off bargains (line 28)

5 What does the writer imply by the phrase 'trends in friends' (line 2)?

   A She worries about keeping up with a changing social scene.
   B She doesn't place much importance on the opinions of others.
   C She fears that her friends may be disloyal in her absence.
   D She doesn't meet her friends unless she goes shopping.

6 The word **it** in line 10 refers to the writer's

   A experience of online shopping.
   B reason for disliking online shopping.
   C wish to try things on before buying them.
   D need for advice when choosing things to buy.

2 The following extracts come from the texts. Do you agree with them? Why?/Why not?

- ... she constantly buys things that she doesn't really need ...
- Actually, designer brands in general are for mugs.
- For me, shopping is a social thing.

Grammar 1: defining and non-defining relative clauses

1

1 Which sentence in each pair below contains a relative clause that gives

- essential information about a noun? (defining relative clause)
- extra information about a noun, but could be omitted? (non-defining relative clause)

1 a) People who use mobile phones on trains really annoy me.
b) The man, who spoke in French, used his mobile phone all through the journey.

2 a) The man gave his money to charity, which he preferred.
b) The man gave his money to the charity which he preferred.

3 a) My sister whose flat is in central London, is a charity worker.
b) My sister, whose flat is in central London, is a charity worker.

2 Complete the sentences about defining and non-defining relative clauses.

1 .... relative clauses are separated from the rest of the sentence by commas.

2 In both defining and non-defining relative clauses we use .... for people and .... for things.

3 In .... relative clauses the relative pronouns *who* and *which* can both be replaced by *that*.

4 .... is a possessive relative pronoun and can only be used before a noun.

2 Rewrite the sentences using *where* or *when*. Then complete the rule below.

1 The school at which I first studied Economics was in London.

2 Wednesday is the day of the week on which I always have a meeting.

3 It was a conference in Rome at which I met my future husband.

4 Two o'clock is the time at which I always have a cup of coffee.

With relative clauses of place and time, use *where* or *when* instead of ....

▶ **Grammar reference p.196 (13)**

3 In non-defining clauses we can use *which* with other *wh-* words. Rewrite the sentences using *which* and another *wh-* word.

Example:
I went to Paris last month, and *it was then that* I met my new boss.
I went to Paris last month, <u>*which was when*</u> I met my new boss.

1 She gave me her email address, and that was the way we managed to contact her later.

2 I spent the money on a new car, as I had always planned to do.

3 Her face was red, and that was the way we knew she was upset.

4 He left at six, and that was the time she arrived.

5 The actor forgot his words, and so at that moment they brought the curtain down.

6 I had a holiday in Spain, and that was the place I learned to swim.

4

1 Read the text quickly and find:

a) two reasons why celebrities support charities
b) how celebrity endorsement of a charity is 'mutually beneficial'.

What's in a name?
·························

Behind every modern-day celebrity there is a network (1) .... is what helps them to maintain their image. This network could include an agent, a manager, a personal trainer and a full-time assistant, and quite often there is also a 'significant other' (2) .... may have similar celebrity status. But equally important to celebrities nowadays is the particular charity to (3) .... the celebrity chooses to give financial and promotional support.

This is because it is involvement with charities (4) .... offers celebrities the potential for image and career enhancement, (5) .... is an opportunity not to be missed. Of course, their motivation is good, but it is also useful if the public thinks of a celebrity not just as a beautiful person, but as someone (6) .... is willing to share some of their good fortune with others.

The thing (7) .... also makes celebrity-charity relationships very positive is the fact that they are mutually beneficial. People attending a charity event (8) .... a celebrity is present will remember it and may then support the charity themselves. A charity (9) .... publicity includes pictures of a celebrity will encourage more sponsors, many of (10) .... will then want to donate more money to their cause.

2 Read the text again, and complete the gaps using a relative pronoun.

5

1 Choose two items from the list below. Write down one example of
- a thing you use every day
- an object you couldn't live without
- a charity you would like to support
- a time of day you enjoy
- a period of the year you like best.

2 Now work with a partner. Define each word using relative clauses, but do not use the word itself. Your partner must guess the word.

Example:
It's something which I use for contacting my friends.

6 Discuss these questions.

1 Do you think it is important to give money to charity?
2 What types of fund-raising events do you think are most successful?

Use of English: word formation (Part 3)

1 Work with a partner. Discuss these questions.

1 Have you ever:
   a) bought anything in an online auction?
   b) sold anything in an online auction?
2 What are the advantages and disadvantages of buying and selling things in this way?

2

1 Read the text. Do not worry about the missing words for the moment. What does the writer say about a) selling and b) buying online? What solution to possible problems does the writer suggest?

2 Read the text again. Use the word given in capitals below the text to form a word that fits in the numbered gap. There is an example at the beginning (0).

Sell your stuff online –
without the hassle!

It seems to be a feature of today's **(0)** *throwaway* society that we accumulate **(1)** .... that we do not really need. Impulse buys and **(2)** .... gifts begin to clutter up our homes, and objects that began as a source of **(3)** .... turn into a source of frustration. Too good to put in the bin or donate to a charity shop, these items are, quite **(4)** ...., just in the way!

Online auctions, such as eBay, provide a ready-made **(5)** .... But as anyone who has tried it knows, buying goods online is **(6)** .... easy, whereas selling them can be a complex and time-consuming business. You need to take digital photos of the items from a **(7)** .... of angles, write an enticing description to attract **(8)** .... bidders, negotiate insurance costs and then queue up at the post office to despatch the thing. It hardly comes as a surprise, therefore, to learn that over 90% of auction users are buyers rather than sellers.

Enter a new breed of service provider: the online auction facilitator, who in return for a **(9)** .... of the sale price as **(10)** .... will do all the work for you. Basically, you just take the thing you want to sell to them and they do the rest.

0	THROW		
1	POSSESS	6	REMARK
2	WANT	7	VARY
3	PLEASE	8	POTENT
4	FRANK	9	PERCENT
5	SOLVE	10	COMMIT

3 Would you ever use an online auction facilitator? Why?/Why not?

Vocabulary 1: compound adjectives

1

1 Match the two parts of the compound adjectives.

1	old	a)	fetched
2	self	b)	fashioned
3	last	c)	headed
4	far	d)	centred
5	air	e)	term
6	long/short	f)	produced
7	level	g)	made
8	quick	h)	minute
9	so	i)	standing
10	long	j)	tight
11	mass	k)	called
12	self	l)	witted

2 Which of the compound adjectives you've created might describe a) a person b) a plan c) an idea d) a thing? Some adjectives fit in more than one category.

2 Complete the sentences using compound adjectives from Exercise 1.

1 He made a .... decision to take the job, and only just notified the company in time.
2 The economist was a very .... man, not inclined to get over-excited by unexpected developments.
3 It was a very .... idea – completely impractical and unworkable!
4 Maria was a very .... person who never thought about how other people might feel.

3 Work with a partner. Underline the full collocation (compound adjective and noun) and explain why the last part of the sentence is wrong. Suggest a correct version.

> **TIP!** A compound adjective may or may not be hyphenated, so look carefully at all groups of words.

1 I have a long-standing agreement with Anna to buy the flat – we decided yesterday.
2 I bought a mass-produced car – I'm very pleased with it, because it's completely unique.
3 She's a very quick-witted person – it takes her ages to think of a reply.

4 This is a completely airtight container, so you have to be careful that food doesn't go dry in the air.
5 He was a totally self-made millionaire – he started with a loan from his parents.

4 Listen to the five short extracts. Which speaker mentions:

1 a short-term plan made?
2 a last-minute decision reached?
3 a long-standing agreement broken?
4 a long-term strategy followed?
5 a so-called expert proved wrong?

5

1 Many compound adjectives are made with prepositions. Choose the best alternative to complete the adjectives in these sentences.

Example:
It's dangerous to drive fast in built- *up* / *off* areas of cities.

1 She was too hard *down* / *up* to buy expensive new clothes.
2 After a long period of hard work and poor sleep, I was feeling very run- *out* / *down* and quite ill.
3 Compensation given for accident or injury is often just a one- *off* / *down* payment, and not an income.
4 I'm so tired – I've been working so hard I'm worn *off* / *out*.
5 Many older people who take care of their money are well- *up* / *off* when they retire.
6 People who work too hard often get burnt *down* / *out* when they are young.
7 I get so fed *off* / *up* when politicians talk too much!

2 Choose two sentences that you agree with, and tell a partner why you agree with them.

Listening 2: multiple choice
(Part 3)

1 Discuss these questions.

1 When you buy consumer goods such as electrical goods and clothes, do you:
a) look for the best value?
b) look for the best quality?
c) look to see what other people are buying?
2 How do you get information about:
a) how good products are?
b) whether products are good value or not?

2 You will hear part of a radio programme in which a sociologist, Graham Styles, and a journalist, Sally Greengrass, are discussing the effects of consumerism in society. Choose the answer (A, B, C or D) which fits best according to what you hear.

1 In relation to the research he describes, Graham feels

   A unsure what conclusions to draw from it.
   B disappointed at how ungrateful people seemed to be.
   C concerned about how people interpreted the questions.
   D unconvinced that increased income leads to contentment.

2 Graham gives the example of a fridge to show how

   A consumer goods have gone up in price.
   B people have unreal expectations of consumer goods.
   C people are influenced by the conspicuous consumption of others.
   D consumer goods that were once luxuries have now become essentials.

3 Sally feels that the desire to own luxury goods is

   A not necessarily related to status.
   B not as unusual as Graham thinks it is.
   C not actually related to personal happiness.
   D not growing as much as Graham suggests.

4 According to Graham, what is the main problem that consumerism brings?

   A people becoming more selfish
   B natural resources being wasted
   C environmental problems getting worse
   D people getting into financial difficulties

5 What point does Sally make about the production of luxury goods?

   A It is good for the economy.
   B It has seen a decline in quality.
   C It has changed a lot since the 1950s.
   D It is not doing as well as it once was.

6 Graham feels that family life is suffering as a result of

   A the demands of employers.
   B the effects of the media.
   C the attitude of children.
   D the cost of basic items.

3 Discuss these questions.

1 To what extent do you desire luxury goods?
2 When you buy consumer goods, are you influenced by a) the media b) celebrities?
3 Who do you think is right, Graham or Sally?

4 Imagine that you are looking for a present for a friend in your town. Discuss a) what to buy and b) where to buy it. Then think about why you made these choices. What actually influenced you most?

Vocabulary 2: advertising and marketing

1

1 Think of an advertisement on television you think is particularly successful. Which of the following techniques does it use? Why do you think it is successful? Describe it to your partner. Do you like it? Why?/Why not?

memorable jingles   a continuing story
celebrities or famous people   humour
moral judgements or standpoints   cartoons
beautiful scenery   unusual events

2 What techniques used in advertisements annoy you? Why?

3 How do you think an advertisement on the printed page works? What makes it different from one on television?

2

1 Read the title and text below. Why does the writer suggest starting and finishing the advertisement with a clear mental image?

What makes a great written ad?

My advice to potential ad writers is this:
(1) .... the following approach that I have always found very effective. Memorable ads always begin with good opening lines that involve the reader immediately. They
(2) .... a powerful initial mental image, and don't leave readers in any doubt about what they are reading. OK, these ads are not great literature, because their purpose is to
(3) .... the reader's attention immediately. I use verbs, because they (4) .... vivid and vibrant images to mind, but I avoid adjectives, as these remind people of poetry. An effective ad makes a full circle, and (5) .... with a mental image that is just as effective as the first one. This last image reinforces the first, and so (6) .... the advertising message deep into people's memory which makes it an effective selling tool.

2 Read the text again, and decide which verb from the box best fits each gap. There are two verbs you will not need to use, and you may need to change the form of the verb to fit the gap.

run   adopt   grab   create   drive
finish   cause   bring

3 Many collocations are strong, i.e. the words are usually found together, although they are not fixed phrases, e.g. *involve someone* (in something). Make a note of four strong verb/noun collocations from the text above.

3

1 Do you notice advertisements? Make a list of where you can see them. Then read the text and compare your ideas.

Ads are *everywhere!*

Overt commercial advertising is found everywhere, and includes hoardings in the streets as well as ads taking up whole pages in newspapers and magazines. Targeted advertising uses printed flyers which are put through people's doors and (1) *pop- / hold- / get-*ups on websites that people visit on the net. Television commercials are generally thought to be the most effective format for (2) *huge- / great- / mass-*market advertising, and companies pay extremely high prices to advertise in commercial airtime during popular events such as (3) *top- / high- / long-*profile football games or (4) *highly / greatly / importantly* regarded soap operas. However, there is another form of advertising which is more covert, the (5) so-*named / -called / -considered* 'product placement'. In this form of advertising, which is found in films and on television, a character uses a product on screen with a (6) clearly *identifiable / known / familiar* brand name. Viewers may not think they notice the name, but the effect can be subliminal. Controversially, virtual billboards may also be inserted into (7) *actual / authentic / real-*life settings where none exists.

2 Read the text again, and choose the correct alternative to complete each compound word. Which one is a compound noun?

4   Discuss the questions.

1 Would you buy something because it was well-advertised? Why?/Why not?
2 Do you think there is too much advertising nowadays? Why?/Why not?
3 Do you think that advertising gives the consumer more or less choice? Why?/Why not?
4 Think of your least favourite advertisement. Why do you dislike it? Do the rest of the class agree?

Grammar 2: articles

1 How many brand names can you think of for the following?

coffee   jeans   hamburgers   computers
shoes   bicycles   orange juice

2 Read the text. What is the writer's overall purpose?

a) to introduce the concept of branding
b) to criticise the spread of branding

The power of the brand name

What is a brand? It's something that is special in some way, something that you can distinguish from other products of a similar nature, and it usually has a special name, whether it's a car, a chain of fast-food restaurants or a pair of jeans. The brand name, and the design or packaging, will have been carefully chosen to reflect the special features of the product.

By the time you arrive at school or work in the morning, you will already have been exposed to a huge number of brands and brand names. And this isn't just a local phenomenon. Indeed, if you visited any major city in the world, you would be surprised at how many familiar brands you'd see. In such situations, branding can provide a sense of security. Yet brand names also have a huge financial impact on the consumer, who may think that satisfaction can only be obtained by paying extra for a well-known name.

Copyright Guardian News & Media Ltd 2001

3 Look at the rules below for the use of articles. Fill in each gap with an example taken from the highlighted expressions in the text.

We use the **indefinite article** (*a/an*) for singular countable nouns

- when we mention something for the first time (1) ....
- when it doesn't matter which particular person or thing we are referring to. (2) ....

We use the **definite article** (*the*) for singular and plural countable nouns, and with uncountable nouns

- when something has already been mentioned (3) ....
- when we already know from the context which person or object is being referred to (4) ....
- when the following clause makes it clear what person or thing is being referred to (5) ....

- when only one thing or person exists (6) ....
- in generalisations with singular countable nouns. (7) ....

We use **no article** (**zero article**)

- in generalisations with plural and uncountable nouns when we mean 'all' (8) ....
- when we are referring to the general use of an institution rather than a particular place. (9) ....

▶ Grammar reference p.193 (1)

4

1 Choose the correct article in the text below (θ = zero article).

Promoting brand names

What is it that makes the promotion of (1) *a / θ* brand name successful? Advertisements for (2) *an / θ* insurance, for example, play on our need to feel safe; those for clothes may appeal to our need to belong to (3) *a / θ* group or to have (4) *the / a* desirable lifestyle. Many brands appeal to what we would like to be rather than what we actually are. Modern advertising paints the picture of an ideal life – and yet (5) *a / the* world it portrays still feels familiar. Indeed, the more often our self-image matches that promoted by (6) *a / θ* brand, the stronger and more successful (7) *the / θ* brand image becomes.

2 There is a mistake with the article in each highlighted word or expression in the following text. Correct the mistakes.

A SUCCESSFUL ADVERTISEMENT

It is quite difficult to work out whether (1) advertisement has been successful. If someone buys (2) car from a particular company, you can't be sure whether it was (3) a company's advertisement, the price or (4) a poor quality of the cars on sale elsewhere that was (5) determining factor. So how does any advertisement succeed in making (6) the people buy one product rather than another? There is one clear message – it must generate (7) the strong response from consumers because, surprisingly, it is almost impossible to get people to change their attitude towards (8) product that they feel indifferent about.

3 Did anything surprise you about the information in these two texts?

Writing: informal letter
(Part 2)

About the exam: In Paper 2, Part 2, you may have to write a letter, an article, a proposal, a competition entry, a report, a review, an information sheet, an essay or a contribution to a longer piece of writing (e.g. a book). You should take careful note of what kind of text you have to write. You will be given guidance on what to write about in the task itself.

1

1 Read the following writing task, and underline the four things that you have to do in your letter.

You recently tried to sell an old camera on an Internet auction site, but had some problems. You want to share your experiences with a friend. Write a letter to your friend, explaining what happened, what you did about it, how it affected you and advising your friend about using auction sites in the future.

Write your **letter** in 220–260 words.

2 Work with a partner, and discuss these questions.

1 What sort of problems might have occurred?
2 What possible courses of action could you have taken?
3 How do you think you might feel in a situation like this?
4 What advice would you give your friend?

2

1 Read the following letter, which was written in answer to the task. Answer the questions.

1 Has the writer included ideas similar to yours?
2 Has the writer included all the information necessary for the task?

Dear Pedro,

How are you doing? I thought it would be a good idea to catch up on any news, and something happened to me recently that I'd like to tell you about.

I was hoping to sell my old digital camera on the Internet, and I had a go, but it was a bit of a disaster. In the first place, I hadn't realised that I'd have to pay the Internet site – that was a definite downside! I wrote a really persuasive ad but it was impossible to include a photograph of the camera, which was a shame. The advert was on the site for five days, and at first there were no bids but then on the last day there were five! I thought I was home and dry, but the buyer really let me down because his cheque bounced. With hindsight, I was naive – but now I've lost confidence in the whole thing. At least I didn't send him the camera!

I complained to the website, but what they said was that they couldn't control bidders, and it was up to the sellers to watch their backs. They weren't very sympathetic really. So I'm fed up because I was looking forward to updating my camera once I got the money – and it is still sitting in the cupboard! I'm at a loss to know what to do now unless you know anyone who wants one! It's still in pretty good condition, and I'm sure that it would be a good buy for someone. You remember that it was the camera I took when we went on holiday together last year.

Have you ever tried to sell anything on the net? Drop me a line and tell me if you've got any tips!

Regards to Helen and hope to see you soon.

All the best

Jon

2 Underline informal expressions that mean the same as:

1 tried (para 2)
2 very unsuccessful (para 2)
3 a disadvantage (para 2)
4 successful (para 2)
5 take care (para 3)
6 unsure what to do (para 3)

> **TIP!** Remember to add any useful expressions to your vocabulary lists and include information about register.

3

1 The writer has written too many words, but has omitted part of the task. Rewrite the last two paragraphs so that any unnecessary information is left out and the missing information is included.

2 Exchange your rewritten paragraphs with a partner. Did you have the same ideas?

4 Write an answer to the task on page 191. Make sure that you use an informal register and include all the necessary information.

▶ Writing reference p.202

1 Read the text below. Use the words given in capitals at the end of some of the lines to form a word that fits in the gap in the same line. There is an example at the beginning (0).

Dirty money

Sooner or later it's something that everyone does; you put your jeans into the washing machine, having completely **(0)** *forgotten* about the   **FORGET**
money in the pocket. Coins, on the whole, survive the experience
relatively **(1)** ...., but the same is not true of banknotes.   **HARM**
These have a **(2)** .... to disintegrate as a result of prolonged   **TEND**
(3) .... to the forces of heat, water and detergent. If you live   **EXPOSE**
in Britain, however, all may not be lost. It is possible to send
damaged banknotes, **(4)** .... for use as payment in shops and   **ACCEPT**
other retail **(5)** ...., to the Bank of England's 'Mutilated Notes   **LET**
Section' (BEMS) in Leeds. Here experts will give the note a
thorough **(6)** .... and, if they are convinced that it is indeed the   **EXAMINE**
remains of a valid banknote, they will send you a **(7)** .... – or   **REPLACE**
at least a cheque of the equivalent value.
And it's not only washing machines that destroy notes. According
to BEMS staff, who receive up to 500 **(8)** .... per week, toddlers   **APPLY**
and puppy dogs also figure high on the list of offenders, as do people
who hide their savings in rather **(9)** .... places, such as microwave   **FORTUNE**
ovens or damp cellars. Sometimes, even banks make use of the service,
as happened during last year's spring floods when a number of branches
found that their burglar-proof and fireproof safes sadly were not
(10) .... waterproof.   **EQUAL**

2 Complete the second sentence so that it has a similar meaning to the first sentence, using the word given. **Do not change the word given.** You must write between three and six words, including the word given.

1 Tom's house is the one with the blue door.
  WHICH
  Tom lives .... a blue door.
2 Life without music would be very difficult for me. **LIVE**
  I would find .... music.
3 Lidia is a supporter of several wildlife charities.
  NUMBER
  Lidia gives .... wildlife charities.
4 Spring is my favourite time of the year. **BEST**
  The time of year .... spring.

3 Choose the correct article or cross out both if there should be no article.

Self-belief and strong nerves are essential if you're going to make your mark as (1) *a / the* salesperson. Take 21-year-old Leonora Pearl for example. She's (2) *a / the* sales consultant for (3) *a / the* Cabouchon Collection of (4) *a / the* jewellery. She works from (5) *a / the* home or wherever she happens to be. Not only is Leonora skilled at selling jewellery, she is also good at selling (6) *a / the* job. She says she fell in love with (7) *a / the* company's range of products as soon as she saw it, and signed up to be (8) *a / the* sales consultant 'within five minutes'. Leonora finds (9) *a / the* prices 'fantastically reasonable' and (10) *a / the* availability of stock 'absolutely fabulous'. She is, in (11) *a / the* other words, a walking, talking advertisement for (12) *a / the* products. 'In many ways, I'm never really off (13) *a / the* duty,' she says. 'When I go out, I always take (14) *a / the* duplicate set of whatever jewellery I'm wearing, so that if anyone expresses interest in, say, my necklace, I can sell it to them on (15) *a / the* spot.'

3 What makes us tick

Vocabulary: adjectives of character

1 A television company is planning another 'Big Brother' reality show in which a group of people who are strangers to each other are locked into a house for a given period of time. Cameras record how they react to each other, and viewers vote for who they want to stay in the house. The person who stays the longest wins a money prize.

What do you think the producers look for when choosing people to go into the house? Why?

- strong, conflicting personalities
- strange appearance
- interesting hobbies
- varied background or experience
- sense of humour

2

1 Read the profiles of hopeful contestants, and underline the adjectives they use to describe themselves.

2 Which of the adjectives you underlined do you think best sums up each person? Do you think it is positive, negative or either?

Example:
Alain: idealistic – could be positive as long as it's not taken too far.

Name: Alain   Describe yourself below:

I'm idealistic and conscientious – I've got a strong sense of right and wrong. Everything has to be correct. I'm well-organised and have high standards. I'd bring a sense of order to the house, though some people say I'm difficult to live with.

Name: Cris   Describe yourself below:

I'm extremely ambitious. It doesn't matter what others think of me and I'll do anything to get on in life. Being in the house will give me a high profile and get me where I want to be. I'll make sure the others don't take advantage when I'm not looking, though.

Name: David   Describe yourself below:

I'm pretty quiet, really – and if I'm honest, sensitive. I'm a bit self-conscious, and what I need is something different to take me out of myself, though I don't really mind. Being in the house would be good for me and make me more confident.

Name: Ella   Describe yourself below:

I'm curious and I want to be part of an experiment. I'm independent and I like to think for myself – I'll try anything once. I'm quite taciturn though, and I'm happy with my own company. I don't have to join in everything going on if I don't want to, though I like to watch.

Name: Franz   Describe yourself below:

I'm trustworthy and supportive. I'm an excellent trouble-shooter so I can stop arguments in the house – I love working with others and I'm totally reliable. I don't like jokes much, so I'll keep it serious – but that doesn't mean that I'm not supportive.

Name: Gina   Describe yourself below:

I'm playful and high-spirited though teachers say I'm undisciplined. I can be impatient - I don't suffer fools gladly - and so I annoy people sometimes. I'm extrovert. I want to enjoy myself and I'd bring fun to the house.

Name: Harold   Describe yourself below:

I'm a bit quick-tempered, and quite assertive - maybe too much! I say what I think and people may think I'm self-opinionated but why should I let people get away with things I don't like? I know I'm right, and people will agree when I'm in the house bringing everyone in line.

Name: Iva   Describe yourself below:

I'm pretty normal, really. I think positively and I'm sociable, not confrontational - I'd rather agree with people. I like everyone to get on. I hate people who trample over others. I want to be in the house because I love meeting people I can empathise with, and chatting to them.

Name: Brita   Describe yourself below:

I'm caring, empathetic, sincere and warm-hearted. I know I can be sentimental and I try to please others too much, but that means I'd be able to make the others feel at home. I'll organise games and things like that - get everyone involved.

Watch Out! *sensitive/sensible; sympathise/empathise*

Choose the correct alternative.

1. a) It's *sensible / sensitive* to keep a note of your passport number when you travel.
   b) She is rather *sensible / sensitive* and is easily upset if people criticise her.

2. a) She's willing to listen to people's problems and to *empathise / sympathise* with them when they are upset.
   b) It's easy to *empathise / sympathise* with someone who has been through the same experience as you.

3

1. Highlight the reason each person gives for wanting to be in the house. Do you think that their reasons are sensible or valid?

2. Decide on five people who would make the most interesting programme for viewers, and why. Compare your ideas with the rest of the class. Do you all agree?

Grammar 1: modal verbs 1

1   Match the sentences to the ideas they express.

1. You mustn't tell anyone about it, not even your best friend.
2. I must phone Julie to tell her where to meet us.
3. I might be able to go out tonight but I'm not sure.
4. I think you should tell Josh exactly how you feel.
5. We don't have to go everywhere together, you know.
6. My mobile's not in my bag – it must be somewhere at home.
7. Can I bring a friend with me to the party?
8. You can always tell what Tessa is thinking from her expression.

a) possibility   e) prohibition
b) logical deduction   f) advice
c) obligation/necessity   g) permission
d) lack of obligation/necessity   h) ability

▶ Grammar reference p.196 (10)

2 Complete the second sentence so that it has a similar meaning to the first sentence, using the word given. Do not change the word given. You must use between three and six words, including the word given.

1 It would be great if taking exams were voluntary for students. **HAVE**

It would be great if students .... exams.

2 It's possible that this book might help you in your research. **HELPFUL**

You .... for your research.

3 He'll probably be very successful. **CHANCES**

The .... be very successful.

4 Joe promised to call tonight, so I'm sure that's him on the phone now. **MUST**

Joe promised to call tonight, so .... on the phone now.

5 Working on the shop floor is a compulsory part of the training for everyone. **HAS**

Everyone .... on the shop floor as part of their training.

3

1 Complete the advice below, using modal verbs from the boxes for each section. There are two verbs you do not need to use each time.

2 Think of some more advice on how to be a good friend, using the modal verbs from the boxes.

3 Tell a partner about a time when you
- ought to have asked for help, but didn't
- could have helped a friend, but didn't.

How to be a good friend

Be aware

| couldn't | can | might | ought to | shouldn't |

The problem is that as we get older we feel we (1) .... be able to sort out our own problems, and we keep these to ourselves, rather than talking about them. So if one of your friends suddenly becomes more withdrawn than usual, it (2) .... mean that they have a problem, but don't feel they (3) .... tell you about it.

Listen

| could | mustn't | have to | can't | couldn't |

If your friend wants to tell you about their problem, you (4) .... listen! In most cases, you (5) .... actually do anything about it, but allowing them to talk about their feelings (6) .... help them to work it through.

Wait for the right time

| shouldn't | couldn't | must | may | can't |

You (7) .... be able to get practical information that can help your friend. You probably think you (8) .... tell them straightaway – but there's a right time for everything. So you (9) .... force the information on them; instead, wait until they actually ask for it.

Don't bring it back to you

| mustn't | can't | can | might | don't have to |

You (10) .... talk about your own experiences to show you understand your friend's problems. If your friend doesn't ask if anything similar has happened to you, you (11) .... go on about your own problems, past or present. Remember, the most important thing you (12) .... do for your friend is just be there for them.

Exam focus

Paper 4 Listening: multiple matching (Part 4)

About the exam: In Paper 4, Part 4, you will hear five short extracts on the same theme. In each extract you hear one person speaking. You have to do two tasks as you listen, and these will focus on different things in the texts, for example, the speaker's reason for doing something and their feelings.

> **TIP!** Remember that there are **two** answers for each speaker – one in task one and another in task two. You hear all five speakers once, then the sequence is repeated.

Suggested procedure

1 Listen to the instructions and follow the wording on the page.
2 Read both sets of options in the pause before the listening is played.
3 Underline the most important word in each option.
4 As you listen for the first time, focus mainly on task one. Write in the letters of any answers you are sure of.
5 As you listen the second time, focus mainly on task two.
6 Don't leave any questions unanswered. If you're not sure, guess. Although you may be unsure, you have probably understood more than you think, so your guess may be right.

1 You will hear five short extracts in which people who have changed their names talk about why they did this. Remember that you must complete both tasks as you listen. You will hear the recording twice.

TASK ONE

For questions 1–5, choose from the list A–H each person's reason for disliking their original name.

A People couldn't remember it.

B It felt rather old-fashioned.   Speaker 1 [1]

C Someone couldn't pronounce it.   Speaker 2 [2]

D It hadn't been carefully chosen.   Speaker 3 [3]

E It didn't sound right for my career.   Speaker 4 [4]

F People used to laugh at it.   Speaker 5 [5]

G It made me sound too serious.

H It wasn't individual enough.

TASK TWO

For questions 6–10, choose from the list A–H where each person got the idea for their new name.

A a friend's suggestion

B online research   Speaker 1 [6]

C a fictional character   Speaker 2 [7]

D a family joke   Speaker 3 [8]

E an overheard conversation   Speaker 4 [9]

F a magazine article   Speaker 5 [10]

G a television programme

H a colleague's mistake

2 Match each phrase from the extracts to the closest meaning.

to laugh it off (1)   to stand out in a crowd (1)   really fed up (2)
I happened to (2)   to get his tongue round (3)   to split up (3)
made redundant (4)   did the trick (4)   a snap decision (5)
to tease (5)

end a relationship   achieved its aim   be distinctive   make fun of
not take too seriously   pronounce   happened quickly   lost a job
very unhappy   by chance

3 Discuss these questions.

1 Do you like your name? Why?/Why not?
2 If you could change all or part of your name, what would you choose? Why?
3 What disadvantages might there be to changing your name?

Reading: multiple choice (Part 3)

1 Look at these two well-known sentences and answer the questions.

1 Do you know where each one comes from?
2 Do you think they are wise sayings or not?

> Sorry seems to be the hardest word.

> *Love means never having to say you're sorry.*

2 Look at the situations below.

1 In which of these situations would you apologise?
2 What would you say in each case?
3 Which situation needs the most sincere apology?
4 How would you make your apology more sincere?

- You tread on someone's toe.
- You borrow something without asking.
- You arrive late for something.
- You say something which upsets a friend.
- Someone complains about your behaviour.

3

1 Look at the title of the article on page 35. In what ways could saying sorry be powerful?

2 Read the article quickly to compare your ideas. There are six paragraphs; make a note of which one deals with:

A cultural attitudes⁻
B gender differences
C the writer's own experience

D personal relationships
E a work context
F people of different ages

4 Now read the article more carefully. Choose the answer (A, B, C or D) which you think fits best according to the article.

1 In the first paragraph, the writer is acknowledging that

A she is less arrogant than she used to be.
B she owes a debt of gratitude to her father.
C her boyfriend is more self-righteous than her.
D her apologies for past mistakes were unsuccessful.

2 The writer feels that British people nowadays

A tend to feel uncomfortable when others apologise.
B tend to say sorry much more often than they used to.
C tend to regard apologies as a sign of weakness in others.
D are becoming more sincere in their apologies.

3 In the third paragraph, Paula Hall is quoted to illustrate

A how men and women apologise to each other.
B how men's attitude to apologising has changed.
C how men and women apologise in different ways.
D how women now apologise in a more confident way.

4 Ben Renshaw feels that modern children

A may learn inappropriate behaviour from their parents.
B should not be made to apologise to their parents.
C have to learn that their parents make mistakes.
D need help to interpret their parents' apologies.

5 Beverley Engel feels that office workers tend to

A ignore minor disagreements in the workplace.
B find it hard to complain about their colleagues.
C blame their employers for interpersonal difficulties.
D allow small arguments to grow into major problems.

6 Which phrase used earlier in the fifth paragraph introduces the idea of 'sulking' (line 91).

A too insecure to admit when they are wrong (line 79)
B minor office feuds (line 82)
C wars of anger and silence (line 84)
D to get back at him or her (line 88)

7 Why does the writer mention the film *Love Story*?

A It misled her about something.
B It led her to question something.
C It taught her the value of something.
D It helped her to understand something.

The power of saying sorry

Saying sorry is not something that comes easily to many people. I know I couldn't for a very long time. I was too self-righteous and arrogant to be able to apologise. I learned how to behave like this from my father, and then I met my match – a boyfriend who made me look at my own actions. Now I've learned that not only do we all make mistakes but what a magnificent gift it is to be able to admit them, and then apologise as well.

Of course, not all apologising is powerful. The British tend to say sorry too often, as a way of pleasing other people. It's glib and without any real feeling, but it's a polite formula in certain social situations. Powerful saying sorry is about real communication – it's honest and heartfelt. Traditionally, in Britain, saying sorry has been taken to mean backing down, losing the argument or being weak – I've certainly been guilty of thinking this in the past. But there are real signs that times are changing. 'As a society we know more about psychology,' says counsellor Paula Hall. 'We are learning that saying sorry is about allowing yourself to be vulnerable, which is actually a sign of strength, not weakness. You learn from experience that saying sorry increases people's respect for you, rather than diminishing it.'

Men used to be particularly bad at saying sorry, but that is changing too. 'Men were encouraged to be committed and single-minded,' says Paula. 'But now it is seen as OK for men to change their minds, which means more of them are able to admit they were wrong and say sorry.' On the other hand, women tended to say sorry too often because they were afraid of hurting people's feelings. 'That's not the case any more either,' says Paula. 'Women are getting more confident so they are less eager to rush into the position of saying sorry when they have done nothing wrong.'

When it comes to apologising, the balance of power is also changing between parents and children too. In the past, saying sorry was a one-way street. Children said sorry and parents did not. However, a new generation of parents have re-evaluated apologising. 'We're far more willing now, as a culture, to say sorry to our children,' confirms relationship expert Ben Renshaw. 'It's a model for them. I certainly apologise to my son. For instance, when I am too angry with him over something which doesn't merit such an outburst, I say sorry. I hope that I'm preparing the terrain for him to be able to admit his mistakes more readily than I ever did.' So it is very healthy for parents to be able to admit they get it wrong and children learn that even their parents are fallible.

Yet in some situations saying sorry, as Elton John pointed out, seems to be the hardest word. Psychotherapist Beverly Engel, who conducts apology seminars for companies, believes apology is probably the most effective means of resolving business disputes. 'A large percentage of lawsuits against businesses, employees or co-workers would not be filed if a simple apology were given. Unfortunately, many people are too proud, stubborn or too insecure to admit when they are wrong,' she says. Considering how long we spend each week with co-workers, it's not surprising to find that minor office feuds arising out of trivial matters can escalate into wars of anger and silence. But, says Engel, it would be far easier if someone upsets you, 'to ask for an apology instead of complaining to other co-workers or planning to get back at him or her. By the same token, when a co-worker apologises, be big enough to accept the apology instead of sulking.'

Unfortunately, the 1970s film *Love Story* is responsible for promulgating a lie about relationships and apologies. Its famous slogan is 'Love is never having to say you're sorry'. At first I took this to mean that if you love someone, you'll never hurt them, therefore, you'll never need to use the word. But I've come to realise that's not true – the ones you love are the ones you're most likely to hurt, so this is misinformation. Love, as in enabling a loving relationship to survive, is all about being able to say sorry. In relationships, the path to a powerful apology is obvious then – when you say it you have to really mean it. That's why explaining, 'I didn't realise I'd hurt you so much when I was ...', increases the potency of your apology. So what are you waiting for? The hardest word to say is also the most rewarding.

5

1 Look at these adjectives from the article. Are they used positively or negatively?

self-righteous (line 5)	honest (line 19)
vulnerable (line 29)	arrogant (line 5)
heartfelt (line 20)	committed (line 36)
glib (line 16)	guilty (line 23)
single-minded (line 37)	trivial (line 83)
powerful (line 105)	rewarding (line 111)
proud (line 78)	stubborn (line 78)
insecure (line 79)	fallible (line 67)

2 Complete the sentences with one of the adjectives above.

1 Any problems you have, come and tell me, however .... they may seem.

2 We are .... to providing a high level of service for our clients.

3 I'm afraid I may be .... of giving you some misleading information.

4 Nobody should ever be too .... to apologise when they're in the wrong.

5 I'm afraid I found most of his comments rather .... and insincere.

6 He's a very .... man, you'll never get him to change his opinion.

6 Talk about a time when:

- you had to make an apology
- somebody made an apology to you
- an apology might have helped a situation

Grammar 2: gerunds and infinitives

1 What would you do in these situations?

A Your neighbour plays 60s rock music very loud every evening.
a) ring them up to complain
b) go round and try to work out a compromise
c) play heavy metal music even louder in the middle of the night

B A classmate tells the teacher that you copied your last assignment off the Internet.
a) tell the teacher about something that your classmate has done wrong
b) resolve never to speak to your classmate again
c) decide not to cheat again

2

1 Read the text opposite and decide which statement best sums up the main point.

People who take revenge on others are
a) acting naturally.
b) behaving badly.
c) rarely justified.

2 Read the text again and complete it using the gerund or infinitive form of the verbs in brackets (in one case it could be either).

3 Find a verb in the text which has the pattern verb + object + infinitive. Which of the other numbered verbs could be followed by an object in this way?

> **TIP!** Note down verbs that are followed by the gerund or infinitive in your grammar checklist, together with examples.

3

1 Sometimes a verb may be followed by either the gerund or the infinitive, but the meaning changes. The meaning may also change when the tense changes.

   Look at the pairs of sentences and answer the questions.

1 a) John remembered to tell her about the change of arrangement.
   b) Peter remembered telling her about the change of arrangement.

REVENGE IS SWEET

Why do some people take revenge on others? Why aren't we (1) able .... (*sort*) out our problems without (2) seeking .... (*get*) even with those who have hurt us?

Well, apparently we are simply experiencing a deeply rooted part of human nature. Our desire for revenge comes from the brain's limbic system, the most primitive part of the brain and one that we share with all animals. So when someone confronts us, we often (3) prefer .... (*attack*) verbally or physically rather than (4) try .... (*work out*) a solution together.

However, unlike animals, we also possess a highly evolved cerebral cortex which (5) allows us .... (*plan*) and analyse – and this can make revenge more than just an instinctive reaction. A person who feels they have been wronged may even (6) enjoy .... (*plan*) a creative and appropriate act of revenge.

When they consider they have been wronged in some way, practically anyone may (7) attempt .... (*get*) revenge, although it appears that older people are more (8) prepared .... (*forgive*) and forget than the young and (9) prefer .... (*settle*) their personal problems through negotiation rather than through confrontation.

Some people suggest that taking revenge can be seen as a positive move, allowing you to work though your negative emotions. However, it can also be dangerous, and you may (10) risk .... (*find*) yourself in a situation which rapidly gets out of hand.

- Who remembered something they had to do?
- Who simply remembered that they had done something?

2 a) Carlos tried sending an email to Alina to explain his feelings, but she didn't respond.
   b) Jose tried to send an email to explain his feelings, but the network was down.

- Who couldn't send an email?
- Who sent one, but did not get a good result?

3 a) Andrew would like to finish it.
   b) Jane would like to have finished it.

- Who can still finish it?

4 a) Jack meant to do the job on Saturday.
   b) Jon meant to have done the job by Saturday.

- Who intended to do the job at the weekend?
- Who wanted it done before the weekend?

2 One group of words connected with observation (*notice*, *see*, *observe*, *sense*, *feel*, *hear*, etc.) can be followed by either a gerund or the bare infinitive.

Look at this pair of sentences and answer the question.

a) I saw Sara reading a book during the lesson.
b) I saw Susan read a book during the lesson.

- Who finished the book?

▶ Grammar reference p.197 (15)

4 Complete the sentences in a way that is true for you. Use a verb in the gerund or infinitive form. Then compare your sentences with a partner, and explain your answers.

1 When I was young I generally wasn't allowed ...
2 On Saturday afternoons I generally like ...
3 I generally avoid ...
4 I really regret ...
5 In the future I hope ...
6 If someone wants to stop smoking, I suggest ...
7 I remember ... last week.
8 I noticed ...

Speaking: language of possibility and speculation

1 Work with a partner. Look at the three photographs below. Discuss what you think the relationship between the people in each photograph might be.

colleagues   strangers   good friends
acquaintances   siblings   family
boyfriend/girlfriend

1 How long do you think they've known each other?
2 How well do you think they get on with each other?
3 Why do you think this? Explain your reasons to your partner.

2 Listen to some students discussing their ideas. Did they have the same ideas as you?

3 Listen again and complete the sentences with expressions from the recording.

1 Well, ... the young couple are probably quite close.
2 My .... that it's a long-term relationship.
3 I .... that they know one another very well.
4 On .... they seem to be closer than that.
5 I .... if they were in a relationship outside the office.
6 I .... that she is a friend of the family.

4 Work with a partner. Look at the photographs on page 178. Take turns to compare two of the pictures, and say what you think the relationship between the people might be, and how good the relationship seems to be.

Use of English:
multiple-choice
cloze (Part 1)

1

1 What do you notice first when you meet someone for the first time?

- hair
- smile
- voice
- personality
- clothes
- something else.

2 How do you think someone can make a good impression

- on you?
- on your parents?

2

1 Read the title of the text. What do you think it will be about?

2 Read the text quickly to check.

The truth behind a smile

People smile a **(0)** ..*B*.. deal, and we seem to know instinctively that some smiles are more genuine than others. But is there any scientific **(1)** .... for this? Recent research suggests that a mechanism in the brain can help us **(2)** .... whether a smile is really heartfelt – or whether it is just being **(3)** .... on for show.

(4) .... to various long-held traditions, a genuine smile involves the eyes as well as the mouth. In the nineteenth century, a French anatomist **(5)** .... to prove this. He used electrodes to stimulate the facial muscles of volunteers, **(6)** .... creating false smiles. He found that real smiles were always **(7)** .... with the contraction of a muscle around the eye, but that his artificially induced ones were not.

During more recent research, volunteers were shown a variety of human facial **(8)** .... and their reactions to these were monitored. When they were shown a happy face, 35% of the volunteers immediately started looking at the eye area, checking for tell-tale crinkles that would **(9)** .... that the smile was genuine; but when shown a sad or neutral face, they did not. So why did the human brain evolve to **(10)** .... between real and false smiles? It could be that this ability to **(11)** .... a quick assessment of a smile has an important role to play in successful communication. A genuine smile **(12)** .... as a gesture of conciliation in conflict, and it's important to know whether we are really being offered a truce or not.

3 Now read the text again more carefully and decide which answer (A, B, C or D) best fits each gap. There is an example at the beginning (0).

0	**A** big	**B** great	**C** large	**D** huge
1	**A** sign	**B** basis	**C** root	**D** fact
2	**A** recollect	**B** accept	**C** admit	**D** recognise
3	**A** put	**B** brought	**C** created	**D** stuck
4	**A** Providing	**B** Considering	**C** Relating	**D** According
5	**A** got down	**B** set out	**C** went off	**D** carried out
6	**A** despite	**B** thereby	**C** however	**D** nonetheless
7	**A** associated	**B** mixed	**C** joined	**D** accompanied
8	**A** exhibitions	**B** resemblances	**C** appearances	**D** expressions
9	**A** assure	**B** confirm	**C** justify	**D** approve
10	**A** decide	**B** tell	**C** distinguish	**D** reckon
11	**A** make	**B** earn	**C** do	**D** hold
12	**A** aims	**B** serves	**C** portrays	**D** applies

4 Complete these sentences using the correct form of a word or expression from the text.

1 She arrived at the meeting very late, but her apology was sincere and h................. .
2 Using electrodes to stimulate the facial muscles of volunteers led to the c................. of false smiles.
3 When we genuinely smile, the muscles around our eyes c................. .
4 The e................. of the human brain enables people to differentiate between a real and a false smile.
5 Most people can a................. whether a smile is sincere or not quite quickly.
6 A genuine smile is seen as a c................. gesture during a time of conflict.
7 A smile is one of the most successful ways of c................. a friendly attitude.
8 An a................. smile can be spotted by most people easily.

5 Apart from what they say, how else can you tell when someone is:

• not reacting honestly to something?
• telling a lie?
• (un)happy about something?
• angry about something?
• unsure about something?

6 Discuss these questions.

1 Do you think that it is important to do scientific research into things such as smiling? Why?/ Why not?
2 What effect can body language have on communication? How can it cause misunderstandings?

Writing: information sheet (Part 2)

1 Are the following statements about writing an information sheet true or false?

1 You should always use full sentences.
2 You can use bullet points and headings.
3 The aim of an information sheet is to catch the reader's eye and make points clearly.
4 You should use a formal style.
5 You should plan the information sheet carefully.
6 An information sheet is the same as an article.

2

1 Read the task.

> Your school wants to help its students prepare themselves better for job interviews by helping them to become more aware of things to do or not to do to make a good first impression. The Principal has asked you to draw up an information sheet that he can display on the careers notice board which will help students. Write your **information sheet** in 220–260 words.

2 Discuss ideas that you can include in the sheet and make notes under these headings.

• Appearance
• Manner
• Behaviour
• Dos and Don'ts

3 Work with a partner. Look at the information sheet in the Writing reference on page 201. Make sure that you read and understand all the Dos and Don'ts. Plan your information sheet and discuss these questions.

1 What title will you give your information sheet?
2 How many sections will you have and what headings will you use for each one?
3 Will you use a formal or informal style?
4 What is the purpose of the information sheet?

4

1 Look at the information sheet below, which was written in answer to the task, and compare your own ideas. Then discuss these questions.

1 What is wrong with the general heading? Choose a better one from the options below.
   a) The art of making a good impression
   b) Useful interview techniques
   c) Behaving better in formal situations
2 Is the introduction helpful? Why?/Why not?
3 Are the different paragraphs clear and complete? Does each paragraph have its own heading?
4 Does the information sheet *inform* and *advise* readers in a clear and useful way? What technique does it use to do this?
5 Why can bullet points be useful? In the exam, what must you be careful about if you use bullet points?

2 The writer has made eight spelling mistakes. Find the mistakes and correct them.

3 The writer has also made one mistake with modal verbs and one mistake with gerunds and infinitives. Find the mistakes and correct them.

5

1 Use the ideas that you discussed in Exercise 2.2 and write your own answer to the task. Use the questions you discussed in Exercise 4.1 to help you.

2 Exchange your answer with another student. Check each other's information sheets and make comments on layout and style. Remember to also look for spelling and grammar mistakes.

▶ Writing reference p.201

Information about job interviews

People say 'you only get one chance to make a good first impression'. Wat can you do to improve your chances of achieving this?

Appearance

Dress smartly but don't go over the top. If you are overdressed, you creat an impression of formality, but you couldn't dress down too much because you give the impression that you couldn't care less. However – a word of warning. Always be yourself – if you wear clothes that are unfamiliar, you will feel uncomforetable and will not project the right image of yourself. Be natural.

Manner

When you are meeting someone for the first time, try to acheive a balance between friendlyness and formality. Listen politely, don't interrupt, but give full answers when necessary. Never be monosylabic. Remember you want conveying an impression of quiet confidence, not shyness or nervousness.

Behaviour

Smile! A genuine smile establishes a relationship, says that you are happy to be there. What people often remember of others is their smile.

Dos and Don'ts

Don't
• talk too much or too quickly. This gives the impression that you are nervous.
• forget that you can ask questions too. It is good to give the impression that you are interested in other people.

Do
• maintan eye contact. There is nothing worse than talking to someone who won't look you in the eye.
• relax.

If you follow this advise, you will make a fabulous first impression.

1 Read the text below. Use the words given in capitals at the end of some of the lines to form a word that fits in the gap in the same line. There is an example at the beginning (0).

Control your anger

When a celebrity, a (0) _politician_ or other person in the media	POLITICS
spotlight loses their temper in public, they run the risk of	
hitting the headlines in a most (1) .... way. For such	EMBARRASS
(2) .... outbursts of anger are often triggered by	CONTROL
what seem to be trivial matters and, if they are caught on	
camera, can make the person appear slightly (3) .... But it's	RIDICULE
not only the rich and famous who are prone to fits of rage.	
According to recent surveys, ordinary people are (4)	INCREASE
tending to lose their cool in public.	
Yet anger is a potentially (5) .... emotion that uses up a	DESTROY
lot of energy and creates a high level of emotional and	
physical stress – and it stops us thinking rationally. (6)	CONSEQUENT
angry people often end up saying, and doing, things they	
later have cause to regret.	
So, how can anger be avoided? Firstly, diet and lifestyle may be	
to blame. (7) .... and irritability certainly come to the surface	TOLERANT
when someone hasn't slept properly or has skipped a meal, and	
any (8) .... of caffeine can make things worse.	TAKE
Taking regular exercise can help to ease and diffuse feelings	
of (9) ...., however, reducing the chances of an angry response.	AGGRESSIVE
But if something or someone does make you angry, it's (10)	ADVISE
not to react immediately. Once you've calmed down, things won't	
look half as bad as you first thought.	

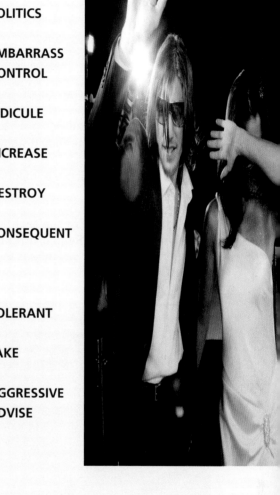

2 Choose the correct alternative in each of these sentences.

1 As we get older we *should / ought* be able to deal with our own problems!
2 You *must / could* tell the truth at all times otherwise someone will find you out.
3 I *must / have* to go now otherwise I'll be late.
4 You don't *have / should* to tell anyone about this – it *can / may* be our secret.
5 Of course you *could / can* go now – but leave quietly, please.
6 The chances are that he *will / would* be very successful when he starts his new job next week.

3 Four of these sentences have mistakes in them. Find the mistakes and correct them.

1 Our brains allow us planning our lives well, which animals can't do.
2 I always try to working out the best solution to problems by talking them over with friends.
3 I don't want to suggest that planning revenge is in any way a positive move!
4 When people take chances, they can risk to find themselves in difficult situations.
5 I intended to have finished this by Sunday, but now I'm so late there's no chance.
6 I really regret not to have studied harder when I was at school.

UNIT

4 Pushing the boundaries

Vocabulary 1

1 Discuss these questions.

1 What do you think of science? Is it interesting or boring? Why?
2 Did you study science at school? Did you enjoy it? Why?/Why not?
3 Is science a popular subject in schools?
4 Do you think everyone should study science? Why?/Why not?
5 Do you think that science is important for you personally?

2 Look at the title of the text below. What do you think it will say? Read it quickly to find out. What does the writer say makes science interesting?

3

1 Read the text and think of the word which best fits each gap. Use only one word in each gap. There is an example at the beginning (0).

2 Read the complete text again. Find short phrases that mean the same as:

1 produced unexpectedly
2 to reach an understanding of something
3 separate something into smaller parts
4 on the whole

4 Do you agree with the writer that scientific knowledge has the potential for both good and bad? Why?/Why not?

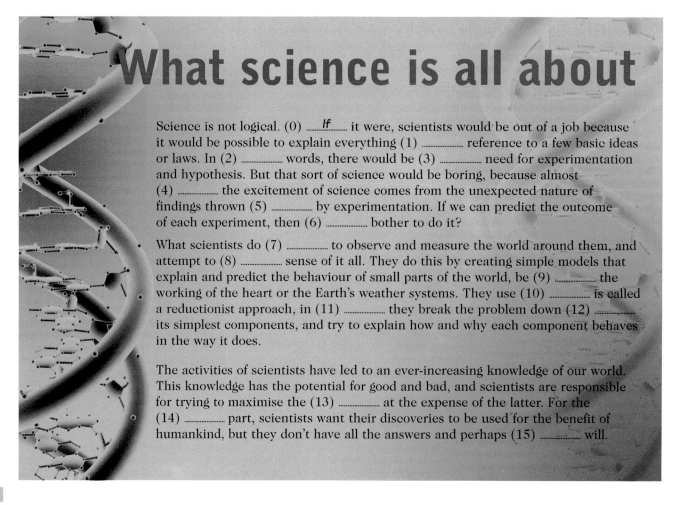

What science is all about

Science is not logical. (0) ___If___ it were, scientists would be out of a job because it would be possible to explain everything (1) .... reference to a few basic ideas or laws. In (2) .... words, there would be (3) .... need for experimentation and hypothesis. But that sort of science would be boring, because almost (4) .... the excitement of science comes from the unexpected nature of findings thrown (5) .... by experimentation. If we can predict the outcome of each experiment, then (6) .... bother to do it?

What scientists do (7) .... to observe and measure the world around them, and attempt to (8) .... sense of it all. They do this by creating simple models that explain and predict the behaviour of small parts of the world, be (9) .... the working of the heart or the Earth's weather systems. They use (10) .... is called a reductionist approach, in (11) .... they break the problem down (12) .... its simplest components, and try to explain how and why each component behaves in the way it does.

The activities of scientists have led to an ever-increasing knowledge of our world. This knowledge has the potential for good and bad, and scientists are responsible for trying to maximise the (13) .... at the expense of the latter. For the (14) .... part, scientists want their discoveries to be used for the benefit of humankind, but they don't have all the answers and perhaps (15) .... will.

42

Speaking: Parts 3 and 4

1 In Part 3 of the Speaking test you will be given a problem-solving task to do with your partner. After you have completed the task you will be asked some general questions on the same topic.

1 Look at the pictures and listen to the interlocutor's instructions. What two things do the students have to do?

2 Listen to two students talking about two of the pictures. What mistake are they making with the task? What should they be doing?

3 Look at the following phrases. How and when do we use them? Match them to the functions below.

> So what you mean by that is …
> What I mean is …
> I feel that …
> So you're saying that …
> I'm trying to say that …
> How do you feel about …?
> It seems to me that …
> Do you feel the same as …?
> What do you think about …?

a) clarifying what someone has said
b) asking for an opinion
c) explaining your point of view

4 Listen to two different students talking about the other two pictures. How many of the expressions above do they use? What difference does it make to their discussion compared with the students in Exercise 1.2?

5 Work with a partner and complete the task. Discuss the pictures on page 178 and try to reach a decision.

2

1 Think about how you would answer these questions.

1 Do you think we depend on science too much nowadays?
2 Was life easier or more difficult without gadgets?
3 Do you think that life is generally better now than it was for our grandparents?
4 If you were a politician, what changes would you like to introduce to the way we live nowadays?
5 What's the best age for children to start studying science in school?
6 How can we get more young people interested in following a career in science?

2 Listen to two people discussing the first question. Do they have similar ideas to you? Discuss any similarities and differences with a partner.

3 Listen again. Do they use any of the phrases from Exercise 1.3? What phrases do they use to add information?

3 Work in groups of three. Discuss all the questions in Exercise 2.1. Use phrases you have heard to clarify, explain, ask for opinions and add information.

Grammar 1: conditionals
(overview)

1

1 Complete sentence b) in each pair so that it has a similar meaning to sentence a).

1 a) You won't pass your science test unless you do some serious revision.
   b) If you .... some serious revision, ... fail your science test.

2 a) We didn't know then what Oliver would do with the chemistry set, but later on we wished we'd never given it to him.
   b) If we .... what he would do with it, we'd never have given Oliver the chemistry set.

3 a) I don't have access to the Internet, so I don't use my computer very much.
   b) I .... my computer more if I .... access to the Internet.

4 a) Every time you press this button, extra milk is automatically added to your coffee.
   b) The machine .... to your coffee when you ....

5 a) I want everyone who comes from London to stand up.
   b) If .... from London, ...

6 a) Don't touch this light switch because it is very unstable and might give you an electric shock.
   b) If .... this light switch, it .... give you an electric shock.

2 Complete these rules about conditional sentences.

1 To give additional meaning such as possibility and ability we use a modal verb such as ...., ... and .... instead of .... or ....

2 To express a general truth, we use *if/when* + present simple + ...

3 To talk about something that is contrary to a fact in the past we use ....

4 To talk about something that is unlikely or contrary to present facts we use ....

5 We can use the imperative form in the .... part of the conditional structure when we want to tell someone to do something.

6 To talk about something that is possible we use ....

▶ **Grammar reference p.194 (3.1)**

2

Each of these sentences has a mistake with the conditional form. Find and correct the mistakes.

1 If you really want to keep up with scientific developments, you would have to read more!

2 If there were more information about science on television, there's a chance that young people should get interested in it.

3 There is a great offer on sci-fi books on the Internet – if you buy two, you got one free.

4 I would have done better at science when I was at school if I worked harder.

5 If I promised to take care of it, will you lend me your video mp3 player?

6 I wouldn't take that job unless I were you!

7 If he went to the party, he might have seen her there.

8 If you had taken up her offer of a lift, you might got home sooner.

3

1 Here are some areas of life in which major changes could happen in the near future. Discuss possible changes with a partner. Then make a sentence for each one beginning *If …* and describing a probable consequence.

Example: *If cosmetic surgery becomes cheaper, more people will want to have it.*

cosmetic surgery: cheaper? more generally accepted?
television broadcasting: on mobile phones? on computers? more advertising?
medicine: transplants? genetic engineering?

2 Here are some areas in which major changes are possible, but may be unlikely. Discuss possible changes in each of these areas with a partner. Then say what changes you think could happen and what the results would be.

forms of transport   ways of keeping in touch
ways of saving information

Example: *If cars were banned from city centres, there would be less pollution.*

3 Think how your life would have been different if these things had not been invented.

mobile phones   cars   computer games

Example: *If mobile phones hadn't been invented, I wouldn't have been able to call my friends so easily.*

4 Work in a group. First complete the sentences in a way that is true for you, then compare your answers with others in the group.

1 If I have some free time tonight, I …
2 If I become completely fluent in any other language, I …
3 If I won a lot of money, I …
4 If I could live anywhere in the world, I …
5 When I was younger, if I had known …

Exam focus

Paper 4 Listening: multiple choice (Part 1)

About the exam: In Paper 4, Part 1, you listen to three short extracts of about one-minute each. As you listen, you answer two multiple-choice questions.

The three extracts are not linked in any way and you will hear a range of different speakers, contexts and topics across the three texts. You hear each extract twice before moving on to the next one. This part of the exam tests your ability to understand the gist of what people say, their opinions, feelings and attitudes and whether or not speakers are agreeing with each other.

Suggested procedure

1 Read the two questions for each extract before you listen. Use the information on the page to help you. Remember the context sentence on the page will give you information about the speakers, context and topic, and the questions themselves give you some information about what you're going to hear.
2 The first time you listen, mark the answer you think is correct for both questions, even if you're not sure.
3 The second time, listen to check your answer and to be sure that the other two options are wrong.
4 If you're not sure, then guess. You've probably understood more than you think and you don't lose marks for wrong answers.

You will hear three different extracts. For questions **1–6**, choose the answer (**A**, **B** or **C**) which fits best according to what you hear. There are two questions for each extract.

Extract One

You overhear two friends, Phil and Miranda, chatting at a science conference.

1 How does Miranda feel about her job?

  A disappointed with the salary
  B keen to start doing more practical work
  C optimistic about her chances of promotion

2 What drawback of his current teaching job does Phil mention?

  A the constraints he works under
  B the attitude of students
  C the lack of facilities

Extract Two

You hear a married couple talking on the radio about their family life.

3 The man says that the only disadvantage of having such a large family is

  A it restricts their ability to make long-term plans.
  B it's hard to respond to each child's particular needs.
  C it makes it difficult to do things on the spur of the moment.

4 The woman tells us about their holiday plans in order to stress that

  A problems can occur wherever you go.
  B children should be included in activities their parents enjoy.
  C it's better not to be overambitious in planning family activities.

Extract Three

You overhear two work colleagues talking.

5 What is the man doing?

  A apologising for something
  B blaming someone else for something
  C explaining how something happened

6 How does the woman react?

  A She admits that she's had similar experiences.
  B She advises him on a sensible course of action.
  C She reassures him that he's done the right thing.

Reading: gapped text (Part 2)

1   Are you an optimist or a pessimist? Do you think that things happen randomly, or for a reason?

2

1 Read the first paragraph of the article below. Do you think the writer is going to be positive or negative about life? Explain what you think 'Murphy's Law' is.

2 Read the whole article. Six paragraphs have been removed from the article. Choose from the paragraphs A–G the one which fits each gap (1–6). There is one extra paragraph which you do not need to use.

MURPHY'S LAW

If you were to spread some jam on a piece of bread and then accidentally drop it, Murphy's Law dictates that it would fall, annoyingly, on the side coated with jam. Or, if you were driving hastily to reach an important date, Murphy's Law dictates that your car, for the first time in years, would, of course, break down.

1

Edward Murphy was an engineer with the US Air Force. He coined the term during a project to test the tolerance of human beings to ejection from the latest jet aircraft. The project involved shooting a rocket-sled across the base, accelerating volunteer passengers to speeds in excess of 630 miles per hour, which then stopped in 1.4 seconds. For one of the experiments, sixteen sensors had to be glued to the volunteer's body. There were two ways these could be attached and, of course, each tended to get stuck on the wrong way round.

2

Moreover, the project manager kept a list of 'laws' that he deemed vital to the success of future experiments. He added the new Murphy's Law, thus making it integral to the aviation industry. Other manufacturing industries picked up on the useful new term and soon it was being quoted in newspapers and magazines and, in 1958, was included in *Webster's Dictionary.*

3

You do not, for example, make a two-pin plug symmetrical then label it 'This way up'. If it matters which way it is plugged in, you make it asymmetrical in shape. This is not to say that the law has no use away from manufacturing industries or that it is irrelevant to everyday life.

4

There is another name for such examples – 'Sod's Law'. This title is derived from the fact that if something catastrophic is likely to go wrong, it will go wrong for the poor soul who needs it least. There are countless other examples, among them: Lotto Law, in which you have been playing the same numbers since draw number one. You fancy a change, and then your original numbers are drawn. Plus, Tots' Law, which states that if you need to carry a child, he or she will want to walk. It follows that if you need a child to walk, he or she will want to be carried.

5

But despite this long pedigree, there is no scientific evidence to support Murphy's Law itself – it's all down to perception. The alarm clock that failed to go off when you needed it most has probably been ultra-reliable for many years. The fact is that you only register the occasions that cause problems and not the dozens of times your day starts smoothly.

6

But while it is possible that Edward Murphy's announcement has saved a lot of lives, the sad fact is that he was killed by his own law. One evening Murphy's car ran out of petrol. He hitch-hiked to a petrol station, correctly facing the oncoming traffic, but was struck from behind by a British tourist who was driving on the wrong side of the road.

A However, there is a scientific application in that basic premise, 'If something can go wrong, it will.' By working on this basis, scientists try to eliminate any possibility of disaster or failure, rather than trust probability.

B In reality, Murphy's Law has been around long before humans walked the planet. You can imagine a wounded dinosaur making his way home and being confronted by two different and unknown routes. One leads to home and safety, the other to an ambush – and we all know which one he would take.

C In short, if anything can go wrong it will, or, as Edward A. Murphy first said in 1949: 'If there are two or more ways to do something, and one of those can result in catastrophe, then someone will do it.' This sad truth was the basic premise of Murphy's Law.

D So, we should remember that Murphy's Law is not just a throwaway comment to explain why bread would fall jam-side down. It is an integral part of a wide spectrum of technical cultures and only by employing Murphy's Law and acting upon it can engineers be almost certain that nothing will go wrong. In some circles this principle is known as 'defensive design'.

E This is what led Edward Murphy to pronounce the 'law'. Shortly afterwards, at a press conference, the team's good safety record was put down to a firm belief in Murphy's Law and to the necessity of checking everything twice and twice again to circumvent it.

F The most popular of these is: 'If anything can go wrong, it will'. This 'folk' variant is sometimes referred to as Finagle's Law, as popularised in the science-fiction novels of Larry Niven. He depicted a frontier culture of asteroid miners who worshipped the dread-god Finagle and his mad prophet, Murphy.

G Today, Murphy's Law is generally looked upon as being less associated with precise and sensible manufacturing techniques and more to the stresses of our modern life and its new-fangled technology. Take the alarm clock – is it not the case that whenever you have something important to do the next morning, the alarm will not go off? Or escalators – can it be that the first one you find is always going the wrong way?

3 Match the words and phrases to the closest meaning. Look back at the text to see if you were right.

1 coated (para 1)
2 hastily (para 1)
3 coin a term (para 2)
4 accelerating (para 2)
5 deemed (para 3)
6 wounded (option B)
7 ambush (option B)
8 new-fangled (option G)
9 escalators (option G)

a) a trap
b) with an injury
c) increasing speed
d) moving staircases
e) name something
f) in a hurry
g) covered with
h) considered
i) confusingly modern

4 Discuss these questions.

1 Do you have a term for Murphy's Law in your language? What is it?

2 Do you believe in it, or do you think that things happen by chance and you only remember the bad ones?

Listening: sentence completion (Part 2)

1 You will hear part of a radio programme in which a science book called *The Red Canary* by Professor Tim Birkhead is being reviewed. Complete the sentences.

The Red Canary

Professor Tim Birkhead's field of study is .... **(1)**

The speaker feels that Prof. Birkhead's book falls into the category known as .... **(2)**

The speaker praises the quality of Prof. Birkhead's .... **(3)**

The book is mostly about a man called Hans Duncker, who worked as a .... **(4)** in Germany.

Hans Duncker set out to prove that he could breed a canary with red .... **(5)**

The speaker feels that the .... **(6)** of the book makes a rather exaggerated claim.

Hans Duncker's work is not what would be called .... **(7)** today.

The fact that flamingos eat .... **(8)** explains their pink colour.

2 Would you be interested in reading a book like this? Why?/Why not?

Do you think that scientists should interfere with the genetics of plants and animals?

Vocabulary 2: word formation

1 Look at the text. Can you work out which medical discovery is being described in each section? Write the name of the discovery as a heading A, B, C or D.

Medical discoveries made by chance

Not all medical mishaps have a bad end. In fact, the history of science is full of stories of how people made really important scientific (1) .... by accident.

A ....
For example, it's well known that this drug was discovered when Dr Fleming spotted some mould growing on a Petri dish. Less well known is that this was not the only fluke in the drug's discovery. Six years (2) ...., one of Fleming's own tears fell onto a bacteria sample. He found that the spot where it fell remained sterile. It was this that gave him the idea that certain compounds might show some (3) .... to bacterial (4) ....

B ....
Another medical discovery came about when carnation farmers asked why their flowers wouldn't bloom. (5) .... discovered that the gas that was being used to light the greenhouses was the reason. The gas was then found to have even more (6) .... properties when humans were exposed to it.

C ....
According to legend, this drug was discovered when a South American man with the disease (7) .... drank water from a bucket contaminated by the sap from a particular tree. His fever then (8) .... disappeared.

D ....
This vital medical (9) .... tool was discovered when a physicist was studying whether cathode rays could escape from a glass tube wrapped in paper. When they showed up on a fluorescent screen a metre away, he realised this new type of ray could even record a human skeleton on a (10) .... negative.

2

1 Read the text again. Use the word given in capitals to form a word that fits in each numbered gap.

1 BREAK	6 CREDIBLE
2 PREVIOUS	7 ACCIDENT
3 RESIST	8 MIRACLE
4 GROW	9 DIAGNOSIS
5 BOTANY	10 PHOTOGRAPH

2 Write the words from above. There is sometimes more than one word.

1 a compound noun made from a phrasal verb
   breakthrough
2 an adverb made from an adjective
3 an adjective made from a noun
4 an adverb made from a noun
5 a noun formed from a verb
6 a noun formed from another noun
7 an adjective formed from another adjective

3 Discuss these questions.

1 What do you think have been the most significant medical discoveries in history?
2 What medical discoveries do you think will be made in the future?

Grammar 2: conditionals (advanced)

1

1 Which of the options below are grammatically possible to complete each sentence? Tick all the possible options.

1 He would never have become famous
   a) had he been a typical scientist.
   b) if he had been a typical scientist.
   c) if he must have been a typical scientist.

2 Please ask the doctor for my test results
   a) if you happen to see her.
   b) if you should see her.
   c) if you see her.
   d) were you to see her.

3 a) Supposing people could live for two hundred years,
   b) Even if people could live for two hundred years,
   c) In case people could live for two hundred years,
   d) Imagine that people could live for two hundred years,
   how many would really want to?

4 a) If you were to find some of his DNA,
   b) If you had found some of his DNA,
   c) Had you found some of his DNA,
   d) Provided that you found some of his DNA,
   it's still unlikely that you could clone William Shakespeare.

5 I'll see if the doctor is free
   a) if you'll wait here.
   b) if you wait here.
   c) if you were to wait here.

6 I would be delighted for him to participate in the research
   a) unless he would agree to share the costs.
   b) were he to agree to share the costs.
   c) as long as he would agree to share the costs.

2 Look at all the conditional clauses you ticked, and highlight their structure.

Which correct sentence/option uses:

1 another linker with a similar meaning to *if*: _3a_ ,
   ....

2 *were to* (stressing that something is hypothetical) in the conditional clause: ....

3 a modal verb (suggesting that something is unlikely) in a conditional clause: ....

4 *happen to* (suggesting that something is unlikely) in a conditional clause: ....

5 an inversion in a conditional clause: .... ,
   ....

6 *will* (meaning 'are willing to') in the *if* clause:
   ....

3 One of these statements is false. Find the false statement.

a) Using an inversion is more formal than using *if*.
b) *Supposing* and *imagine* are more polite than *if*.
c) Using *if* + *was/were to* stresses that we are talking about a hypothetical event.
d) *If* + *will* is used in polite requests.

▶ Grammar reference, p.194 (3)

┌─ **Watch Out!** *in case* and *if* ◀─

In case does not have the same meaning as *If*.

In case is used to talk about precautions – something we do to prevent or avoid a problem.

Take some suncream with you *in case* you need it.

Use your suncream *if* you sunbathe.
└─

2 One word is missing in each of these sentences. Put it in the correct place.

Example:
   Were
   ⟨You to continue with your studies, I am sure you would become a competent scientist.

1 We spent more time studying, we might have been more successful.
2 If you just be patient, I'm sure the teacher will be here soon.
3 If I were say that I wanted to become a scientist, what would you say?
4 If you happen see the film before I do, please don't tell me the end!
5 Supposing I changed the date of your appointment, that be a problem?

3 Rewrite the sentences using the words in brackets.

1 I won't use wireless connection to the Internet if I'm not sure it's safe. (*unless*)
2 You wouldn't have this problem if you'd taken my advice. (*had*)
3 Imagine that someone found a cure for the common cold, they would be famous! (*were*)
4 I can't find my car keys – if you find them by chance, could you call me? (*happen*)
5 The game tonight will not be cancelled if the weather improves. (*provided that*)
6 If she works hard, she will be successful. (*as long as*)

4 Work with a partner. Look at the dilemmas below, and discuss what you think the solutions could be. Then think of another dilemma to ask other students in the class to discuss.

If you happened to think that your friend was spending too much time playing computer games, what would you do?

If you happened to see someone travelling on a bus without a ticket, what would you do?

Vocabulary 3: collocations, fixed phrases and idioms

Collocations

A collocation is a combination of words that are usually used together, e.g. *catch a cold*.

1 The verbs in the following sentences have similar meanings, but only one will collocate with the following noun. Choose the best verb to complete the sentences. Then underline the full collocation.

1 Some people can *hold / maintain / keep* their breath under water for a long time.
2 Footballers are at risk of injury, and often *bend / curl / twist* their ankle or knee.
3 Athletes can *pull / drag / haul* a muscle if they don't warm up properly before they run.
4 Scientists can *get / make / have* a good living, especially if they write books.
5 People *hack / probe / look* into computers to get personal information illegally.
6 If you use the Internet a lot, you should always *note / bookmark / book* your favourite web pages.
7 It's important to *prioritise / rank / order* your work so that you can make the best use of your time.
8 Scientists *conduct / control / check* experiments on animals before trying new drugs on humans.

2 Choose the adverb which collocates best with the adjectives in these sentences.

1 The play was *utterly / mainly* hilarious – I couldn't stop laughing.
2 She was *bitterly / completely* disappointed with his reaction to her news.
3 The project was *hugely / greatly* successful, and changed the company's approach to sales.
4 He felt *totally / deeply* grateful for having been given the opportunity to do the job.
5 He was *absolutely / enormously* impressed by her knowledge of technology.
6 She was *completely / exactly* absorbed in her work and hated taking holidays.

> **TIP!** When you learn new vocabulary, write down all possible collocations. This will make it easier to remember and use correctly.

Fixed phrases

A fixed phrase is a combination of words that are always used together, e.g. *a matter of opinion*.

3 Match the sentences halves. The expressions in bold make fixed phrases which follow the pattern noun + *of* + noun.

1 You have every right to express your own **point**
2 Everyone has to provide **proof**
3 Everything she said was **a pack**
4 When something goes wrong in the science lab it may be an accident, **a twist**
5 Children should be encouraged to develop **a sense**

a) **of lies**, and I didn't believe a word of it.
b) **of view**, but I am entitled to disagree with it.
c) **of identity** when they set up a mobile phone contract.
d) **of curiosity**, as this will help them develop scientific skills.
e) **of fate** or just an unforeseen chemical reaction.

Idioms

An idiom is a group of words that has a different meaning from the usual meaning of the separate words, e.g. *a piece of cake* = something that is easy to do.

4 Look at what people have said. Which sentence answers the questions below? They are not in the same order.

Example:
1 – d) *Designing a website isn't rocket science.*

1 I'm sorry – I just don't think that designing a website is that difficult!
2 I've just bought a new computer and I'm hoping that my father will pay for it!
3 I hadn't heard from her for years, so her email was totally unexpected.
4 I think that the way they talk to each other is the real issue.
5 You're always taking a risk with advertising – it's impossible to be precise with your predictions of profit.

a) What's at the root of the problem?
b) What came out of the blue?
c) Who will have to foot the bill?
d) What isn't rocket science?
e) What isn't an exact science?

Exam focus

Paper 3 Use of English: gapped sentences (Part 4)

About the exam: In Paper 3, Part 4, you are given six sets of three separate sentences, each one with a gap. For each set you have to find one word which can fill all three gaps; the word will always be in the same form and will always be used as the same part of speech.

This task tests your knowledge of vocabulary. Different words will fit in the gaps in the sentences, but only one word will fit in all three. So it is not possible to base your answer on only one sentence, or even on two of them.

The best way to prepare for this exam task is to record vocabulary in phrases rather than single words, and to check all possible meanings and collocations of words in a dictionary such as the *Longman Exams Dictionary*.

Suggested procedure

1 Read through the three sentences. If you think of a possible word to fill the gaps, do not write anything until you have read all the sentences and you are sure that the word fits all three contexts.
2 If you cannot immediately think of a suitable word, check what part of speech is required, e.g. noun, verb or adjective. You will probably already know the main meaning of the word, but you may not recognise it immediately in these contexts. Look carefully at the other words in the sentence and see if they suggest any collocations or grammatical patterns (e.g. look at prepositions).
3 If you still can't think of a possible word, leave the question and go back to it later.
4 Check the dictionary definition of the word you have chosen. Does it fit all three uses?

For questions **1–5**, think of **one** word only which can be used appropriately in all three sentences. Here is an example (0).

Example:

0 The aim of this task is to ..*test*.. your knowledge of vocabulary.

The drug company has decided not to ..*test*.. its products on animals in future.

In order to ..*test*.. out his new theory, the scientist has taken over the university laboratory.

1 In the .... term, there is very little chance of funding for further research into the matter.

There will be a .... break after the next lecture to give students the chance to grab a coffee.

After climbing to the top of the stairs, the elderly professor was rather .... of breath.

2 The scientist's proposal to do further research into his subject has been .... by the finance committee.

When there was a total eclipse, the moon completely .... out the light of the sun.

The road to the airport has been completely .... by an overturned lorry.

3 If the college buys its computer equipment in bulk, it may get a special .... from the supplier.

There has been a great .... of money invested in research into global warming in recent years.

Some people complain about having to walk home in the dark, but for me it's no big ....

4 As the weather deteriorated, it became obvious that we would have to .... back and find a hotel in the town we'd just passed through.

When you see the hotel on your left, you need to .... right immediately afterwards.

If you .... the piece of paper over, you'll see my address on the back.

5 Terry's in the .... of applying for a new job with a pharmaceutical company.

Scientists are developing a new .... that will allow minerals to be extracted from waste.

You must check the temperature at each stage in the cheese-making ....

Writing: article (Part 2)

1 In Paper 2, Part 2, you may be asked to write an article. This can be on a range of topics for different types of reader, but there are some features that are true of any article.

1 Look back at the article on page 46. Which of the following statements about articles is not true?

An article:

- should have an interesting title
- should have an engaging opening paragraph to catch the reader's interest, which can include (or begin with) a question to involve the reader
- should have bullet points and headings
- can be in a formal, informal or neutral style depending on the target reader
- should finish with a statement or conclusion which sums up and gives the writer's opinion
- can talk to the reader directly, using 'I'.

2 What other ways can you think of to make an article interesting for readers? Choose the most important from the list.

- include structures to provide emphasis
- provide specific examples to illustrate points, not just general statements
- use direct speech where appropriate
- use paragraphs
- use a range of interesting vocabulary and a variety of structures

2

1 Look at the writing task below and answer the questions.

1 How many things do you have to do? Underline them.
2 Who will read your article?
3 What style would be best for the target reader?

An international magazine for young people has asked readers to send in articles on the topic of 'Computer games – a complete waste of time and money'. Write an article supporting or disagreeing with the statement, and give your reasons.

Write your **article** in 220–260 words.

2 Look at the two introductory paragraphs. Which one is

1 more formal?
2 more suitable as the introduction to an article for a student magazine? Why?

A

Some people say that computer games are a waste of time and money, but others hold the opposite point of view. There are clearly factors that can be cited on both sides, and they need to be balanced in order to assess the true position.

B

Do you love computer games or hate them? Whatever your point of view, you are not alone! Such games tend to bring about extreme reactions in people, and there is little middle ground. Why is this? Let's find out.

3

1 Decide whether you agree with the statement in the task, and write down three main points that you want to make.

2 Starting with the introductory paragraph you chose in Exercise 2.2, write three new paragraphs, one for each point you want to make. Remember to support each point with extra details, and to link your paragraphs together.

3 Write your conclusion. It can be a whole paragraph, or just one or two lines. Remember to return to the topic, and to summarise your own opinion.

4 Use your grammar checklist to make sure you have not made mistakes, then exchange your article with a partner. Does your partner find your article interesting? Do they have any suggestions for making it more interesting?

▶ Writing reference p.208

1 Read the text below and think of the word which best fits each gap. Use only one word in each gap. There is an example at the beginning (0).

How you can help science

Granny finds evidence of alien life using the PC her daughter bought her so (0) __that__ they could keep (1) .... touch via emails. An accountant discovers a cure for cancer while taking a break (2) .... processing tax returns on his laptop. A teenager spots a comet heading (3) .... Earth and warns government scientists about it. Do you think these stories are true or false?

Although they sound (4) .... the unlikely plots of Hollywood blockbusters, they could all become real-life stories thanks to a quiet revolution that may change (5) .... face of science.

An American computer scientist realised that most PCs spend a lot of time doing nothing except displaying screensavers, and decided to put the technological power of these idle PCs (6) .... use. He set up the SETI@home project, in (7) .... PC owners agreed to allow their idle computers to scour radio astronomy data for signs (8) .... life on other planets. (9) .... expertise was required on the (10) .... of the PC owner, and millions have signed (11) .... worldwide. Suddenly the idea of someone's grandmother becoming the first to find Extra Terrestrials doesn't look quite (12) .... silly.

(13) .... a result there is now growing public involvement in genuine, living science. For years, the word 'amateur' has been shorthand for 'sloppy' and 'muddle-headed', but the word comes from Latin where it means 'one who loves something'. Maybe science is not (14) .... for professionals after (15) ...., and we should all learn to love it.

2 Read the text again. Answer the questions.

1 Where do you think the text was written?
   a) in a trendy magazine for teenagers
   b) in a serious scientific journal
   c) in a popular science magazine for general interest

2 Who do you think are the target readers?
   a) scientists
   b) anyone
   c) teachers

3 What style is the text written in?
   a) mostly formal
   b) mostly informal

3 Find words or phrases in the text that mean the same as the words in italics in the following sentences. Which words are more formal?

1 She wanted to *maintain contact* with her. (para 1)
2 He was *relaxing*. (para 1)
3 A teenager *observes* a comet. (para 1)
4 He *established* the project. (para 3)
5 Millions of people have *registered*. (para 3)
6 *More people are taking part*. (para 4)

4

1 Find these words in the text. What part of speech are they? What are the other forms of the same word?

technological   warn   revolution
expertise   evidence   genuine

2 Complete the sentences using the correct form of a word from the box above.

1 A teenager emailed a .... to the government about the dangers of an approaching comet.
2 I'm not very good with using .... manuals, I'm afraid gadgets unnerve me!
3 He's a real .... on astronomy – there's nothing he doesn't know about the stars.
4 When the mouse mat was first introduced, it was regarded as a .... new idea.
5 I was .... surprised by the success of the project.

UNIT
5 Thrills and skills

Listening 1: multiple matching  2
(Part 4)

1

1 Answer the questions.

1 How would you describe yourself?

a very fit

b averagely fit

c unfit

2 When was the last time you:

a played tennis?

b went swimming?

c ran a kilometre?

d took part in a team sport?

this week   last week   last year   never

3 How do you feel about sport?

a I like watching sport but not playing it.

b I like watching and playing sport.

c I hate sport because …

2 Compare your answers with a partner and the rest of the class. Is sport generally popular? Why?/Why not?

1 How do you think the world of sport has changed since your parents were young? Listen to five people talking. Match each speaker (1–5) to one of the topics (A–F). There is one topic you do not need to use.

A reasons for taking part in sport	Speaker 1	1
B the sporting facilities available	Speaker 2	2
C innovations in sport	Speaker 3	3
D attitudes towards health and fitness	Speaker 4	4
E the cost of buying sports equipment	Speaker 5	5
F the income and status of sports stars		

2 Do you agree with what these people say? Would you add anything? How do you think these things might change in the future?

3

1 Now listen to two people talking about sport. Using points A–F above as headings, make short notes about their ideas, and compare them with yours.

2 Listen again. What unusual sports do the speakers mention?

4

1 Work with a partner. Imagine that you are developing a new sport, and are going to combine two different sports in the way that Boxercise or Bouncy Boxing do. Choose from the sports below, and think about:

- which two sports you want to combine
- how you would play your new sport
- why people would enjoy it
- what you would call it.

tennis   hockey   horse-riding   basketball   cycling
trampolining   baseball   any other

2 Tell other students about your new sport. Make sure you give reasons why people would enjoy it. Then vote for the new sport the class would most like to try.

Grammar 1: intensifiers/modifiers

1

1   Look at these two sentences from the listening. Underline the modifier and the adjective in each sentence. Can you think of any other intensifiers you could use with each adjective?

a)   To be perfectly honest
b)   Professional sport is very conservative at heart

2   Read the text below. Decide if you can use one or both of the alternatives in each case.

EXTREME SPORT

Alex Thompson is a bobsleigh rider. Why does she do it? Because she is addicted to speed. This becomes (1) *hugely / absolutely* clear when she describes what a bobsleigh run is like. 'The start of a slide run is often (2) *fairly / completely* gentle, but then the track falls away and it's (3) *very / really* steep. That's when the speed picks up, and some (4) *really / absolutely* amazing thrills kick in.' How long does it take? The answer she gives is (5) *quite / utterly* mind-blowing – about 49 seconds. The average speed she reaches is 120kph, and the only thing separating Alex's body from the ice is essentially a flat piece of metal on skates. Lying head-first, her visibility is (6) *extremely / totally* limited and she can see only about one metre ahead. When she's travelling at speed the time she has to make decisions is (7) *very / utterly* short. When it goes well, the whole experience can be (8) *absolutely / totally* overwhelming. Asked whether she feels upset that her sport is less well funded than others, Alex is (9) *slightly / completely* honest: 'I'd like more money – of course I would. But I'd do it anyway – it's (10) *extremely / terribly* important to me, and I just can't imagine how boring life would be without it.'

2

1   Decide which of these adjectives from the text are gradable, e.g. *interesting*, and which are ungradable, e.g. *impossible*. Write G (gradable) or U (ungradable) next to each one.

1   clear   6   limited
2   gentle   7   short
3   steep   8   overwhelming
4   amazing   9   honest
5   mind-blowing   10   important

2   Look at the following modifiers/intensifiers. Using the text to help you, decide which you can use with gradable adjectives and which you can use with ungradable adjectives. Write G or U next to each one.

very	terribly	absolutely	really	rather
completely	extremely	totally	fairly	

3   Which modifier from the box above can be used with both gradable and ungradable adjectives?

3   There are four mistakes with modifiers in the sentences below. Find the mistakes and correct them.

1   I found the whole situation absolutely embarrassing.
2   I felt very resentful about having to work at the weekend.
3   Everyone in the team was quite confident about winning the game.
4   She felt utterly nervous before going on stage.
5   I was completely disgusted by his bad behaviour.
6   It should be very clear that the situation is totally difficult.
7   His suggestion is absolutely ridiculous!
8   I find the plan rather acceptable.

▶ Grammar reference p.195 (8)

4   Tell another student about the last time that you felt:

•   really hot
•   quite satisfied with something you'd done
•   totally amazed
•   extremely happy
•   rather annoyed
•   absolutely exhausted
•   fairly surprised.

Exam focus

Paper 1 Reading: multiple matching (Part 4)

About the exam: Paper 1, Part 4 is a multiple-matching task. The text is on one topic, but may be divided into different sections. You have to match 15 questions to a particular piece of text.

Suggested procedure

1 Read the instructions carefully.
2 Read all the questions, highlighting key words and phrases.
3 Read the whole text quickly to get an idea of the content of each section.
4 Look at each question in turn. Find and highlight the pieces of text which talk about these ideas (there will probably be more than one).
5 Read the sections of text carefully to decide which is the best match.
6 If you're not sure of an answer, move on to the next question – this will save time. Go back to those you're not sure about at the end.
7 At the end make sure that you've answered all the questions, and that you've used all the possible keys (A–D). If you're still unsure of some answers, then guess. Remember, there are no penalties for wrong answers in the exam and your instinct may be right!

1 You are going to read an article containing information about four different sportsmen. For questions 1–15, choose from the sections (A–D). The sections may be chosen more than once.

Which sportsman ...

admits to enjoying the competitive aspects of his sport? `1`

gets pleasure from doing something that wouldn't normally be allowed? `2`

feels that some people watch the sport in the hope of seeing accidents? `3`

suggests that people may have a wrong impression of his lifestyle? `4`

has the occasional mishap when taking part in his sport? `5`

has recently cut back on his expenditure in the sport? `6`

has recently fulfilled a long-held ambition? `7`

helps other people when they're having difficulties? `8`

is modest about the level of success he's attained? `9`

is looking for the right combination of factors to increase his speed? `10`

remembers the moment when he decided to have a go at the sport? `11`

mentions the unpredictable conditions affecting his performance? `12`

says that he achieves greater speeds than participants in similar sports? `13`

spends his free time on the upkeep of his equipment? `14`

lacks the financial resources to take part at the level he aspires to? `15`

2

1 Compare your answers with another student.
- Did you look at the same pieces of text for each answer?
- Did you make the same final choice?

2 **Double-check any questions to which you have different answers.**

3 Look at these words and expressions from the text. Match them to the word which is closest to the meaning in context.

1 to get told off (A)	a) to be excited by
2 to topple (B)	b) to feel busy
3 to get in the way (B)	c) to fall
4 to whizz about (B)	d) to make small adjustments
5 to tweak (C)	e) to tolerate
6 to put up with (C)	f) to complete a race
7 to get a buzz from (D)	g) to obstruct
8 to cross the finishing line (D)	h) to move quickly
9 to be hectic (D)	i) to be reprimanded

4 Discuss these questions.

1 Which, if any, of these sports would you try? Why?/Why not?
2 Why are people attracted to activities like these?
3 Are there any disadvantages to people doing sports like these? For participants? For others?
4 Should these sports be allowed?

Thrills and skills

Our reporter Jo Malone talked to four men of speed

A ROGER: Formula Four catamaran speedboat driver

Like our other speed lovers, Roger's middle name could actually be adrenalin. The record for his class of boat is 165kph and they normally race at around the 152kph mark. Roger's raced all sorts of powerboats since falling in love with the sport in 1993 and is involved with everything from racing himself to manning the rescue and recovery boat at his club. He would love to race the Formula One powerboats which hit speeds of about 240kph, but can't afford this at present. As in the world of motor-racing, as you move down the ratings from four to one, so the cost of taking part rises astronomically. Roger races all over Europe, enjoying the thrill of the race as well as the chance to go incredibly fast. 'Where else in the world can you drive a boat as fast as you like and not get told off for it? It is an incredible feeling to drive fast on water. 110kph feels like travelling at 320kph. Every inch of water is different, there's the wind, and the waves from the bank and from other craft. It's never the same,' he says. Quite the action man, Roger's other interests have included navigating in a rally car, canoeing and sailing: 'I've sailed for 30 years and all I've done is raced.'

B STEVE: Parakiter

Steve's sport may be one of the slower fast-man activities, but it gets his heart pumping. He rides a wind-powered kite buggy, also known as a parakite, at about 56kph. In his three-wheeled machine, Steve sits virtually on the ground and yes, he does topple out sometimes. 'We're only a couple of inches off the ground and it feels very quick indeed,' says 29-year-old Steve. The record is just over 95kph and Steve has so far touched 72kph, and is hoping to find the wind and surface conditions that will allow him to go even quicker. 'The stronger the wind the smaller the kite we use,' he says. Steve recalls the day he spotted the enormous kites and buggies and decided it was a sport he had to try. 'I've never looked back since. I like the adrenalin of it and the feeling of control.' says Steve. 'It feels so fast. Wind's an amazing thing,' he says. He and his fellow parakiters need large areas of flat hard ground such as a beach or a park with mown grass where there aren't too many goalposts to get in the way. He says the parakiters are quicker than the kitesurfers, who use similar kites but whizz about on surfboards on the waves: 'I couldn't afford that, and we are going faster.'

C JAMIE: Motorbike speedster

Jamie loves the sheer thrill of going extremely fast, extremely close to the ground, on his motorbike. He recently left the powerful Superbike class of monster 1000cc bikes for the cheaper-to-run, but just as much fun, super mono motorbike class. That's four stroke single cylinder 720cc bikes which easily reach speeds of about 225kph on the track. He rides for a racing team and competes virtually every other weekend in the racing season from April to September, practising or tweaking his bikes several nights a week. 'It's just the thrill. It's something that I've been into that gives me the excitement I like,' he says. His wife Amanda goes to watch and generally puts up with masses of motorbike talk. One of the fastest riders on the circuit, Jamie doesn't ride a road motorbike. 'I'm not interested. I want to go fast and race,' he says. He admits that some spectators are partly watching to see the crashes. 'No-one wants to see anyone hurt, but it is quite spectacular when they fall off,' he says.

D RALPH: Formula One racing driver

Racing driver Ralph adores burning rubber at 320kph on the Formula One racetrack. 'I started when I was ten years old. It was my birthday and I had a day's go-karting as a surprise treat. I did that for six years and achieved quite a bit of success.' This is an understatement as he won virtually every race around. By the time he was fourteen, karting had become more than a hobby, and he was travelling all over Europe to compete. 'I wanted to go for Formula One from that first day I started racing, so getting the chance this year is like a dream come true. The first time you drive the car it's amazingly quick, but after that you get used to the speed and don't notice it. What I get a real buzz from is going round in a good time or crossing the finishing line ahead of my opponents. People think motor racing's a very glamorous situation with lots of things going on, but the races are very busy with the team and the media, so you don't get to see so much of whatever else is going on. Maybe at the end of the year, I'll be able to sit back and reflect a bit, but for now it's pretty hectic.'

Vocabulary 1: word formation
(prefixes)

1   Look at the prefixes in the box. Although they do not mean anything by themselves, they are used to make words negative or opposite.

Work with a partner and write down two adjectives for each one using the prefix. They may be negatives or opposites. You can use a dictionary if you need to.

un-   dis-   im -   il-   ir-

2   Work with a partner. Take turns to read one of the following statements so that your partner can contradict it using a word with a prefix from Exercise 1. Remember to stress the prefix.

Example:
A: *I think the new stadium has very comfortable seats.*
B: *Oh, really – I think the seats in the new stadium are very <u>un</u>comfortable.*

1   That information is completely relevant to this discussion.
2   When I read it, I thought the ideas in his proposal for a new sports club were totally logical.
3   The young footballer interviewed on television last night seemed very mature for his age.
4   Children nowadays seem to be more obedient than in the past.
5   I found that last statement quite believable.

3

1   Some prefixes have a dictionary definition. Look at the prefixes in bold in each of these sentences. Match them to their meanings below.

1   You'll have to **re**run the race, as the result wasn't clear. *b)*
2   The English team were completely **out**played by the Australians.
3   I completely **mis**heard the trainer's instructions, and ran ten miles instead of ten kilometres.
4   He **over**ate and put on so much weight that he was dropped from the team.
5   I am very **anti**social when I'm training for a competition – I never go out with friends because I always have early nights.

6   I've read Lance Armstrong's **auto**biography six times – I think it's really inspiring.
7   The player was not feeling well, and **under**performed in the final.
8   There was a kind of **post**mortem after the team lost the game, to try to find out what went wrong.
9   Do you use a **mono**lingual dictionary in class?
10   I find it easier to use a **bi**lingual dictionary when I'm travelling – it's quicker!

a)   less of an action or quality than is correct, needed or desired
b)   again
c)   opposite
d)   after
e)   badly/wrongly
f)   two/double
g)   too much
h)   being or becoming bigger, further, greater, etc.
i)   one/single
j)   of or by yourself

2   How does knowing the meaning of the prefix help you understand the word?

4   Decide which prefix(es) from Exercise 3 can be used with each of the words below. Then write a sentence using each one to bring out its meaning.

graduate (n)   instate (v)   clockwise (adj)
understand (v)   statement (n)   active (adj)

Use of English: word formation
(Part 3)

1

1   Look at the title of the text on page 59. What do you think 'counterfactual thinking' might involve?

a)   seeing things in an unnecessarily negative way
b)   not setting yourself high enough goals in life
c)   convincing yourself that false things are true

2   Read the text quickly to see if you were right. Do you believe that people really think in this way? Why?/Why not?

2 Read the text again. Use the words given in capitals below the text to form a word that fits in the numbered gap. There is an example at the beginning (0). Remember to look out for negative prefixes.

Counterfactual thinking

Sometimes the way we view life seems to be determined not by what really happens to us, so much as by our (0) _perception_ of what happens. This is sometimes called counterfactual thinking. Let's look at the example of sport. For those who come second in a race, their (1) .... to winning creates an intense feeling of (2) ...., and they need to find an excuse for their 'failure'. Conversely, bronze (3) .... often feel lucky because they nearly didn't win anything at all. It's the same feeling you get when a traffic hold-up leads you to miss a flight. Missing it by an hour is much less (4) .... than missing it by just a few minutes.

Another type of counterfactual thinking occurs when we regret doing things that cause problems far more than we regret doing nothing, even though (5) .... can lead to just as many problems as (6) .... actions. Counterfactual thinking also happens when we think about the past and wish that something had or had not happened. This desire can be so (7) .... that we can even change our own memories of the past, making (8) .... to the actual facts to create new memories that suit us better. We do this, for example, when we want to avoid facing up to (9) .... truths.

If we're not careful, therefore, counterfactual thinking can lead us to (10) .... history, and so lose sight of real events altogether.

0	PERCEIVE		
1	CLOSE	6	WISE
2	SATISFY	7	POWER
3	MEDAL	8	ADJUST
4	FRUSTRATE	9	COMFORT
5	INACTIVE	10	WRITE

3 Discuss this question.

Are you a positive thinker or a counterfactual thinker? What about people you know?

Speaking: agreeing and adding information (Parts 3 and 4)

1 Read the following speaking task.

I'd like you to imagine that your town council wants to encourage local people of different ages to take part in competitive sports. These are some of the ideas that they are considering. Talk to each other about how effective these different ideas might be in encouraging people to take part in competitive sports. Then decide which two would be the most effective in encouraging people of different ages.

2

1 Listen to two people discussing one of the pictures on page 179. Make a note of:
- which picture they are discussing
- what points they make.

2 Listen again and complete the table with expressions used in the discussion.

Make an additional point	Indicate partial agreement	Agree with a point
On top of that		I take that point on board.

> **TIP!** If you keep a note of these expressions and try to use them regularly, they will sound natural and you will use them effectively.

3 Work with a partner. Discuss the rest of the pictures, and reach a decision.

4 Discuss these questions. Where appropriate, use the expressions you made a note of in Exercise 2.

1 Why do you think people enjoy taking part in competitive sports?
2 Do you think that it is a good idea for people to support a particular team? Why?/Why not?
3 What is the difference between watching sport on TV and watching it live in a stadium?
4 Do you think that major international sporting events have any real value?
5 Do you agree that business is too involved in sport?
6 Should children be encouraged to take part in competitive sport? Why?/Why not?

Grammar 2: intensifying comparative forms

1

1 Complete the text using expressions from the box.

| by far the | considerably |
| great deal | much more |

PILATES EXERCISES are named after Joseph Pilates, who was born in Germany in 1880. He was very frail as a child, but was determined to overcome his ill health and worked out a programme of rigorous exercise, using ideas from a variety of sports. Not only did his health become a (1) .... better than it had been, but he developed a body that was strong and fit. In the 1930s he set up a studio in New York where his exercises became popular with dancers and actors as well as athletes. In recent years Pilates has become (2) .... popular with the general population than it was in the past. Pilates puts (3) .... less impact on the joints than other types of exercise, and many doctors say it is (4) .... best type of exercise for older people.

2 Choose the correct alternatives in the following dialogue.

James: I was wondering whether to enrol on a Pilates class – you do it, Anne, what do you think about it?

Anne: Well, it's certainly (1) *not nearly as / no more* exhausting as something like aerobics or jogging. And I know they say 'no pain, no gain', but I'm (2) *many more / a lot more* likely to keep on with an exercise class if I'm actually enjoying it.

James: What sorts of things do you do?

Anne: Well, the basic idea's what they call 'drawing your navel up to your spine'. It's actually (3) *quite / rather* more complicated than that, but you do lots of exercises to strengthen what they call the core muscles – the abdominals, basically. They're all very slow and controlled – (4) *loads / less* slower than aerobics, for example – and they're supposed to improve your balance and your posture as well as things like muscle tone.

James: And do you think it works?

Anne: Well I've not had (5) *half as many / slightly more* problems with my back as I used to before I started the classes. And I must say I feel (6) *a bit / a bit more* fitter generally. It's not a dramatic improvement – they say that really you should combine it with aerobic exercise to get the best results. But it's certainly very popular. There were (7) *hardly any / nothing like as many* classes when I started as there are now. There seem to be (8) *more and more / fewer and fewer* opening up all the time now.

James: And is it all middle-aged people?

Anne: No, there are (9) *slightly / scarcely* more people in their thirties and forties in my class, but there are all ages really. Why don't you come along to a class and give it a go?

James: OK, maybe I will.

▶ Grammar reference p.194 (2.2)

3 Look at the expressions in the two exercises above. Choose three which are formal, and three which are informal.

2 Work with a partner. Compare:

- your feelings about exercise
- how you spend your free time
- two places you have visited on holiday
- two films you have seen recently
- the music you listen to.

Be ready to report a summary of your results to the class.

Vocabulary 2: sports idioms

1

1 Look at the expressions a–f below. They originally came from the world of sport, but are now commonly used in other situations. Match each statement to its non-sporting context 1–6.

Which of the people 1–6

a) has just made a comeback? d) has set a record?
b) has suffered a setback? e) is an also-ran?
c) has fallen at the final hurdle? f) is a team-player?

1 Maggie is the most unselfish person I've ever worked with – she's so supportive of her colleagues.

2 James can't win anything – he'll always come last whatever he does!

3 Petra has finally started dancing on stage again – it took her ages to get back to fitness after having her second baby.

4 Peter was on course to win salesman of the month award, but on the very last day a customer cancelled a big order and Simon won it instead.

5 Jane's final exam marks were the highest the college has ever awarded.

6 Erica had hoped that she could record her new album in two weeks, but she got a bad throat and was forced to postpone the session.

2 How are the expressions used in sport?

2

1 The highlighted common idioms and expressions in the following sentences come from sport. Match the sentence halves, and decide what you think the idiom means.

1 He made sure that everything was completely above board so

2 I never expected him to win because he had had so many problems, but

3 He guessed completely right and

4 I can't do anything else to help you, you must make the next move –

5 He's got such a short temper and

6 He got the information so quickly that when the time came to close the deal he

7 He took unfair advantage and started before anyone else so in fact

8 They moved the goalposts

9 They seem to have changed their minds about what they want us to do, so in fact

a) scored a bullseye with his accusation.
b) there was nothing illegal or wrong about the deal.
c) really goes off the deep end if anyone argues with him.
d) was in pole position.
e) he came first against all the odds.
f) he jumped the gun.
g) by changing the rules of the competition without warning.
h) it's a different ballgame now.
i) and so the ball is in your court now.

2 What sport or kind of sport do you think each idiom comes from?

3 Choose the best idiom to complete the dialogues.

1 A: It's so difficult to discuss anything with him because he gets angry so easily.
   B: I know – one disagreement and he *jumps the gun / goes off the deep end*.

2 A: I've done all I can and so it's up to you – *the ball is in your court / it's a different ballgame*.
   B: I know – I'll have to decide soon.

3 A: Are you sure that everything is legal?
   B: There's nothing illegal about it – it's all completely *in pole position / above board*.

4 A: She's overcome so many difficulties to win the competition.
   B: I know – I have to admire her, because she's *scored a bullseye / succeeded against all the odds*.

3 Choose two idioms from the box below and write a short dialogue for each one to bring out the meaning. Use a dictionary if necessary. Compare your dialogues with a partner.

Be a good/bad sport   Don't count me out
Go the distance   Make up ground

4

1 Tell a partner about

• something you did against all the odds
• someone who is a good sport
• someone who set a record.

2 Discuss a sportsperson who

• has had a number of setbacks in their career. How did they overcome them?
• has made a comeback. How well did they do?
• has made a lot of money out of their sport.

3 Why do you think some sportspeople are so driven to win?

Use of English: open cloze
(Part 2)

1   What do you know about the sport of gliding? Discuss these questions.

1 Who does it?
2 How much does it cost?
3 What do you think it feels like?
4 Why do you think people do it?
5 Do you think it is a competitive sport? Why?/Why not?

2

1 Read the title of the text below. What connection do you think computers could have with gliding? Read the text to find out.

a) Do people fly using computers to help them navigate?
b) Do people use computers and the Internet to see who flies furthest?
c) Do people only fly using virtual reality like computer games?

2 Now read the text to find out about the sport. Think of the word which best fits each gap. Use only one word in each gap. There is an example at the beginning (0).

3 Discuss these questions.

1 Would you like to go gliding? Why?/Why not?
2 Would you want to join a competition like OLC?
3 Do you think people's enjoyment of gliding could be enhanced or reduced by the competition?

4 What other sports do you think could be organised in a similar way to OLC?

Online gliding

It is **(0)** ......*by*...... no means unusual for teenagers to use their video-game consoles to compete over the Internet with opponents from around the world; people they have never met and **(1)** .... names they barely know. It was only a matter of time **(2)** .... the idea was transferred to other competitive activities. Indeed, the latest online competition has thousands of grown men and women using toys costing **(3)** .... to $150,000 to compete via the Internet worldwide. What's more, it involves those elegant engineless aircraft known **(4)** .... gliders.

The key to **(5)** .... is called 'Online Contest' (OLC) is a combination of global positioning-system receivers, someone to record the data and the power of the Internet. Glider flying requires the pilot to **(6)** .... advantage of thermals, air currents **(7)** .... rise up from hot spots on the land. Skilful pilots learn to identify these thermals and by moving from **(8)** .... to another, they can travel huge distances. The world record for the longest glider flight stands **(9)** .... 3,017 kilometres – which is not bad for an aircraft with **(10)** .... engine!

In OLC, glider pilots gain one point for every kilometre flown, but the competition is completely flexible, with pilots free to fly from the airfield of **(11)** .... choice, to use any glider at any time and fly in any weather conditions. It is **(12)** .... flexibility that has allowed the sport to take **(13)** .... in such a big way. Last year, competitors logged as **(14)** .... as 58,800 flights, performing 17.4 million miles of cross-country gliding **(15)** .... the process.

Listening 2: multiple choice
(Part 3)

1 Discuss these questions.

1 What do you know about the sport of indoor or wall climbing?
2 Why do you think it has become increasingly popular in recent years?
3 How do you think it is different to outdoor rock climbing?

2

1 Find words or phrases in the questions below that mean:

a) basic training
b) beginners
c) a social grouping
d) not very willing
e) support one thing at the expense of another.

2 Are there any other words in the questions that you don't know or are not sure of? Check them in your dictionary.

3 You will hear part of a radio discussion about the sport of indoor climbing. Choose the answer (A, B, C or D) which fits best according to what you hear.

1 According to Tom, young people are attracted to indoor climbing in the USA because

A they have been specifically targeted by gyms.
B there has been a growth in available facilities.
C it isn't regarded as a highly competitive activity.
D it offers a grounding in traditional climbing techniques.

2 What does Amy see as the main benefit of the game she describes?

A It gives climbers of varying abilities the chance to climb together.
B It helps climbers remember specific moves they have to make.
C It keeps more experienced climbers focused on a clear goal.
D It allows novice climbers to build up their strength.

3 Amy feels that in London, indoor climbing

A appeals to people with time on their hands.
B attracts people who dislike outdoor activities.
C is more of a social activity than a serious sport.
D is part of a wider sub-culture including other activities.

4 Tom is keen to point out that, in his experience, indoor climbing

A is just as demanding as traditional outdoor rock climbing.
B offers the thrill of outdoor climbing in a safer environment.
C lacks the element of fear present in traditional rock climbing.
D requires a higher level of concentration than outdoor climbing.

5 Amy feels that compared with other kinds of workout, indoor climbing

A focuses on one particular group of muscles.
B does not require such a regular commitment.
C represents more than solely a physical challenge.
D offers a more appropriate form of training for other sports.

6 When asked which type of climbing he prefers, Tom is

A keen to stress that he enjoys both types equally.
B careful to avoid saying which he actually favours.
C reluctant to admit that he likes outdoor climbing better.
D critical of people who feel a need to take sides on the issue.

4 Which do you think would be more enjoyable – indoor or outdoor climbing?

Which do you think will become more popular in the future? Why?

Writing: a reference (Part 2)

1 In Paper 2, Part 2, you may choose to write a reference. This will be a job reference for a friend.

Before you plan your reference, think about:

• who you are writing to
• what the job is
• what points you need to include in your reference. Imagine you are interviewing someone for the job – what would you want to know about them?

Then organise the information clearly into paragraphs, and use a semi-formal style. Finish with your recommendation.

2

1 Look at the task below.

The organiser of a sports camp for children has asked you to provide a reference for a friend of yours who has applied for a summer job as an activities supervisor at the camp. The reference should include relevant information about your friend's skills and interests and suitability for the job.

Write your **reference** in 220–260 words.

2 Think about what to put in the reference. What should you **not** include?

• how long you have known your friend
• what you and your friend have done together
• your friend's character
• reasons why you like your friend
• your friend's skills and interests
• details of previous experience your friend has
• reasons why your friend is suitable for the job
• informal or colourful language

3

1 Read the reference on page 191, which was written in answer to the task. It is too long. Cross out two sentences that contain irrelevant information.

2 Underline semi-formal expressions in the reference that mean the following:

1 polite (para 2)
2 is used to (para 2)
3 good at (para 3)

4 also (para 3)
5 previously (para 3)
6 at a really good standard (para 3)
7 so (para 3)
8 so (para 4)
9 put in (para 4)
10 I think she would be good for the job (para 5)

4 Complete the paragraph plan with the information the writer has included in each paragraph. What tenses or structures have been used in each paragraph? Add these to the plan.

present   present perfect   past   hypothesis
skills and qualifications   future plans
recommendation   her character

Paragraph 1: opening
Structures used: ....
Paragraph 2: your relationship with your friend +

....
Structures used: ..../..........................
Paragraph 3: .... + your friend's interests and suitability
Structures used: ..../.........................../

....
Paragraph 4: ..../reasons why she would be good for the job
Structures used: future/hypothesis
Paragraph 5: ....
Structures used: ....

5 Complete the following task. Remember to use semi-formal language, and to organise your reference clearly in appropriate paragraphs.

You have been asked to provide a reference for a friend who has applied for a summer job in an adventure holiday camp. The person appointed must have good social skills and enjoy sports. They must be reliable and have some knowledge of first aid.

You should include information about your friend's personal qualities, skills and relevant work experience, and give reasons why you recommend them for the job.

Write your **reference** in 220–260 words.

Use of English: multiple-choice cloze (Part 1)

1 For questions **1–12**, read the text below and decide which answer (**A**, **B**, **C** or **D**) best fits each gap. There is an example at the beginning (**0**).

Chiptunes

When the pop singer Imogen Heap was looking for (**0**) ..**A**.. bands to go on tour with her, she searched through *My Space* to find exactly what she was looking for. Two of her selected acts are part of what's (**1**) .... as the 'chiptune' scene which cannibalises old toys and computers and turns them into strange musical instruments. Imogen herself (**2**) .... use of a modified *Speak&Maths* toy on her album and gets it to (**3**) .... things like 'sexy baby' which obviously it wouldn't have done under other (**4**) ....

Much of the (**5**) .... of using these modified toys – which would (**6**) .... have been thrown away – is nostalgia. While she's ripping the back off them, rewiring their contact points and (**7**) .... sinister looking switches to make weird noises, she's not above getting sentimental about them. As she says: 'They have a (**8**) .... in our hearts and I like the idea of (**9**) .... them back to life.'

The golden age of chiptunes was the early 1990s when the sound chips of video game consoles were the only (**10**) .... available means of creating music on computers. But the scene now has devotees all over the world, and sites such as *My Space* have (**11**) .... them to share their music. As one fan says: 'There's so much sound production around now that's hi-tech, clean and polished; this music is the (**12**) .... of that.'

0	**A** support	**B** assistant	**C** partner	**D** help
1	**A** named	**B** termed	**C** called	**D** known
2	**A** finds	**B** makes	**C** seeks	**D** gets
3	**A** talk	**B** sound	**C** utter	**D** speak
4	**A** circumstances	**B** situations	**C** instances	**D** cases
5	**A** reason	**B** attraction	**C** explanation	**D** motive
6	**A** therefore	**B** otherwise	**C** nonetheless	**D** meanwhile
7	**A** putting	**B** sticking	**C** attaching	**D** joining
8	**A** place	**B** point	**C** seat	**D** zone
9	**A** giving	**B** taking	**C** bringing	**D** sending
10	**A** greatly	**B** widely	**C** largely	**D** wholly
11	**A** facilitated	**B** promoted	**C** granted	**D** enabled
12	**A** opposite	**B** alternative	**C** contrast	**D** diversity

Use of English: open cloze (Part 2)

2 For questions **13–27**, read the text below and think of the word which best fits each gap. Use only **one** word in each gap. There is an example at the beginning (**0**).

Does skiing have a future?

In recent years, the sport of skiing (**0**) ..*has*.. been having a tough time in Europe. A series of warm winters has meant skiers arriving at their destinations to find grass and daisies (**13**) .... there should have been snow. All over the continent, people have been questioning the wisdom (**14**) .... developing any more low-level ski resorts, when even World Cup races at high levels have (**15**) .... to be postponed for (**16**) .... of snow.

Environmentalists might consider this rough justice, however. Ski resorts have always been considered (**17**) .... best ecologically unfriendly. They cause forested mountainsides to be levelled and use up huge amounts of energy. (**18**) .... guaranteeing snow for skiers means more resorts at higher levels, then this will put even (**19**) .... pressure on fragile mountain ecosystems.

(**20**) .... artificial snow may be the answer to some of the ski industry's problems, this too has its drawbacks. It weighs five times as (**21**) .... as real snow, something which can't be that good for the mountain, (**22**) .... to mention the energy used up in creating the stuff; twenty million dollars worth was used in one US resort in one year alone.

So (**23**) .... can environmentally conscious skiers do? Well, first of (**24**) .... , don't even consider going to a resort without an environmental policy. You (**25**) .... to be able to find out things (**26**) .... whether each slope is given a day off to recover, and whether your accommodation is heated by a renewable source of energy, as (**27**) .... as all sorts of other details.

Copyright Guardian News & Media Ltd 2007

Use of English: word formation (Part 3)

3 For questions **28–37**, read the text below. Use the word given in capitals at the end of some of the lines to form a word that fits the gap **in the same line**. There is an example at the beginning (**0**).

An old phone never dies

The mobile phone is fast becoming the world's (**0**) ..*favourite*.. gadget, with	**FAVOUR**
nearly a billion (**28**) .... sold annually around the globe. But what	**HAND**
happens when the screen stops flashing, the battery dies, or people simply	
start laughing when you fish it out of your pocket?	
In Britain, people (**29**) .... replace their mobiles every two years, with	**TYPICAL**
25% of people (**30**) .... their equipment each year. So where do all the	**GRADE**
old phones go? According to Nokia, most get stuffed in a drawer and	
forgotten. Although about 30% are traded in or inherited by a family	
member, only 2% end up back at Nokia for recycling.	
Markus Terho, director of environmental affairs at Nokia says: 'We've	
been doing a lot of (**31**) .... research into what would convince	**CONSUME**
people to recycle their phones. The biggest obstacle seems to be	
that people have very strong (**32**) .... bonds to their mobiles, and	**EMOTION**
so are (**33**) .... to part with them.'	**WILLING**
One answer is turning your old mobile into a charitable (**34**)	**DONATE**
About 70% of mobiles sent for recycling still work, and these can be	
(**35**) .... and sold in developing countries, where they provide an	**CONDITION**
(**36**) .... alternative to new equipment. In many places in Africa,	**AFFORD**
for example, where there are few landlines, having a (**37**) .... mobile	**RELY**
phone can make a real difference to people's lives.	

Use of English: gapped sentences (Part 4)

4 For questions **38–42**, think of **one** word only which can be used appropriately in all three sentences. Here is an example **(0)**.

Example:

0 Naomi is a very approachable woman and people find her _easy_ to talk to.

My grandmother thinks that I have a very _easy_ life compared to her experience of being a teenager.

It's _easy_ to see why so many people support the local team who have done so well in recent seasons.

38 I suspect that the new tax on airline fuel is really aimed at raising revenue rather than at .... the planet!

If you buy goods online, you will be .... yourself the effort of going to the shops.

Fiona was rather extravagant and .... regularly did not come easy to her.

39 Rules about the use of kitebuggies on the beach only .... during the tourist season.

If you want to get good results at the end of the year, you need to .... yourself to your studies.

Anyone interested in the job is invited to .... before the last day in June.

40 Your keyboard needs to stand on a .... surface a comfortable distance away from the screen.

Whichever type of car you hire, with this deal you pay a .... rate of £30.00 per day.

The landscape to the south of the resort is rather .... and uninteresting compared to the hilly area to the north.

41 According to a recent ...., the number of science graduates is likely to fall in the future.

Rolf decided to turn one room in his new flat into a ...., so that he could keep his work and his family life separate.

In the 19th century, it was not unusual for wealthy people to devote themselves to a life of ....

42 It is .... to find a shop that gives a truly personal service these days.

One CD by that group is no longer available in the shops and was classed as .... in one online auction.

I have joined an organisation that is dedicated to helping preserve .... species of butterfly.

Use of English: key word transformations (Part 5)

5 For questions **43–50**, complete the second sentence so that it has a similar meaning to the first sentence, using the word given. **Do not change the word given.** You must use between **three** and **six** words including the word given. Here is an example.

Example:

0 The two friends were sitting on their own looking at a computer screen. **FRONT**

The two friends were sitting by _themselves in front of_ a computer screen.

43 The pianist performed beautifully and received a standing ovation. **GAVE**

The pianist .... and received a standing ovation.

44 The group's popularity increased thanks to word-of-mouth recommendations. **LED**

Word-of-mouth recommendations .... popularity of the group.

45 That young man is the organiser of the charity concert I told you about. **HAS**

That's the young man .... the charity concert I told you about.

46 Why are some brands more successful than others? **MAKES**

What is .... some brands more successful than others?

47 Unfortunately, I didn't have enough money to go to the theatre regularly. **ABLE**

If I'd had more money, ... to go to the theatre more regularly.

48 Damian is sure to finish the race in first place. **CROSS**

Damian is sure to be the first person to .... in the race.

49 It is quite usual for boys to begin playing football at the age of five. **MEANS**

It is by .... for boys to begin playing football at the age of five.

50 Had he spent more time at home, he wouldn't have made so many friends. **GONE**

If he .... often, he wouldn't have made so many friends.

UNIT
6 Family ties

Reading 1

1

1 What sort of things do parents and teenagers have arguments about? Work with a partner and make a list. Decide whether the points on your list are either:

a) typical everyday arguments, or
b) serious issues that need to be resolved.

2 Do you think that parents and teenagers have the same ideas about what is a serious issue and what is not? Why?/Why not?

2

1 Read the article quickly. Which of the points on your list in Exercise 1.1 are mentioned? Is the style of the article formal or informal? How do you know?

2 Now read the article more carefully. Match each statement to one of the sections of the article.

In which section are the following mentioned?

1 an argument that's unlikely to impress parents ☐
2 an unreasonable condition being imposed by parents ☐
3 an argument where neither side will give any ground ☐
4 an indication that you may be winning an argument ☐
5 a strategy for reducing parental anxiety ☐
6 countering a suggestion with logical arguments ☐
7 convincing parents of a continued need for something ☐
8 getting parents to recall their own teenage attitudes ☐
9 reaching a compromise solution in a dispute ☐
10 remaining calm when parents do not ☐

'Be home by 9.30'

A This always happens. You persuade your parents to let you go to a party, then they make you come home before most people even get there. If you try to argue, they'll say something like, 'You're lucky we're letting you go out at all.' In order to win this one you have to get inside their heads and work out why they don't want you to go in the first place. Then come up with a sensible solution. If they think staying out late is dangerous, reassure them it isn't. Tell them where the party is, who you're going with and who's going to be there, because parents like to know stuff like that. Also, tell them you'll get a cab home (yes, it's expensive, but much safer than walking or getting the bus). This is exactly the sort of thing your parents want to hear.

'As long as you live under my roof you'll live by my rules!'

B This is a classic angry parent phrase, used whenever they're losing an argument. Make them realise they're laying down the law for no reason. Don't go mental, just stay cool and say, 'If you're not going to be reasonable, I'm not going to argue with you.' That way you sound sensible and mature, and your parents don't and are much less likely to continue screaming at you. The only problem is, sometimes they are being reasonable and say annoying things like, 'If you don't do your homework, you'll get into trouble.' Then you have to try and strike a deal, like 'OK, if I get all my homework and chores done tonight, can I go to the cinema with my mates tomorrow?'

'You're not going out looking like that!'

C   Obviously girls get this more than boys, but my mum hates it when I wear ridiculously baggy jeans. Whether it's midriff-baring tops or enormous jeans, it comes down to the same thing – they worry about what people who don't know you will think. It's not that big a deal when you think about it, but it still causes big fights because neither of you wants to back down. Changing your clothes is the obvious way to avoid an argument, but you shouldn't have to. Right? No matter what you look like, you're the same person and you'll act the same way. You need to make them realise this. If you have any old photos of them when they were teenagers, dig them out. They're sure to be wearing just as unsuitable clothes as you, so they'll feel hypocritical not letting you wear them, and they'll know exactly what it feels like to be judged by their appearance.

'Why should we raise your allowance?'

D   This is tricky. You've spent all this time trying to persuade your parents you're independent, then you ask them for money. They'll probably say something like, 'If you're so independent, why don't you get a job?' or something equally annoying. You could try getting a job, but jobs are hard, boring and leave you with less time for partying. And what's the point if you can just get money off your parents? What you need to do is persuade your parents getting a job is a bad idea. Weigh up the advantages and disadvantages, so you sound like you've thought it through and know what you're talking about. If you say jobs are too hard and boring and you'd rather be out partying (even though that's true), you'll sound irresponsible and you're much less likely to get a raise. Instead, say a job would interfere with your schoolwork. You'll score major points with your parents, as it sounds like you've got your priorities right.

Listening 1

1   Listen to two extracts from a radio programme about family life. Choose the answer (A, B or C) which fits best according to what you hear.

Extract One

You hear a married couple talking about their children.

1   What surprises people about their children?

   A   They have a good influence on the behaviour of other children.

   B   They still behave well when their parents are not around.

   C   They appear unaffected by social pressures.

2   They feel that their children are

   A   sensitive to the feelings of others.

   B   unusually quiet and well-mannered.

   C   unaware that their behaviour is untypical.

Extract Two

You hear a teenager talking about her family.

3   Why does she tell the story about the babysitter?

   A   It changed the way she viewed her brothers and sisters.

   B   It provided her with an opportunity to challenge authority.

   C   It marked a turning point in her relationship with her parents.

4   She was upset that her offer was turned down because

   A   her parents gave no reason for their decision.

   B   she felt it revealed her parents' true attitude towards her.

   C   her parents accused her of giving them false information.

2

1   Work with a small group of other students. Imagine that you have been asked to draw up a set of rules for making family life run more smoothly. Think about both practical and emotional issues.

   Write down two rules for each of the following:

   parents   siblings   grandparents

2   Compare your rules with other groups. Draw up a set of four rules for each group that the class can agree on.

Grammar 1: hypothetical meaning – *wish*

1

1 There is a mistake in some of these sentences. Find the mistakes and correct them.

1 I wish my dad couldn't always be so cross with me.
2 I wish I have an older brother.
3 If only I could spend more time with my grandparents!
4 Would you rather I will call back later?
5 It's definitely time the children go to bed.
6 Don't you wish you had spent more time with your great-grandmother?
7 I wish I would stop eating chocolate!
8 Suppose nobody will come to the party – I'd be really disappointed!
9 I really wish I can play the guitar!

2 Match each of the (corrected) sentences above to one of the following rules.

a) We use *wish* + past simple to express a wish that is not true in the present. We also use it to express wishes that might come true in the future.
b) We use *wish* + *would* to talk about other people's irritating habits, not our own.
c) We use *wish* + *could* to talk about our own irritating habits.
d) *If only* is used with the same verb forms as *wish*, but can be used when your feelings are stronger.
e) *It's time* or *it's high time* is used with the past simple to talk about the present or the future.
f) *I'd rather* is used with the past simple when we say what we want to happen in the present or future.
g) *Suppose* means *what if*? We use it to describe something that may possibly happen or that may have happened.
h) We use *wish* + past perfect to refer to things we are sorry about in the past or that we regret.
i) We use *wish* + *could* to talk about an ability we would like to have.

▶ Grammar reference p.195 (7)

2

1 Work with a partner.
Student A look at the text on page 189.
Student B look at the text on page 190.
Read your text quickly and find out what the family connection is. Then choose the best alternatives to complete the text.

2 Now tell your partner what you have read about. Exchange texts and check each other's answers.

3 Complete the following sentences so that they are true for you. Tell another student your answers, and answer any questions they may have about your ideas.

1 I wish I was …
2 I wish I wasn't …
3 I wish … wouldn't …
4 I wish I could …
5 It's high time I …

4 Discuss these questions.

1 What advantages might there be in living with a grandparent?
2 Do you think it might be easier to live with someone older or someone younger than you? Why?
3 Is it better to live in a large family or a small family? Why?/Why not?

Exam focus

Paper 5 Speaking: collaborative task/ discussion (Parts 3 and 4)

About the exam: In Paper 5, Part 3, you and your partner discuss a situation or task outlined by the interlocutor. You are given some pictures to base your discussion on, and asked to reach a decision. In Part 4, you and your partner discuss questions from the interlocutor which extend the topic of Part 3.

Suggested procedure

1 Listen carefully to the instructions for Part 3. If you don't understand what you have to do, ask the interlocutor to repeat the instructions.
2 Discuss the visuals with your partner. Remember the task you have been given – it will also appear as prompts on the visuals sheet to remind you. As you have to talk for about three minutes, you should discuss each visual in turn in some detail, and don't reach a decision too quickly. You don't have to agree with your partner, but remember to take turns when you discuss and to use a range of language.
3 In Part 4, try to initiate discussion as well as answer the interlocutor's questions.

1 You will hear two students doing part of a Part 3 task.

1 Look at the pictures on page 180 and listen to the interlocutor's instructions. What two things do the students have to do?

2 Now listen to the students, Pascale and Fernando, doing part of the task. Which one:

a) initiated discussion as well as responding?
b) used the best range of vocabulary and grammar?

2

1 Work in groups of three.
Student A is the interlocutor. Turn to page 182 and read the interlocutor's instructions.
Students B and C are the candidates. Look at the pictures on page 180. Remember to keep to the time given by the interlocutor.

2 Discuss the activity. How well did the candidates perform? What did they find difficult?

3 Form new groups, change roles and do the task again.

Vocabulary 1: word + preposition(s)

1 Group these verbs according to the preposition they are usually followed by.

refer   congratulate   pay   apologise   result
concentrate   boast   benefit   coincide
refrain   suffer   specialise   insist   confide
confess   react   apply   compare   contrast
worry   learn

2

1 Read the text. According to Brian Firstall, whose influence is the strongest?

2 Read the text again and complete the gaps with the missing preposition.

3 Who has the greatest influence on you, friends or family? Whose influence lasts the longest?

CHILDHOOD INFLUENCES

It's often claimed that the kind of childhood we have, and what our backgrounds are, both play an important role (1) .... how successful our future relationships are. But is this so? Isn't it up to us as individuals to decide (2) .... the truth of this – whether to let our upbringing, good or bad, determine the way we relate to those around us? According (3) .... relationship expert Brian Firstall, although a difficult family life can impact (4) .... later relationships, this does not mean that the rest of our life has to be dictated (5) .... it. So are you convinced (6) .... his theory? Or do you think that the way you are brought up inevitably leads (7) .... the kind of friends you make, and results (8) .... the partner you choose? And should your family have a say (9) .... your decisions or should they simply be satisfied (10) .... the choices you make? Can you benefit (11) .... their advice? The bottom line according to Firstall is that it's up to you – you don't need to suffer (12) .... things that happened in your past.

4 Some verbs can have more than one preposition, but the meaning changes. Choose the best preposition to complete these sentences.

1 The photograph reminded me *about* / *of* a picture I had seen in India.
2 It was such a bad design that I complained *to* / *about* the architect the next time I met her.
3 I hadn't heard *about* / *from* my friend for ages so I sent her a card to make sure she was all right.
4 We all agreed *on* / *with* the time and place to meet before the show.
5 I arrived late for the dinner party, but when I apologised *for* / *to* my host she was very understanding.
6 I saw the job advertised on the web and I immediately decided to apply *to* / *for* it.

5 Discuss these questions.
1 How important do you think the opinion of your family should be in your own relationships?
2 Have you ever dated someone or had a friend whose family you did or didn't like? What happened?

Reading 2: multiple choice (Part 1)

1

1 Look at these sentences. Which describes a nuclear family and which describes an extended family?

a) It was a large rambling old house in which four generations of the same family lived together, including an unmarried aunt and two cousins who had come to the city to study.

b) It was a small surburban villa, typical of the area, and inside lived an equally typical family: mother, father and two school-age children.

2 What are the advantages and disadvantages of living in either a nuclear or an extended family; for parents, children and other family members?

3 Which is typical of your country? Are things changing? Why?/Why not?

2   Read the three texts which are about families in different parts of the world. Choose the answer (A, B, C or D) which fits best according to the text.

India's youth moves out

When Pooja Arya got married nearly three years ago, there was no question of moving in with her in-laws, as most young women in
5 India do following their wedding day. 'My husband and I are both independent-minded,' she says. 'I thought it would be more fun to live on our own.'
10 After renting a place for 18 months, Arya, a camera operator for a popular television channel, and her financial journalist husband were able to purchase a brand new
15 flat in Gurgaon, a suburb of New Delhi that has sprung up over the last decade, as multi-national companies set up headquarters and call centres in what had been
20 an undeveloped area south of the capital.

And they are not alone among young Indian couples in forsaking the joint-family system.

25 A combination of shifting social mores and economic changes has pushed Arya's generation towards a more modern lifestyle that includes home ownership.

30 One of the main drivers of the trend is an evolving credit business, which now gives young Indians access to home loans, not previously available. Rising
35 employment and the need for a more mobile workforce means that professionals must frequently move to a city different from **the one** where they grew up to pursue a
40 career – Mumbai for finance, say, or Bangalore for technology. Women have also taken on jobs in droves in the past decade, giving rise to India's own Dinks – double income,
45 no kids – who have enough money to leave the home they once shared with mummy and papa and cover a monthly mortgage payment.

1 For the writer, Pooja Arya provides an example of a woman who

A was unusual in deciding to go against convention.

B was determined to break with established tradition.

C was influenced by peer pressure to change her lifestyle.

D was instrumental in starting a trend that is now widespread.

2 In the text as a whole, the writer is

A accounting for social changes that he regrets in India.

B arguing in favour of a more flexible family structure in India.

C providing an explanation for a marked change in some Indian lifestyles.

D blaming foreign influences for undermining traditional Indian family patterns.

More isn't always merrier

So the extended family is set to make a comeback in Britain, research * carried out by a building society reveals. It is easy to see why: grown-up children can't afford to move out of the family home, what with
5 booming property prices and student loans to pay back; grandparents are living longer and can't afford the cost of residential care.

Some might see **this** as a good thing: children can bond with their grandparents, who are so much wiser and
10 more patient than their parents. And if there is childcare to be done, the old folks are there to do it, in return for being looked after themselves. Think of all the money to be saved.

But as someone who spent the early years of childhood
15 in just **such** a set-up, believe me, it's not all good news. For the first four years of my life I lived in the villa in Budapest that my mother had built during her heyday as a popular singer in the late 1930s. Her father, a village headmaster, had contributed to the building costs and
20 planned to move there with his wife, my grandmother, when he retired. This they did, in 1948. By then my parents had married and soon they had two children.

I learnt much later – when I was old enough to understand **such** things – that as soon as my
25 grandparents moved in, life got worse for my father. My stern Victorian grandfather felt that as he had paid in part for the villa, he was a rightful owner, the real head of the household, and my father * little more than a tenant. He answered the phone with the words 'Racz
30 residence' (his own name), and when a friend of my parents gave them a handsome wrought-iron nameplate bearing both their surnames, it vanished from the front gate within days, never to be seen again.

Guest speaker Charlotte Allen brought a wholly unexpected message to the College in her talk on March 29. Traditional extended families allowed women more freedom, privacy, power and self-worth than they gain from the fragmented families and
5 communities produced by the modern 'cult of self-fulfilment,' she argued.

Extended families have been the basic social unit worldwide and throughout history, even when people physically reside in nuclear households Allen claimed, citing several studies. People in **such**
10 families have important relationships with different family members, so that their self-worth and contentment do not depend on a lifelong emotional and intellectual romance with their spouses.

Allen described a way of life that is now largely abandoned in the West. **It** was characterised by families * bound by duty and
15 necessity rather than by a quest for self-fulfilment. **They** were economically productive units in which women did socially respected work in or near the home, children helped with chores, and older people helped raise children.

Allen read an excerpt by feminist author Germaine Greer that
20 described a mid-20th-century Italian family. The married couple grew apart as their romance wore off, but maintained a web of relationships with in-laws, siblings and parents. In contrast, Allen explained, American women who moved to the suburbs after World War II found themselves isolated from any extended family or
25 community. Their only long-term relationships were within the household, and they were forced into inescapable intimacy with only one person. Their husbands became their only source of adult conversation. Suddenly, women began noticing that men weren't 'supportive', or 'responsive', and didn't share their feelings. **Their**
30 discontent focused on the only family relationships they had left.

3 In this article, the writer is seeking to

A challenge certain predictions made by researchers.

B explain why recent research may be inaccurate in its findings.

C provide a counter argument to some conclusions reached by researchers.

D highlight possible consequences of social changes identified by researchers.

4 What does the writer's anecdote about the nameplate illustrate?

A how unaware the family's friends were of their difficulties.

B how unreasonable she feels her grandfather's behaviour was.

C how aware she was as a child of tensions within the family.

D how hard her father tried not to offend his wife's family.

5 The writer thinks that the theme of Charlotte Allen's talk may

A come as something of a surprise to his readers.

B confirm his readers' negative feelings about the nuclear family.

C contradict his readers' positive ideas about the extended family.

D make his readers reconsider other beliefs they have about family life.

6 Charlotte Allen mentioned Germaine Greer's work to emphasise the point that the nuclear family

A has reduced the status of women in the community.

B has changed the attitude of men to their families.

C never really existed until the last fifty years.

D puts too much pressure on one relationship.

3

1 Look again at your list of advantages and disadvantages from Exercise 1.2. After reading the texts, do you want to add any points? Have you changed your mind about any of them?

2 Find the words in column A in the texts. Match them to their meaning in the context of the article in B.

A	B
1 in-laws (text 1 line 3)	a) customs
2 forsaking (text 1 line 23)	b) large numbers
3 mores (text 1 line 26)	c) get close to
4 droves (text 1 line 42)	d) best times
5 is set to (text 2 line 1)	e) broken up
6 booming (text 2 line 5)	f) reduced
7 bond (text 2 line 8)	g) increasing
8 heyday (text 2 line 17)	h) giving up
9 fragmented (text 3 line 4)	i) brothers and sisters
10 spouses (text 3 line 12)	j) looks likely
11 wore off (text 3 line 21)	k) husbands or wives
12 siblings (text 3 line 22)	l) husband's or wife's family

Grammar 2: substitution/ellipsis

1

1 Look back at the texts on pages 72 and 73. What do the following words in bold in the texts refer to?

1 the one (text 1, line 38)
2 this (text 2, line 8)
3 such (text 2, line 15)
4 such (text 2, line 24)
5 such (text 3, line 9)
6 It (text 3, line 14)
7 They (text 3, line 15)
8 Their (text 3, line 29)

2 Look at the texts again. Three places are marked with a *. In each place, a different word or phrase is understood by the reader but has been left out of the text by the writer. What word or words have been missed out in each case?

Substitution

We often try to avoid repeating a word or expression that has already been used, as it improves the style of what we are saying. To do this, we can use other words instead, e.g. *it, one, do, there, that, so, neither, not*. These connect phrases and sentences.

2 Complete the sentences using a substitute word from the box. Underline the word(s) the substitute word replaces.

it   one   do   there   that   so   neither   not

Example:
Do you think Joe will <u>remember</u> Kath's birthday?
I'm not sure – he might _do_ .

1 I'll be at the theatre at 7 p.m. tonight.
Good – I'll meet you ....
2 Are you going to go out with Jim again?
I think .... – he was very nice!
3 I can't decide whether to buy a new car or a second-hand .... There are pros and cons on both sides!
4 Jack asked me whether I was going to the dance or ....
5 Nils lost his job on Friday. .... was a real shock as his employers gave him no warning.
6 They aren't going to the party, and .... are we.
7 It's a difficult decision, but I think I'll take the job – .... means I can move to be nearer my family.

Ellipsis

We often leave words out to avoid repetition. This is called ellipsis, and it improves the style of the sentence.

3 Which words or phrases have been missed out in each of these sentences? Add the missing words or phrases and compare the two sentences. Which version reads better to you?

1 She was planning to visit her cousin on Saturday, but now she can't ....
2 They feel tired but .... very happy with the decision they reached.
3 Kate is leaving on Thursday, but she will email to tell you why ....
4 Borrow as many books as you want ....
5 That laptop belongs to John. This .... is mine.
6 He promised to email me, but he hasn't ....
7 If you can ...., call me when you get there.
8 I'm sorry I got annoyed – I didn't mean to ....

▶ **Grammar reference p.197 (14)**

4   Each of these dialogues has a mistake. Find the mistakes and correct them.

1   A: Are you going to move house?
    B: No, I'm afraid I can't afford.
2   A: I've managed to fix the broken mp3 player.
    B: Well, I think we should get a new. It'll never be the same again!
3   A: Tell Peter I want to speak to him, please.
    B: No problem. I do.
4   A: Who does this book belong to?
    B: I think it's Karen's one.
5   A: We all seem to have more free time than we used to.
    B: Do you think? I'm not so sure!
6   A: Do you think the traffic will be bad on Saturday?
    B: I expect it because people will be trying to drive to the beach as it's hot.

> **TIP!** Look out for ellipsis and substitution in reading tasks.

5   Work with a partner. Decide how the following text can be improved in style by using substitution or ellipsis.

It is well-documented that relationships between children and their parents fundamentally affect children's behaviour as adults. But now the importance of the relationships between children and their parents is being challenged as new research shows that a child's relationship with its siblings may have a more important effect on a child's future adult behaviour.

Psychologist Francine Klagsbrun says: 'Our relationship with our siblings is unmatchable. Our siblings are there whether we like our siblings or whether we don't like them. Other relationships change – parents die, friends drift away, marriages break up, but the relationship with siblings carries on and the memories of life that has been shared with our siblings remain with us long after childhood has ended.'

6

1   Work with a partner. One of the responses in each of these dialogues is not possible. Cross it out, then read the dialogue together, thinking about the word stress in each response.

1   Do you think Sue will visit the UK again?
    a) She might.
    b) She might do.
    c) She might do it.
    d) She might not.
2   Can I buy you a drink?
    a) No thanks, I've just had.
    b) No thanks, I've just had one.
    c) No thanks, I shouldn't.
    d) No thanks, I don't want one.
3   Were you planning to visit us on Sunday?
    a) No, but I can do.
    b) No, but I can.
    c) No, but I can think about it.
    d) No, but I can so.

2   Write your own two-line dialogues, beginning with the following questions. Then practise reading them with your partner.

1   Do you think you will do that again?
2   Can I help you?
3   Were you planning to come to the party?

Listening 2

1

1   Look at these adjectives. Which do you think describe typically female characteristics and which describe typically male characteristics? Are any of them equally male and female?

sensible   emotional   aggressive   determined   adventurous   cautious   technically-minded   decisive   caring   contrary   reliable   sensitive   stubborn

2   Compare your ideas with another student.

3   Discuss these questions.

1   Do you think people are born with typically male or female characteristics, or are these a result of their upbringing?
2   Would you want your children to have typically 'male' or 'female' characteristics?
3   Should parents consciously try to influence their children's attitudes and behaviour?

2

1 Listen to a mother speaking and decide whether she would agree or disagree with each of these statements.

1 Husbands and wives should share the job of bringing up their children.
2 My daughters seem to have very different interests and characters.
3 I'm worried about my eldest daughter's behaviour.
4 I like my daughters to wear pretty clothes.

2 Listen again. Gaynor describes her daughter as a 'tomboy'. What has she noticed about:

a) Megan's physical appearance?
b) Megan's behaviour?

3

1 Now listen to a second mother speaking and decide whether she would agree or disagree with each of these statements.

1 Girls are easier to bring up than boys.
2 It's wrong to have ambitions for your children – they need to find their own.
3 Husbands and wives should share the job of bringing up their children.
4 I don't want my son to become a typical male.
5 My husband and I have the same attitudes towards our son's upbringing.

2 Listen again. Marie talks about boys behaving differently to girls. What examples does she give:

a) of her brothers' behaviour?
b) of her son's behaviour?

4 Look at these extracts from the listening texts. What do you think the highlighted words mean?

1 My husband Rhodri is the breadwinner.
2 Women who mollycoddle their sons turn them into awful husbands.
3 My husband's afraid he'll be picked on at school if he's too soft.

5 Discuss these questions.

1 In what ways are Gaynor's and Marie's attitudes:

• the same?
• different?

2 Which of them do you think has the best attitude towards bringing up their children?

Exam focus

Paper 3 Use of English: key word transformations (Part 5)

About the exam: In Paper 3, Part 5, you are given a sentence and asked to complete a second one using a 'key word'. The meaning of the second sentence must be similar to the first. You must use 3–6 words, including the key word, which you must not change in any way. This task tests your knowledge of grammatical structures, vocabulary and different ways of expressing the same idea.

Suggested procedure

1 Read the two sentences and the key word. Think about what information included in the first sentence is missing in the second sentence.
2 Fill in the missing words, being careful to keep the meaning the same.
3 Check that you have not:
   • changed the key word
   • changed the meaning
   • written more than six words (contractions count as two)
   • made any unnecessary changes, e.g. to tenses
   • made any spelling mistakes.

For questions **1–8**, complete the second sentence so that it has a similar meaning to the first sentence, using the word given. **Do not change the word given.** You must use between **three** and **six** words, including the word given. There is an example at the beginning (**0**).

Example:

0 What are the chances of the film winning an Oscar? **LIKELY**

How _likely is it that the film_ will win an Oscar?

1 Fewer people live in extended family units in this country nowadays. **COMMON**
It is .... to live in extended family units in this country nowadays.

2 I don't think you'll find it hard to find Cynthia's house. **DIFFICULTY**
I don't think .... finding Cynthia's house.

3 My brother Sam was very surprised to be offered the job. **CAME**
The job offer .... my brother Sam.

4 I don't mind where we decide to go for our family holiday this year. **DIFFERENCE**

It doesn't .... where we decide to go for our family holiday this year.

5 Gaynor's friends persuaded her not to get married in spring. **TALKED**

It was Gaynor's friends .... getting married in spring.

6 Why did nobody tell me that the match had been cancelled? **INFORMED**

Why .... the cancellation of the match?

7 Cindy intends to complain about the service in that restaurant. **GOING**

Cindy .... complaint about the service in that restaurant.

8 Could I could borrow your umbrella this evening, please? **LEND**

Would .... this evening, please?

Vocabulary 2: easily confused words

1

1 Work with three other students. Choose one of the groups of words A–D below. Use your dictionary if necessary to find the differences in meaning between the words in each pair. Check the pronunciation, part of speech and any collocations as well as the meaning of each word.

A compare / contrast; childish / childlike; affect / effect; specially / especially

B prescription / receipt; principle / principal; lonely / alone; memory / souvenir

C lie / lay; raise / rise; practise / practice; loose / lose

D worthless / priceless; imply / infer; hard / hardly; check / control

2 Work with three students who have studied different groups of words. Explain the difference between the words in the pairs in your group.

2 Complete the sentences using the correct form of one of the words from Exercise 1.

1 He booked a table at an expensive restaurant .... to celebrate their anniversary.

2 I had an accident with my sister's car and now it's a write-off – it's completely .... now.

3 Could you .... the table while I get the food ready?

4 Sometimes writers don't state exactly what they think – you have to .... it from their choice of words.

5 I'll have to stop at the bank because I've got .... any cash on me.

6 The story about the homeless family had a tremendous .... on me. I was extremely upset.

7 Immigration officers have to .... the passports of all the members of families entering the country, even children.

8 My clothes feel very .... since I lost some weight.

9 He has no .... and will do anything at all to make money.

10 I have very happy .... of family holidays at the beach during my childhood.

Writing: competition entry (Part 2)

About the exam: In Paper 2, Part 2, you may be asked to write an entry to a competition of some kind. 'Competition entries' are not a separate text type, but can involve writing a description, an article, a review or a narrative. Whatever the text type, it is important to make what you write as interesting and engaging for the reader as possible, and to include reasons why your entry should be chosen. Remember, you are entering a competition, so you have to persuade the judges that you should win!

1

1 How do you think you can make your writing interesting for a competition entry? Choose the best ideas from the list below.

a) use interesting and varied vocabulary
b) think about your target reader
c) use a very formal style
d) use a variety of different structures
e) link ideas logically and clearly
f) use headings and bullet points
g) use direct quotations and anecdotes
h) use rhetorical questions
i) include persuasive argument or explanation of why you should win

2 Which two ideas on the list would not be appropriate for any of the four text types given above? Which one is vital for any competition entry?

2 Look back at section D of the text on page 69. Find an example of:

- a rhetorical question
- a quotation
- informal language.

3 Look at the task, and the competition entry that was written in answer to the task.

1 How is the writing organised? What is the purpose of:

- the first paragraph?
- the last paragraph?

2 Replace expressions marked with * using any one of the three linguistic devices in Exercise 2, or with substitution.

3 Find six spelling mistakes with double consonants.

You see this announcement in an international family magazine.

'Best member of any family ever!' award

We want you to nominate one of the members of your family for our 'Best member of any family ever!' award. Send us your competition entry, telling us about your nomination. Your entry should:

- describe what the member of your family is like
- explain what they contribute to family life and how
- tell us why they deserve to win the award.

Write your **competition entry** in 220–260 words.

I have a fantastic brother, Gianni, and I would like you to consider him for the 'Best member of any family ever!' award because I am sure that there is no-one who deserves it more.

First I'd like to tell you about his personallity. He's kind, thoughtful and never in a bad mood. He looks on the bright side of everything, trying to cheer other people up when they are sad. On one occasion he went out of his way to help a friend who was in trouble, even though he was going through some dificult times himself. He has had some health problems, but always makes light of the problems *.

However, it is what he brings to family life that makes him so special. He is the oldest sibling of the family (there are five of us) and you might think that he would prefer to spend time with his friends. But he doesn't do this.* No, he looks after the young siblings*, acting as a babysiter as well as a role model. When I had problems with bulying at school, he was the first to support me and help me sort it out with the bullies. What he said to the bullies * was incredible!

He deserves to win the award because of his selflesness and his thoughtfulnes. People say that he is a bright light in the world, and for me this is certainly true.

Gianni is definitely the best member of any family anywhere, and I hope that you will see fit to reward him as I know he deserves.

4 Write your own answer to the task. Remember to make your answer interesting by using linguistic devices from Exercise 2, and to persuade the judges to pick your entry by including a final persuasive sentence. Check your spelling when you have finished.

▶ Writing reference p.209

1 Read the text below and think of the word which best fits each gap. Use only one word in each gap. There is an example at the beginning (0).

? What comes first on holiday: phone or family?

Passport, money, tickets; these are all essential items to pack **(0)** _when_ you're off on a family holiday. A mobile phone, **(1)** ...., is a different matter, especially if everyone at work has the number. Theoretically, it **(2)** .... to be possible for stressed-out managers to have a phone-free fortnight without interruptions. **(3)** .... reality, go to any Mediterranean beach hotel where British families stay and you'll be confronted by the pathetic sight of husbands and fathers wandering around the pool **(4)** .... mobile phones clamped to their ears, saying things **(5)** ....: 'It's in the third drawer down, next to the pencils,' or 'I thought that contract went off last Wednesday.'

To the sensitive observer there is a tragic juxtaposition between the beauty of the surroundings, with the family all enjoying themselves together **(6)** .... once, and the dull mundanity of the issues **(7)** .... discussion. To **(8)** .... matters worse, a quirk of mobile phone pricing means these poor fathers probably end **(9)** .... paying for the call that's come between **(10)** .... and quality time with the family.

Some, it's true, do try to resist **(11)** .... pull of the phone; carrying it around with them but leaving it switched off **(12)** .... they get back to the hotel. The trouble **(13)** ...., they spend the whole day wondering who **(14)** .... have called, and then the whole evening in a state of frustration because everyone has now left the office and they can't **(15)** .... back to them for another sixteen hours.

---

2 Find words or expressions in the text that mean the same as:

1 under a lot of pressure
2 everyday and boring
3 a strange feature
4 return someone's call

3 Each of these sentences contains a wrong word. Find the words and correct them.

1 The principle reason for the mistake was carelessness.
2 The doctor gave me a receipt to take to the chemist.
3 I've lost such a lot of weight recently that all my clothes are lose.
4 Although it's not worth anything, that family photograph is worthless to me.
5 When he called he inferred that he would help us, though he didn't actually do anything.

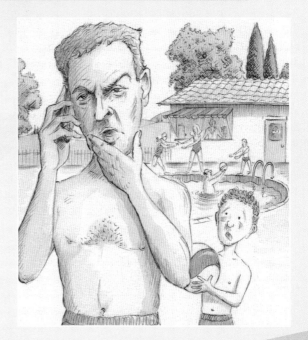

Creative talents

Exam focus

Paper 4 Listening: sentence completion (Part 2)

About the exam: In Paper 4, Part 2, you hear someone giving a talk. A set of eight sentences summarises information from the talk. In each sentence, a word or short phrase is missing. As you listen, you complete the gaps in the sentences with the missing information. You hear the words which you need to write on the recording, but you don't hear the exact sentences in the task. They are a summary of what you hear.

Suggested procedure

1 Look at the rubric and the task heading. Think about who you will hear, the context (i.e. is it a radio programme, a lecture, etc.?) and the topic.

2 After hearing the rubric, you have time to read through the questions. Think about the type of information that is missing in each one. For example, is it an object, a place, a person or a number?

3 Read the whole sentence, including any words after the gap.

4 Listen to the recording. The sentences are in the same order as the talk – use them to follow the speaker. Complete any gaps you're sure of, but remember you'll hear the recording again.

5 Each answer is a single word or a very short phrase (e.g. a noun with adjectives). Don't try to write long answers, or you will miss the next one. You are listening for the missing information – so don't write words already in the sentence.

6 Listen again to check your answers and complete any missing gaps.

7 Check your answers. Do they make complete sense in the sentence? Check, for example, whether answers should be singular or plural and that your spelling is correct.

1 You will hear a local radio announcement about a charitable event called The Cow Parade. For questions **1–8**, complete the sentences.

The cow parade

Tonight's programme is about the city's twentieth annual ....**(1)**

Fibreglass cows, decorated in a wide range of ....**(2)** and colours, will be on show around the city.

The original creator of the cows was a ....**(3)** by occupation.

A zoo, a gallery and a ....**(4)** are given as examples of local firms sponsoring cows.

At the end of the event, up to ....**(5)** of the cows will be sold in a charity auction.

In 2003, a cow decorated with small pieces of ....**(6)** sold for a record price.

One of the main charities benefiting from the event gives aid to ....**(7)** in poor countries.

At events called ....**(8)**, children will decorate a cow with thumbnail photos.

2 Who do you think might buy the cows? Do you think they have any artistic value?

3 Listen again and make a note of words that mean the same as:

1 the entrance hall of a large public building.
2 money raised at a charitable event.

Vocabulary 1: phrasal verbs

1 Look at this sentence from the listening and answer the questions below.

You may even have spotted the odd multi-coloured cow *popping up* in unexpected places.

1 What difference would substituting *standing* for *popping up* make to how interesting the sentence is?
2 What is the difference between the phrasal verbs *pop up* and *pop out*? What idea do they share?

2

1 Read the text. What is henna? What is it used for?

It's Henna
but is it really Art?

While some people deny that body painting is art, others (1) *think of / think up* it as a traditional form of self-expression that is as much art as painting on canvas.

For 5,000 years people have decorated their bodies using a natural product called henna which stains skin a bright red colour. In many countries people believed that having such decoration would (2) *bring about / bring round* good fortune, and traditionally we (3) *come to / come across* examples of henna art on the hands and feet of women on special occasions. However, henna is becoming increasingly (4) *sought out / sought after* in western cultures where young people wanting to try body art (5) *go for / go off* henna because its effect is temporary, and fun. One henna artist says that many clients have outrageous henna art decorations done before they (6) *set off / set about* on holiday; they can enjoy the decoration while they are away, but it will have (7) *worn away / worn off* by the time they have to (8) *go away / go back* to work or college.

2 Choose the best phrasal verbs to complete the text.

3 What is the meaning of the phrasal verbs you did not choose? Check in a dictionary if you are not sure. Then write a sentence to show the meaning of each one.

3 Discuss these questions.

1 Would you like to have henna art on your body? Why?/Why not?
2 Do you think that anything that is temporary has any real value?

Speaking 1: two-way conversation (Part 3)

1 In Part 3 of the Speaking paper you have to work together. It is very important to discuss each picture in turn before negotiating a decision. The expressions in the box are useful for moving the discussion on from one picture to another.

Why don't we talk about them all in turn?
Let's move on …
That's as much as we can say about that. What about the next …?
This one is interesting. What do you think about …?
Have you any other ideas about this?
Let's go back to …

2 Work with a partner. Discuss the following task. Remember to move the discussion on and talk about all the pictures on page 181.

I'd like you to imagine that there is a plan to open an arts centre in a small town. The idea is that this will attract visitors to the area. Here are some of the things the organisers are considering as possible exhibits. Talk together about whether these are appropriate things to exhibit in an arts centre. Then decide which four might attract most visitors.

3 Discuss these questions.

1 Should towns invest money in arts centres, or in new businesses? Why?/Why not?
2 What kind of art do you like? Why?
3 Some people say that all art is a waste of time. What do you think?
4 Do you think art should still be taught in schools? Why?/Why not?
5 Should artists be paid more or less money than singers or actors? Why?/Why not?

Reading: multiple choice (Part 3)

1 Discuss these questions.

1 How have our ideas about what is art been changed by technology?
2 Do you think a computer game could be considered as a work of art? Why?/Why not?
3 What aspects of computer games would you view as a) artistic b) technical?

2

1 Read the article about computer games quickly. Do these people (A–D) believe that the games are an artform or not?

A Nic Kelman   C John De Margheriti
B Roger Ebert   D Steve Stamatiadis

2 You are going to read an article about computer games. Choose the answer (A, B, C or D) which you think fits best according to the text.

1 What is the aim of the Friday afternoon sessions described in the first paragraph?

A to find out if a new game is working properly
B to allow non-specialists to try out new games
C to give the game designers a chance to interact
D to give employees a break from intense concentration

2 What does the word 'it' in line 30 refer to?

A a theory put forward by Nic Kelman
B the total effect a computer game can have
C the video game as a form of entertainment.
D the artistic value of certain parts of computer games

3 In the third paragraph, the writer suggests that the computer games industry

A has a lot to learn from the film industry.
B is fast becoming a part of the film industry.
C is more commercially driven than the film industry.
D has yet to achieve the high status of the film industry.

4 According to the writer, why is Miyamoto compared to the filmmaker D. W. Griffith?

A He has employed a similar style in his work.
B He has gained the respect of film enthusiasts.
C He has introduced ways of working that have influenced others.
D He has pioneered the use of a shifting perspective in computer games.

5 Robert Ebert thinks that computer games should not be considered as art because

A they are essentially interactive in nature.
B they do not present sophisticated ideas to the end user.
C they are created by teams of people rather than by individuals.
D they are created by people with technical rather than artistic skills.

6 For John De Margheriti, the artistic value of a computer game can be measured by

A the complexity of the goals the player is set.
B the degree to which a player gets involved in it.
C the nature of the world that is created by the designer.
D the extent to which the designer's original vision is realised.

7 At the end of the final paragraph, the writer reveals that he agrees with

A Stamatiadis's doubts about the content of most computer games.
B Ebert's reservations about considering computer games as art.
C Kelman's analysis of the state of the computer games industry.
D De Margheriti's point about the functions of artforms.

3 Which of the arguments do you find most convincing? Why?

GOOD GAME: BUT IS IT ART?

In the Micro Forte studio in Glebe, Australia, thirty blokes sit at their computers drinking Coke and twiddling with the glorious, computer-generated landscapes splashed across their screens. Wearing enormous headphones, the computer-game designers look like scruffy koalas intent on their work. The only sounds that emanate from this strange colony are mouse clicks and keyboard taps and the low, steady hum of machines. On certain Fridays at 3.30 p.m., however, when the company is creating a game, the scene changes. That's when the floor becomes animated by the sound of thirty brainiacs playing computer games while they drink beer and suck lollies, searching for the flaws within each other's work.

If American author Nic Kelman is to be believed, the men manipulating monsters onscreen are not just entertainment providers, they're artists engaged in a new artform that surpasses visual and technical abracadabra. 'Individual components of computer games have always had artistic value,' he says. 'But in the last few years, the synthesis of all those parts is producing something that has some kind of deeper experience. It transcends the form.' That's the thesis Kelman presents in his latest book, *Video Game Art*.

It may sound innocuous, but Kelman's assertion that the storylines, complex characters, sound, music and breathtaking visuals in games make them valid works of art is controversial, even among gamers. The film and computer games industries feed off each other, with Hollywood pilfering titles such as *Tomb Raider*, yet the games industry that took off in the 1980s remains the brattier cousin of the movie business. Predictions that the value of the games industry will surpass the film and music industries combined within a few years – increasing in revenue from $US25.4 billion in 2004 to $US55 billion in 2009 – have barely altered the public perception that computer games are the domain of adolescents.

Not only do games have their own grammar and cliches, but a handful of designers have recognisable styles. Among gamers, the names Shigeru Miyamoto and Will Wright induce the same respect that Stanley Kubrick and Robert Altman provoke in movie buffs. *The New Yorker* described the Japanese designer Miyamoto, who created classic games such as *Donkey Kong* and *The Legend of Zelda*, as the D. W. Griffith of game design. Just as Griffith pioneered narrative filmmaking in the early 20th century with cinematic devices such as the flashback and cross-cutting, Miyamoto developed many of the techniques now central to games, such as immersive, coherent worlds and shifting point of view. His work is recognisable for its childlike, joyous style.

Even so, late last year, the influential film critic Roger Ebert, of the *Chicago Sun-Times*, banished computer games from his canon of artforms. 'I am prepared to believe that video games can be elegant, subtle, sophisticated, challenging and visually wonderful,' Ebert wrote on his website in response to a reader. 'But I believe the nature of the medium prevents it from moving beyond craftsmanship to the stature of art. To my knowledge, no-one in or out of the field has ever been able to cite a game worthy of comparison with the great dramatists, poets, filmmakers, novelists and composers.' Gamers everywhere posted feverish blog replies condemning Ebert and asking him to explain himself. Admitting that he rarely plays the games, he says: 'There's a structural reason for that: computer games by their nature require player choices, which is the opposite of the strategy of serious film and literature, which requires authorial control.'

The founder of Micro Forte, John De Margheriti, doesn't agree: 'The author of the game has written some grand plotline, has created the races, the pretext of the stories,' he says. 'He's constrained you in a series of quests you must do, missions you must complete, objects you have to collect.' In De Margheriti's mind, the designer plays god just like the director of a film, but in a slippery, multi-faceted universe instead of a static one. In support of his argument, De Margheriti draws parallels between artforms: great games are as engrossing as great novels or films, and players finishing a game can feel as sad as a reader when they put down such a novel. A great artwork, be it sculpture, film or game, is immersive. 'The artform of games is simply a different artform,' De Margheriti says. 'Artforms have different functions. Some architecture may not be considered art ... a three-bedroom red-brick house in the suburbs isn't art, but the Sydney Opera House is. Most computer games are the three-bedroom house, but others are the Opera House.'

Some who work within the games industry, however, agree with Ebert. Steve Stamatiadis, creative director and co-founder of Brisbane studio *Krome*, which made the *Tasmanian Tiger* game for children says: 'Games can potentially deliver the same stuff as art, changing the way you think about something, but I don't think games are at that stage when about 90 per cent are about people running around shooting at something.' But, let's face it, what are the majority of films about? Whatever the realities of the marketplace, maybe Miyamoto and others have already left the suburbs.

3

1 Find words or phrases in the article that mean the same as:

1 not very well dressed (para 1)
2 concentrating hard (para 1)
3 come from (para 1)
4 lively (para 1)
5 mistakes (para 1)
6 harmless (para 3)
7 very impressive (para 3)
8 stealing (para 3)
9 was the first to try something (para 4)
10 very excited (para 5)
11 makes a comparison (para 6)
12 involving (para 6)

2 Complete these sentences using the correct form of one of the words from the article.

1 An .... discussion followed the talk about computer games.
2 Sandra was so .... on her work that she failed to realise that everyone else had gone home.
3 Petra found a .... in the dress material, so took it back to the shop.
4 The view from the hotel balcony was absolutely ....
5 Toni's grandfather was the first to .... the use of computers in this country.
6 I found that book completely .... and couldn't put it down.

Speaking 2: individual long turn (Part 2)

1 Read the following task.

Here are some photographs of people looking at pictures. Compare two of the photographs and say what the people might be enjoying about the pictures, and how long the pictures might be on show.

2 In the exam you have to talk on your own for about a minute. What do you think you should spend most time on in this task?

a) describing what you can see in the picture
b) speculating on what the people might be enjoying
c) speculating on how long the pictures might be on show

TIP! You should try to use a range of language and functions, so only describe what you can see very briefly otherwise you will not have time to speculate. Try to organise your talk clearly, using the task to help you. The task is summarised on the exam paper to help you.

3

1 Choose two of the pictures on these pages and make a note of everything you want to say about them <u>in order to complete the task</u>. Don't write full sentences.

Example:
Pic 2 people just looking
Pic 3 father and daughter talking about the art

2 Exchange your notes with a partner. Expand your partner's notes into complete sentences, using linking words and phrases from the box.

whereas	although	but	similarly
conversely	in contrast		

4

1 Return your sentences to your partner. Discuss your sentences. Then each complete the task without looking at your sentences again. Speak for about a minute.

2 Discuss how well you each completed the task, and how you could have done better.

3 Do the task again, comparing the picture you have not used with one of the original pictures.

Grammar 1: ways of referring to the future

1

1 Read the following dialogue and decide if one or both of the alternative future forms are possible.

A: So, what (1) *are you doing / do you do* this weekend?

B: Well, there's this brand new purpose-built gallery that I've been reading about – it (2) *opens / is opening* on Friday, so I (3) *'m going / go* there on Saturday. Apparently they (4) *exhibit / are exhibiting* a collection of some amazing animal art.

A: Animal art! What's that? I've never heard of it.

B: Nor me! But I've been checking it out on the Internet, and there is a lot of information about it. I want to find out enough to understand what I (5) *'m going to see / will be seeing* in the exhibition.

A: So do you think that animals can produce real art?

B: Who knows? I'll tell you when I've been to the exhibition! But it's an interesting idea, you have to agree.

A: OK – I give in! What time (6) *do you go / will you be going*? I might even come with you!

2 We can use the following forms to talk about the future. Find an example of each one in the dialogue.

- present continuous
- present simple
- *going to*
- future continuous

3 When do we use each form to talk about the future? Use the grammar reference if necessary. Write a sentence for each form to show its use.

Example:
Present continuous: we use the present continuous to talk about arrangements that have already been made, e.g. *I'm playing in a concert on Saturday evening.*

▶ Grammar reference p.198 (16.3)

2 Read the title of the following text. What do you think it will be about?

The talent of the trunk

For the modest sum of $250, (1) <u>it will soon be possible</u> to buy yourself a painting by one of the art world's next rising stars. If that doesn't sound like very much to you, then this is a good moment to snap up a bargain; because it looks like the art world (2) <u>is in for</u> a bit of a surprise.

Two artists in Thailand have opened three elephant painting schools where they want to train elephants to produce works of art. They plan to sell these paintings but not to make money for themselves – they (3) <u>are to</u> channel the profits back into local elephant projects via the World Wide Fund for Nature (WWF).

The artists (4) <u>are on the point of finding out</u> exactly how viable the project actually is. Some animal art is already a commercial success; paintings by chimpanzees can fetch high prices, and are highly sought after. Apparently elephants have a more abstract style, and by the time their work has been assessed by experts it (5) <u>will already have been</u> on the market for some time. Elephants may not be as smart as humans, but perhaps you don't have to be smart to be a great painter. And after all, who can really say what is or isn't art?

3 Read the text again. There are five future forms that you did not use in Exercise 1. Match each of the numbered examples to its use below. Then note down its form.

A to say that something will be completed at a particular time in the future *(5) will (already) have been*

B to express a prediction
C to refer to the very next moment
D to express an arrangement or a plan that has been formally organised
E to indicate a previously scheduled time

4

1 Read the extract from a review of an art exhibition. What is special about Edward?

An artist of the future?

Is he a complete phenomenon? He dashes off works of art with big, bold confident sweeps of the brush, and his style has been compared with Picasso. Nothing unusual in that, except that Edward Simpson is only six years old. He has become the youngest artist to have his work accepted for the British Watercolour Society's annual exhibition, and his paintings sell for £50 each.

2 Listen to two people who have read the same review, and are planning to go to see Edward's paintings on show. Complete the summary of their conversation.

Sarah thinks that it is a good idea to be part of something new because most people
(1) .... Edward yet. William agrees, and thinks that it is difficult to predict what Edward
(2) .... in the future. Sarah admits that she is (3) .... buying one of Edward's paintings as an investment, because it is possible that in twenty years' time he (4) .... the most popular artist in the country. William thinks that it is impossible to predict what his paintings
(5) .... worth then. Sarah is planning to sell her painting for a fortune, so that she
(6) .... her time working in an office, but instead she (7) .... herself on a beach.

5 Five of these sentences have a mistake in the formation of the future. Find the mistakes and correct them.

1 I've never liked art, and so I'm not about to starting going to art galleries now!
2 I hope we have started our new art course this time next month.
3 Work on the new arts centre due to begin on November 15th.
4 Do you think you'll be going to the exhibition this weekend?
5 Look – those security men have stopped Sue – she won't have been realised that she can't take her camera into the gallery.
6 I was on the point of buy the picture when I realised how much it cost!

7 There's no chance they'll have finished building the new gallery by the end of the month.

8 Security officials at the gallery are to get a 6% pay rise next month.

6   Complete the second sentence so that it has a similar meaning to the first sentence, using the word given. You must use between three and six words, including the word given.

1 I'm just about to buy an oil painting for my new flat. **POINT**
   I'm .... an oil painting for my new flat.

2 The completion of the new exhibition space is scheduled for next June. **DUE**
   The new exhibition space .... completed next June.

3 I'm assuming that you haven't heard the news about the art college yet. **UNLIKELY**
   I think you .... the news about the art college yet.

4 The gallery will not stage another exhibition this year. **INTENTION**
   The gallery has .... another exhibition this year.

7   Work with a partner. Tell him/her:
- what you will be doing at the weekend
- where you are going for your summer holiday
- about something you hope you will have done or achieved in a) three months' time b) one year's time c) ten years' time.

Vocabulary 2: words with similar meaning

1

1 Three of the words in each group below have a similar meaning. Highlight the odd one out in each group. What does it mean? You can use your dictionary if necessary.

Example:
   a custom   a habit   an anomaly   a tradition
   An anomaly is a strange or unusual feature of a situation.

1 collect   hoard   accumulate   build
2 symbol   sign   password   logo
3 obsession   preoccupation   fascination   indifference
4 conceal   display   exhibit   present
5 disincentive   motivation   reason   ambition
6 explore   examine   scrutinise   inspect

2 Find at least one other word with a similar meaning to the odd one out in each group. Show the word to another student. Can they match it to the correct word?

3 Work with a partner. Using a dictionary if necessary, look at the three words that have a similar meaning in each group above. What is the difference in their meaning or use?

2   Choose the most appropriate words from Exercise 1 to complete these pairs of sentences. Use words from the same group for each pair. You may need to change the form of the words.

1 a)   After a detailed .... by experts, the painting was pronounced to be a fake.
   b)   The official .... my passport before allowing me in to the country.

2 a)   Most artists and musicians are not .... and just want to produce wonderful art.
   b)   Sportsmen tend to be .... by their desire to win!

3 a)   There was a successful .... of album covers from the 1960s in London which attracted many visitors.
   b)   The director gave a detailed .... on the future plans for the art gallery.

Use of English: word formation
(Part 3)

1   Discuss these questions.

1 Why do people collect things?
2 What kind of things do you collect, have you ever collected or would you like to collect in the future?
3 What makes a collection of anything valuable?

2

1 Read the text and find two pieces of advice offered to people who have collections.

A case of collection madness

Most people who enjoy shopping as a leisure **(0)** _activity_ sooner or later reach the point where they have to try to reduce the number of superfluous **(1)** .... that they have accumulated. Some things, like clothes that have become **(2)** ...., are easily disposed of, but to others we develop a kind of sentimental **(3)** ...., like souvenirs bought on holidays, or gifts from friends. Most teenagers build up collections; be it CDs by favourite bands, football memorabilia, or whatever, but for some people the urge to collect things continues into adult life.

Such people are the subjects of a new book by Stephen Calloway that looks into the **(4)** .... obsessive world of collectors and their passions. These include all sorts of people, ranging from **(5)** .... who hoard Fine Art to ordinary people whose **(6)** .... for, say, poodle dogs leads them to buy all manner of poodle art and poodle shaped objects.

But whether you're into art, pottery, football programmes or vintage motorcycles, all collections need space. As Calloway points out, with less intrinsically **(7)** .... artefacts, it is often only an **(8)** .... display that stops a collection from becoming just a pile of old junk. Knowing when to stop buying, therefore, and using good **(9)** .... when it comes to deciding what to keep and what to sell on, is **(10)** .... the key to successful collecting.

2   Read the text again. Use the words given in capitals below to form a word that fits in the numbered gap. There is an example at the beginning (0).

0 **ACTIVE**
1 **POSSESS**   6 **FASCINATE**
2 **FASHION**   7 **VALUE**
3 **ATTACH**   8 **IMAGINE**
4 **DENY**   9 **JUDGE**
5 **MILLION**   10 **DOUBT**

Grammar 2: verb patterns

1

1 Read the title and first sentence of the text. Have you heard of Robert Ripley? What do you know about him? Read the rest of the text to see if you were right.

A man who couldn't stop collecting things!

Born in 1893 in California, Robert Ripley was a self-taught artist, who _managed_ (1) .... (_sell_) his first drawing when he was 14. A natural athlete, he _longed_ (2) .... (_have_) a career in baseball, but _failed_ (3) .... (_achieve_) this after breaking his arm in his first professional game. Without _allowing_ this (4) .... (_interfere_) with his other plans, he _began_ (5) .... (_work_) as a professional cartoonist and in 1918 he _started_ (6) .... (_draw_) cartoons featuring odd facts. Their success _encouraged_ him (7) .... (_pursue_) his interest in oddities.

Ripley _loved_ (8) .... (_collect_) but _avoided_ (9) .... (_acquire_) anything normal; he _went on_ (10) .... (_fill_) his houses with odd artefacts. He was an unusual person who _dared_ (11) .... (_wear_) bright colours; he collected cars, but never _learned_ (12) .... (_drive_). He never _minded_ (13) .... (_use_) recording equipment for radio broadcasts, but _avoided_ (14) .... (_communicate_) by telephone in case he _risked_ (15) .... (_be_) electrocuted. He _detested_ (16) .... (_swim_), but owned many boats.

In 1933, he opened his first 'Odditorium', _intending_ (17) .... (_display_) his strange artefacts. He never _regretted_ (18) .... (_do_) this, as it was so successful; there are now over 27 museums in ten countries, and tourists are _encouraged_ (19) .... (_make_) them a holiday highlight.

Reject, recycle or retain?

Do you have a roomful of clutter, or are you tidy? Do you agree with people who (1) _tell you to throw_ (tell/throw) things away as soon as they are no longer useful or do you (2) .... (refuse/get rid of) anything? Of course, we all (3) .... (enjoy/look back) on our lives; everyone (4) .... (remember/have) a favourite toy or article of clothing in the past, but do we (5) .... (mind/see) these things being valued now as part of a nostalgic art motif in a trendy restaurant? If only we had kept them, they would be worth a lot of money! However, few of us (6) .... (imagine/make) money from our memories. We (7) .... (fail/realise) the future value of many of the items we possessed, and threw or gave them away. If only we had (8) .... (plan/develop) a collection of such items at the time, we would not now (9) .... (regret/miss out) on a handsome profit! So my advice to you is this. When anyone – parents, partners, friends – (10) .... (persuade/have) a clearout of your treasures, I (11) .... (urge/reconsider). They may think they are only (12) .... (attempt/remove) unnecessary clutter from your life, but they may be (13) .... (encourage/make) the biggest mistake of your life!

2 Read the text again. Complete it using the correct form of the verbs in brackets.

2 Match each set of verbs a–f to the correct pattern 1–6. Refer to the text if necessary.

a) ☐ avoid, detest, imagine, keep on, mind, miss, put off, risk

b) ☐ beg, encourage, invite, persuade, urge, allow

c) ☐ attempt, deserve, expect, fail, manage, neglect, threaten, dare

d) ☐ forget, go on, like, regret, remember, stop, try

e) ☐ make, let, help

f) ☐ begin, continue, intend, propose, start

1 verbs followed by -ing or infinitive (with to) with different meanings
2 verbs followed by -ing or infinitive (with to) with small or no difference in meaning
3 verbs normally followed by infinitive (with to)
4 verbs normally followed by -ing
5 verbs normally followed by an object and infinitive (without to)
6 verbs normally followed by an object and an infinitive (with to)

3 Choose the correct alternative in each of these rules.

1 Verbs followed by the infinitive, e.g. _I expect to see him tonight_, often refer _back to the past / forward to the future_.
2 Verbs followed by -ing, e.g. _I remember closing the window before I left the house_, often refer to an action or state that occurred _before / after_ the main verb.

▶ Grammar reference p.197 (15)

4 Complete the text using the correct form of both the verbs in brackets. Remember that sometimes you may need to add an object.

5 Discuss these questions.

1 Do you have a roomful of clutter, or are you tidy?
2 What do you think of the advice the writer gives at the end of the text? Why?
3 Do you think that collecting souvenirs could be a good way of making money?

Writing: review (Part 2)

1 Discuss these questions.

1 What kinds of things are reviewed in newspapers and magazines?

2 How much are you influenced by a review? Would a good review encourage you to go and see a film? Would a bad review stop you buying a book?

2

1 Look at the information about writing reviews. Then read the review of Edward Simpson's paintings below. Which element is missing?

Reviews usually include the following elements:

- introduction to catch reader's interest
- background information
- a brief account of what is being reviewed
- any general comments (either positive or negative)
- personal opinion and recommendation.

He comes from a long line of artists, but has been painting seriously for less than a year. Although Edward's grandfather is a professional painter and illustrator of children's books, he was less than anxious to encourage his six-year-old grandson, partly because he didn't want him to damage his paints, but mostly because 'we did not need another struggling and penniless artist in the family'. In his father's eyes, though, Edward's paintings 'are spot on. Edward really is a natural. He may only be six, but he has an eye for art and knows instinctively what he is doing with a paintbrush'.

So what kind of pictures does Edward paint? He enjoys painting animals, especially dogs, and his approach is simple and direct. His bold cartoonish figures have already established a small but exclusive market; people may well be collecting them with an eye to the future. He uses primary colours and a natural approach, and his pictures would add charm to any living room. Some people might find them too simple for sophisticated tastes, but there is certainly something special about the sheep in particular that catches the eye.

When I first saw Edward's work I was surprised at the effect it had on me. I was profoundly moved. I found the clean lines of his paintings remarkable and thought-provoking, a return to the simplicity of Picasso. Will Edward be the Picasso of the future? Only time will tell, but I think his exhibition is well worth a look.

2 Look back at page 86, where the missing element can be found. Then read the whole review again and answer the questions.

1 How would you describe the style of the review – formal, informal or a mixture?

2 Why does the reviewer include direct speech?

3 How does the reviewer catch the reader's interest in the beginning?

4 In which part of the review does the reviewer include

a) a description of the paintings?

b) his own opinion?

c) general comments?

3 The reviewer has varied the language to keep the reader's interest and bring the paintings alive. Find words or phrases in the review that mean the same as:

1 unenthusiastic

2 poor

3 exactly right

4 like funny drawings

5 noticeable

6 strongly affected emotionally

7 the future is uncertain

3 Look at the following task. Write a review, remembering to include all the elements from Exercise 2. Take special care to begin in a way that catches your reader's interest, and use a range of vocabulary.

An international magazine is running a series of reviews of exhibitions and museums called 'It really had an impact on me!' You decide to contribute a review. You should describe the exhibition or museum, explain what had such an impact on you and say whether you would recommend it to others.

Write your **review** in 220–260 words.

▶ Writing reference p.204

1 Read the text below. Use the words given in capitals at the end of some of the lines to form a word that fits in the gap in the same line. There is an example at the beginning (0).

Would you pay over the odds for a private viewing?

How much would you be willing to pay for a few moments
alone with the world's **(0)** _costliest_ painting? The Neue Gallery   COST
in New York hit the **(1)** .... recently with its much publicised   HEAD
(2) .... of the painting *Adele Bloch-Bauer 1* for a record   ACQUIRE
$135 million. The painting is now on public display and the
Gallery charges a modest **(3)** .... fee of $15 to non-members   ADMIT
who want to come in and view the work.

The gallery has come up against a problem, however. Demand
to see this picture has been **(4)** .... high, and there is   EXCEPT
always a crowd of **(5)** .... visitors gathered around it.   ADMIRE
There is, therefore, no opportunity for quiet **(6)** .... of the   CONTEMPLATE
work; no time when you can stand in front of the picture,
(7) .... by the movements and comments of fellow art lovers.   INTERRUPT

The gallery has, however, come up with a **(8)** .... It has   SOLVE
announced that on Wednesday afternoons the price will be
hiked to $50. This means that those willing and able to pay
(9) .... more will be rewarded with a more intimate viewing.   CONSIDER
Let's hope that the experience lives up to their **(10)** ....   EXPECT

2 Choose the correct alternative in each of these sentences.

1 The exhibition is *about to / due to* open on 12th December.
2 By this time next year, I will have *been collecting / collected* football memorabilia for almost 20 years.
3 How long *does / will* it take for the artist to finish this commission?
4 Do you remember *to see / seeing* that website about computer games?
5 I'm really looking forward to *go / going* to the next collector's fair.
6 You're bound *to enjoy / enjoying* that play; it's all about a reclusive collector of fine art.

3 There is one spelling mistake in each of these sentences. Find the mistakes and correct them.

1 Edward's grandfather is a profesional painter, which has given Edward a head start.
2 It is very important to have a good illustrater for a children's book.
3 I found the clean lines of the painting both remarkeable and fascinating.
4 Many artists struggle to make a living, and some remain almost pennyless during their lifetime.
5 I always read the reveiw pages of the newspaper – I find them thought-provoking.
6 My room is full of clutter – I'm always planning to have a tidying sesion but never get round to it!

UNIT

8 What keeps us going

Listening 1

1

1 Look at this job advert.

> **SALES EXECUTIVE** wanted for busy city centre office. Good general education and interpersonal skills are essential and some previous experience is desirable. The successful applicant will be a self-starter with the ability to develop the client base for a new range of online services.
>
> Send your CV to:

2 Which of these words and phrases do you think describe the sort of person the company is looking for?

> sociable   able to work independently
> pushy   has good judgement   reliable
> willing to follow set procedures   imaginative
> cautious   conformist   aggressive   trustworthy
> assertive   has common sense   obedient   courteous

3 What do you think is implied by the term 'self-starter' in the ad? Make notes.

4 Listen to someone talking about self-starters and make notes on what they say about the qualities of such people. Then compare their ideas with your own. Were they the same?

2

1 Do you think you could be a self-starter? Complete the questionnaire, then add up your total score.

Are you a self-starter?

1 I like to have control over what I do and when I do it.   ☐

2 I want to complete tasks in the way I think works best.   ☐

3 I hate being supervised.   ☐

4 I like to set my own goals and deadlines.   ☐

5 I motivate myself to achieve results.   ☐

3 = always; 2 = often; 1 = seldom or never

2 Now listen to someone talking about the questionnaire. What are the characteristics of people who score:

1 twelve or above?   3 five or below?
2 six to eleven?

3 Discuss your scores with a partner.

1 Which type of person do you think would be easiest to work with?
2 Which type of person do you think most companies prefer to employ? Why?

Vocabulary: three-part phrasal verbs

1   Look at these extracts from listening Exercise 2.2.

… they're more likely to *fit in with* accepted methods and procedures …
… just *get on with* what they have to do …

2

1 Match the sentence halves.

1 Some managers really look down on administrative staff
2 People often come up against difficult situations
3 I was so disappointed because I sent off for an amazing special offer of a DVD
4 I couldn't go through with the job
5 I try to go ahead with all my work independently
6 Although children grow out of playing with cuddly toys

a) but I had a letter back from the company saying that they had run out of copies.
b) because I couldn't face up to the responsibility it involved.
c) in their workplace, and often have to put up with a lot of stress.
d) they often don't get round to throwing them away; mine are still in my attic!
e) but expect those same people to get on with them.
f) so that I can cut down on the number of boring meetings I have to go to.

2 Think of a synonym for the highlighted three-part phrasal verbs in the sentences on page 92. Check your ideas in the *Longman Exams Dictionary*. Were you right?

3 Replace the phrases in italics with a three-part phrasal verb from Exercise 2.

1 It's not a great idea *to order* anything on the net without checking that the site is secure.
2 Although people told me I was not very good at football it wasn't until I was dropped from the team that I really *came to terms with* the fact.
3 Teachers often *face* bad behaviour from pupils in the classroom.
4 I don't *have much in common with* my sister – we're always arguing.
5 I get through far too much chocolate – I'm trying *to reduce* the amount I eat!

4 Complete the sentences below so that they are true for you. Then compare your ideas with a partner.

1 I couldn't go through with ... because ...
2 I have to put up with ... because ...
3 The last time I ran out of ... was ...
4 I really want to get round to ... because ...

Use of English 1: word formation
(Part 3)

1

1 Imagine you are going to apply for a job. Which two of the following would be most important in your CV or letter of application?

- details of your experience and qualifications
- examples of your personal qualities
- information about when you could start
- a list of your free-time activities and hobbies
- an indication of how much you expect to be paid
- clear layout and accurate language

2 Read the title and the text quickly. Does it include the two things you chose?

2 Read the text again. Use the word given in capitals below the text to form a word that fits in the numbered gap. There is an example at the beginning (0).

HOW TO MAKE A GOOD INITIAL IMPRESSION

If you're job-hunting in Britain, it's **(0)** _essential_ to know the conventions for writing a good Curriculum Vitae (CV). This is usually a sheet of paper on which you list your personal details, **(1)** .... and experience. Many employers request a CV rather than issuing a standard **(2)** .... form when they are looking to fill **(3)** .... posts. The CV can, however, also be useful if you want to write to employers letting them know that you're available should a suitable **(4)** .... arise. **(5)** .... and simplicity are the key features of a good CV.

Employers may have to look through hundreds of them when they are on a **(6)** .... drive, and any that are overlong or have a poor layout are likely to be discarded immediately, **(7)** .... of the content. It is important, therefore, to make your CV look as business-like as possible. It's **(8)** .... to use good-quality, heavy, plain paper and a clear bold typeface in black ink. Information should be presented in the form of concise sentences, possibly arranged into bullet points under **(9)** .... Another important consideration is **(10)** ...., as nobody is likely to be impressed by CVs containing spelling or punctuation errors. So make sure you check it carefully.

0 ESSENCE	
1 QUALIFY	6 RECRUIT
2 APPLY	7 RESPECT
3 SPECIFY	8 ADVISE
4 VACANT	9 HEAD
5 CLEAR	10 ACCURATE

3 Make a note of the advice given in the text about CVs. If you were a boss, which piece of advice would you think is the most important? Why? What does it tell you about the applicant?

Exam focus

Paper 1 Reading: gapped text (Part 2)

About the exam: In Paper 1, Part 2, you will read a text from which six paragraphs have been removed and placed in jumbled order after the text. You must decide from where in the text the paragraphs have been removed. Only one answer is correct in each case and there is one extra paragraph which does not fit in any of the gaps. The texts in this part will either tell a story, or present an argument in logical steps.

Suggested procedure

1. Read the base text through, ignoring the options A–G for the moment. Most of the information you need to follow the story or argument is in the base text. As you read, pay attention to the information and ideas before and after each gap – start to think about what might be missing. Underline any words and expressions that make direct reference to what has gone before, e.g. *so*, *next*, *it*, *though*, etc.
2. Read paragraphs A–G to get a general idea of their content. Again, underline any words and expressions that make direct reference to what has gone before.
3. Go through the base text again. Stop at each gap and check whether each option A–G fits it or not. Look for vocabulary and grammar links. If you think you've found the key, double check all the references, before and after the gap. If you can't decide between two paragraphs, write both letters and come back to it later.
4. When you've finished, read the whole text with your answers in place. Does it make sense? Double check any points where the sense of the narrative or line of argument doesn't feel quite right.
5. Remember, there is one option which does not fit any gap.

1   You are going to read a magazine article. Six paragraphs have been removed from the extract. Choose from the paragraphs **A–G** the one which fits each gap (**1–6**). There is one extra paragraph which you do not need to use.

My dream job

Preethi Nair tells the story of how she broke into the world of publishing with the help of her publicist, Pru Menon

It all began about five years ago. At that point I'd never even heard of Pru Menon, and nor had anybody else. Frustrated with life in general and with my job as a management consultant, I started writing a story on my train journey to the office. It was about a young woman who wanted to follow her dreams but didn't dare to. Then, in one of those insane moments when the mouth engages without involving the brain, I told my boss I was resigning and why. 'To finish a novel?' she asked with disbelief.

| 1 | |

Once it was complete, I enthusiastically sent off my manuscript to various publishers, imagining the day when I'd be signing copies of my bestseller for admiring fans. Then came the first of many 'thanks, but no thank you' letters. Being rejected felt awful. So, in a moment of sheer madness I decided to spend all my savings on self-publishing my book. I'd come this far, I wanted to see it through.

| 2 | |

My main discovery was that printing the book wasn't the biggest problem; the publicity would be the hardest thing to arrange. I'd need a publicist who knew the business to get me book reviews and press coverage, otherwise I'd never succeed. But I didn't have any budget. It seemed like yet another setback.

| 3 | |

So I installed two phone lines in my spare bedroom and created a competent, extrovert alter-ego, by the name of Pru Menon. So nervous that my hands were shaking, I made my first call. As soon as the journalist answered, my voice faltered and, sensing my angst and inexperience, she practically hung up on the spot. I had my head in my hands. What had I been thinking? But then I thought about the money I stood to lose.

| 4 | |

As the weeks passed, I was amazed at how confident and professional I became in role as my pushy alter-ego. She was the woman I'd always wanted to be. While Pru secured interviews, I was busy doing them. If people said we sounded alike, I'd have a comeback ready: 'That's what happens when you work so closely with someone.'

5	

My next logistical headache was making sure there were copies of the book in the shops. I had to go to every bookstore in London and plead with them to stock the title. By this stage, the stress of it all was getting too much.

6	

I still didn't get a deal with a big publisher, but when I thought about all the work I'd done, I knew I had to keep trying. Being Pru had made me stronger in ways I could never have imagined, and I'd learnt to cope with rejection. What's more, my second novel poured out of me in six weeks and was sold as part of a three-book deal to a publisher. Pru is finally in retirement, but I still maintain that dreams do come true if you really make them happen.

A I thought about asking a friend to do it – after all, I couldn't really phone journalists and say 'Hi, I'm Preethi Nair, and I have a fantastic book you must read … it's by Preethi Nair!' But it was a lot to ask of a friend. Then suddenly I got the idea of doing the job myself. I'd have to change my name, and be much more confident and pushy than my usual shy persona, but it could work.

B I didn't tell anyone quite how much I stood to lose, though, because I didn't want friends or family saying it was a crazy idea. Instead, I told everyone I'd found some freelance work, and did some research into how publishing really worked.

C Nobody said anything and I was relieved. But after all her hard work, I realised that my publicist should get some recognition. Thanking her, however, would only have drawn attention to the fact that my pushy publicist was actually me – she was my alter-ego.

D So somehow I made it through even the trickiest situations. And having secured a reasonable amount of press coverage, I thought the rest would be easier. Then the first boxes of books arrived from the printers, all with page 179 missing. With the press waiting for review copies, I had to spend days and nights gluing the pages in myself.

E There was a pause in which I could have retracted what I'd said. But I didn't. I'd always seen handing in my notice as the hardest step. I had this naïve notion that the rest would follow effortlessly, because I'd taken a leap of faith. But it wasn't quite as simple as that.

F So I told two close friends about my secret. I needed them to stand in for me as directors of my publishing and PR company at the event I planned to launch the book. It was a great success, and when people asked for my publicist, they were told that she had gone down with 'flu.

G To prevent this happening again, I planned out everything a confident extrovert would say, took a deep breath and started again. After about 20 phone calls I got into my stride – chatting to media people as though I'd known them for years – and learnt to be unfazed by rejection.

2 Do you have a dream job? How far would you be prepared to go to get something you really wanted?

Use of English 2: multiple-choice cloze
(Part 1)

1 Discuss these questions.

1 What do you think makes a job enjoyable?
2 Are there any jobs you wouldn't like to do? Why?
3 Would you like to run your own business? Why?/Why not?

2

1 Do you think a teenager could run his/her own airline? Why?/Why not? What problems might a teenage entrepreneur face?

2 Read the text quickly to see if you were right.

TEENAGE AIRLINE BOSS

Martin Halstead is a young entrepreneur, **(0)** ...A.... known for having managed to launch his own airline at the age of eighteen. Martin had started his first business **(1)** ...., making flight simulators for use in pilot training, while he was still a fifteen-year-old schoolboy, and at seventeen he left school to **(2)** .... as a pilot. It was whilst on the course that Martin realised that **(3)** .... of just being a pilot, he'd like to run an airline business, and so he **(4)** .... up with the idea for AlphaOne Airways.

Martin **(5)** .... planned to fly between Oxford and Cambridge, and there was considerable public **(6)** .... in the idea. But when a big investor **(7)** .... out at the last minute, Martin was left with no **(8)** .... but to think again.

But he was not to be **(9)** .... In November 2005, he relaunched the company, this time planning flights from the Isle of Man to Edinburgh. A first flight departed on November 7th, carrying invited guests and media in an aircraft Martin had leased from another company. **(10)** .... the airline suspended operations in January 2006, AlphaOne Airways had carried some forty fare-paying passengers on the route, and Martin had **(11)** .... his dream. It was perhaps his naivety and youth that allowed him to ignore the problems and barriers that someone older may have seen as a brick wall **(12)** .... in the way of achievement.

3 Now read the text more carefully and decide which answer (A, B, C or D) best fits each gap. There is an example at the beginning (0).

0	**A** best	**B** greatest	**C** most	**D** widest
1	**A** task	**B** venture	**C** endeavour	**D** affair
2	**A** study	**B** learn	**C** train	**D** prepare
3	**A** instead	**B** alternative	**C** preference	**D** rather
4	**A** thought	**B** dreamt	**C** hit	**D** came
5	**A** largely	**B** initially	**C** primarily	**D** principally
6	**A** interest	**B** attention	**C** support	**D** attraction
7	**A** held	**B** called	**C** checked	**D** pulled
8	**A** way	**B** option	**C** chance	**D** course
9	**A** sent back	**B** caught out	**C** put off	**D** turned down
10	**A** Although	**B** Despite	**C** However	**D** Nonetheless
11	**A** reached	**B** completed	**C** obtained	**D** fulfilled
12	**A** blocking	**B** standing	**C** stopping	**D** impeding

4 What kind of business enterprises do you think teenagers might be most successful at? Why?

- running a website
- being a DJ
- operating a market stall
- organising sports coaching

Grammar 1: direct and reported speech

1

1 Read the title of the text below.

- What was the prize given for?
- Who do you think might have given him the prize?

2 Read the whole text to see if you were right.

Prize for boss who told staff: Spend less time at work

Ian Barnard, a 36-year-old who works for a London financial firm, was declared the country's best employer by the charity 'Parents At Work'. The reason may be surprising. Mr Barnard explained what happened: 'Having kids made me realise there is more to life than work. I also realised that my staff would be happier if they could see their children more.'

Mr Barnard arranged for his staff to work for only nine days a fortnight, on flexible hours. He said: 'When we started giving people a day off every two weeks they felt uneasy about it at first, but they soon started to appreciate it.' He explained his philosophy very clearly by saying 'I always say that if staff are happy, they work better, are more loyal and less likely to leave the company. Another benefit is that the office is actually open longer than before because of flexible working hours.'

2

1 Answer the following questions using reported speech.

1 Why did Mr Barnard question his own attitude towards long hours at work?
He said that …

2 What did he think about his staff's attitude to work?
He realised that …

3 What did he say about the staff's reaction before he introduced the scheme?
He said that …

4 What does he always say about staff attitude to work?
He always says that …

5 What did he say about the time the office was open?
He said that …

2 In which sentence(s) above:

1 does the modal verb not need to change?
2 does the verb tense not need to change?
3 could the verb tense change (backshift)?

Explain why. Look at the Grammar reference if necessary. Then complete the rules.

a) Modal verbs such as .... and .... do not always change their form when the reporting verb is in the .... tense.

b) When the sequence of events is ...., it is not necessary to backshift from past to past perfect.

c) When the reporting verb is in the ...., present perfect or future, it is not necessary to change the tense.

▶ Grammar reference p.194 (5)

3

1 Read the rest of the text. What did Sarah actually say (1–4)? Tell a partner.

Sarah Jackson, chief executive of Parents At Work, (1) explained that she had awarded the prize the previous month for the example Ian's forward thinking had given to others. (2) She believes many people want to break out of the long-hours culture. (3) She accepted that Ian's company had benefited from higher productivity and greater flexibility. (4) She also emphasised that lower staff turnover should help to convince other organisations that this was the way forward.

2 Complete the rules.

a) When something is always true, the tense of the verb .... change.

b) Reporting verbs that express the importance of an action are often followed by the modal ....

> **Watch Out!** *say* and *tell* ◀
>
> Which sentence is correct in each pair?
>
> 1 a) She told me to talk to the boss.
>   b) She told that I should talk to the boss.
>
> 2 a) She said that I should talk to the boss.
>   b) She said me to talk to the boss.

4 Complete the sentences using the correct form of *say* or *tell*.

1 a) James .... me that you were working in London.
   b) It was James who .... that you were working in London.

2 a) Harry .... goodbye to Sue and walked out of the room.
   b) Harry .... Sue that he was leaving and walked out of the room.

3 a) I .... Jules not to go to the party, but he insisted.
   b) I .... that Jules shouldn't go to the party, but he insisted.

4 a) I .... to Carlo that it was the right thing for him to have done.
   b) I .... Carlo that it was the right thing for him to have done.

5 Work with a partner. Take turns to say each of the reported sentences below, using direct speech. Discuss whether you think you are correct or not, and write down a version you think is correct. Then listen to check.

1 He said that he had been wrong to get angry.
2 She said that she had earned more than ever the previous year.
3 She said that she had never met him before.
4 His father urged Michael to think about what he was doing.
5 She promised that she would work harder the following week.
6 He said he believed that overall performance would improve if they gave bonuses to their staff.

6

1 Listen to someone talking about how they started their career. Then write a brief summary of what was said, using reported speech. Compare your version with another student. Are they the same?

2 Write your own short description of your ideal job. Then read it to your partner. They should write a summary of what you have said. Then check their version with your own notes.

Listening 2: multiple choice
(Part 3)

1   How would you feel if you were offered a part in a TV soap?

What could be the advantages and disadvantages of the job?

2

1 Look at the questions in Exercise 3. Highlight the verbs, nouns and adjectives that seem most important in each option.

2 Find words or phrases in the questions that mean the same as:

1 finding the money to do something
2 feeling pleased because people praise you
3 something you've always wanted to do
4 got used to doing something
5 having arguments
6 told people something
7 be unreliable
8 got worried

3   You will hear an interview with Amy Kyme, a former soap star who now works in the Health Service. Choose the answer (A, B, C or D) which fits best according to what you hear.

1 Amy accepted the part in the soap because
   A one of her friends was already working on the programme.
   B she saw it as a way of financing her further training.
   C she felt flattered to think that she had been chosen.
   D it meant she could fulfil a lifelong ambition to act.

2 Once she had settled into working on the programme, Amy found that
   A she kept falling out with her colleagues.
   B the lifestyle associated with it didn't suit her.
   C acting was more difficult than she had imagined.
   D she wasn't left with enough time for enjoying herself.

3 What prompted Amy to leave her job?
   A something she was told to do
   B increasing feelings of homesickness
   C an aspect of the plot of the programme
   D the fact that she was putting on weight

4 After she announced her decision to leave, Amy
   A felt guilty about letting people down.
   B started to have second thoughts about it.
   C became anxious about her financial commitments.
   D had to convince her family that it was the right thing.

5 Why did Amy take a job in an old people's home?
   A She was looking for less tiring work.
   B She needed to do work of some kind.
   C She wanted to feel responsible for others.
   D She thought it would be useful for her career.

6 In her new work, Amy
   A sometimes regrets that she's no longer a celebrity.
   B is pleased that people remember her TV work.
   C wishes that she had more leisure time.
   D feels greater job satisfaction.

4   Do you think that Amy made the right decision? Why?/Why not?

5   What sort of person does Amy seem to be? Choose three words from the list.

thoughtful   frivolous   indecisive   conscientious
sociable   laid-back   realistic   sensitive

Speaking: comparing (Part 2)

1

1 Work with a partner. Think of the advantages and disadvantages of working in these different environments, and what might make people want to work there.

small shop   garage   hospital   theatre
sports centre   open-plan office

2 Compare two of the places by linking your ideas using words from the box.

whereas   conversely   whilst   though

2 Look at the photographs of people working in different places on page 185. Compare two of the photographs and say what the advantages and disadvantages of working in each place might be, and which might be the easiest to work in.

3 Discuss these questions.

1 Do you think that people work harder or less hard now than in your grandparents' day?
2 Do you think that people work too much or too little nowadays?
3 How much time do you think people should spend at work? Why?

Grammar 2: reporting words

1 Match sentences 1–11 to the appropriate reported statement, question or order a–k below. Highlight the words or phrases that helped you choose the appropriate statement, then complete the rest of the sentence.

Example:

'I've made up my mind – I'm going to finish the report tomorrow'.

He decided to finish the report _the next day_.

1 'Finish the report right now!'
2 'I think you should finish the report otherwise you'll miss the deadline.'
3 'Yes, it was me – I made the mistake with the report.'
4 'Don't forget to finish that report as soon as you can.'
5 'You have to finish the report, because the boss needs the information.'
6 'I plan to finish the report this afternoon.'
7 'You don't have to finish the report because Sue has already done it.'
8 'I'll certainly finish the report by tomorrow morning.'
9 'Well done – you've finished the report really quickly.'
10 'You're right – I have to finish the report today.'
11 'I really don't want to have to finish the report today – it's just not fair!'

a) He congratulated me on finishing the report ...
b) He ordered me to finish the report ...
c) He intended to finish the report ...
d) He admitted making the mistake ...
e) He explained that I had to finish the report ...
f) He advised me to finish the report ...
g) He reminded me to finish the report ...
h) He agreed to finish the report ...
i) He confirmed that I didn't have to finish the report ...
j) He promised to finish the report ...
k) He complained about ...

2 We can report what someone says by using:

- verb + infinitive (with or without an object)
- verb + -ing, (with or without an object)
- verb + that
- verb + preposition + -ing
- verb + object + preposition + -ing

Put the reporting words from Exercise 1 into the correct column according to the way they are used. Then add the words from the box below to the correct column, including the preposition where appropriate.

announce	command	remark	claim
offer	refuse	apologise	propose	ask
threaten	invite	accuse	thank	suggest

Verb + object + preposition + -ing	Verb + infinitive	Verb + preposition + -ing
congratulate (on)		

Verb + that	Verb + object + infinitive	Verb + -ing

┌─ **Watch Out!** *suggest* ◄────

Which sentence is not possible?

a) He suggested going out.
b) He suggested that they should go out.
c) He suggested us to go out.

▶ Grammar reference pp.194 (5), 197 (15)

3 Choose the correct alternative in each of these sentences. Then rewrite the sentence so that the other verb would be possible.

1 She *promised / announced* to attend the meeting.
2 He *expected / insisted* to receive the invoice before he paid for the goods.
3 The manager *agreed / confirmed* to accept the policy decision.
4 She *demanded / ordered* him to arrive on time.
5 The employees *offered / suggested* to take a small pay cut.
6 The manager *thanked / congratulated* me on changing the work ethic in the office.

4

1 Work with a partner. Match the following sentences to one of the reporting words from the box below. There are two you will not need to use.

thank	confirm	advise	congratulate
complain	announce	apologise	remind
refuse	ask	~~invite~~

Example:
Would you like to come and stay with me next week, Carlos?
She invited Carlos to stay with her the following week.

1 Please don't forget to send that email today.
2 If I were you, I would resign immediately.
3 Well done for getting promoted – that's wonderful news!
4 I'm definitely not going to do the training course next year.
5 The food in the canteen is terrible!
6 Michael, please help me write this proposal – I can't do it.
7 This is to let all employees know that the managing director will leave the company next week.
8 I'm sorry that I was late – there was a problem with the train.

2 Take turns to report your sentences to each other using the reporting word you have chosen.

Writing: proposal (Part 1)

1   In Paper 2, Part 1, you may be asked to write a proposal. You will be given a task and some input, but you may have to add some ideas of your own.

Look at the two outline plans below. Which one is the plan for a report, and which one is the plan for a proposal?

A

> Reason for writing
> Background information
> Suggestions or ideas
> Reasons why they should be adopted
> Summary

B

> Reason for writing
> Background information/Outline of
>   current situation
> Recommendations based on current
>   situation
> Summary

2

1   Which of the following statements are usually true of a proposal?

- It is written in informal language.
- It includes suggestions and recommendations.
- It includes direct speech.
- It may use headings or bullet points if appropriate.
- It uses a lot of linking words to promote clarity.
- It proposes a new idea and tries to persuade the reader of its value.
- It uses a range of colourful language.

2   What is the difference between a report and a proposal? Complete the following sentences.

1   A .... looks to the future, giving specific plans for a particular situation.
2   A .... makes several recommendations based on a current existing situation.

3

1   Read the following task.

> Your class is going to write a proposal for the ideal workplace of the future. Read the comments from a survey on the subject and the description of a popular workplace from the Internet. Then write your proposal, identifying the main issues that should be considered and proposing the ideal workplace of the future, with reasons.
>
> Write your **proposal** in 180–220 words.

> I can't stand working near other people – so shut in!

> It's hard to work with noise – it's especially bad with the phone.

> I'm worried about having to take lunch at a specific time!

> I hate the idea of work! I need to be pushed, to feel I'm part of a busy office.

> **workplace.net**
>
> _Very important_
>
> The working space is light and bright, with a large table in the centre, and other smaller working areas with individual desks. There are displays with the latest newspapers, magazines, directories and reference books. Tea, coffee and water are available. The environment is quiet: mobile phones must be on vibrate, and personal conversations must happen outside.
>
> _Excellent_

2 Read the proposal, which was written in answer to the task.

4 Look again at the task in Exercise 3. In which part of the proposal has the writer included:

- comments from the survey
- research from the Internet.

Why is this?

5

1 Read the proposal again. Find formal expressions that mean the same as these informal expressions from the comments in the survey.

1 can't stand
2 especially bad
3 I need to be pushed
4 so shut in
5 I'm worried about …

2 Identify the modal verb that is used most often in the proposal. In what part of the proposal is it used? Why is this?

6 In a Part 1 task you should choose the information you use appropriately, and you can expand the information with ideas of your own if you wish. The writer has said there are four key features, but has omitted one. Complete the proposal, adding the key feature omitted from the input information. You can use up to 20 words. Then compare your idea with a partner.

7 Now write your own answer to the task. Ask your classmates for some ideas, and use these as the results of the survey. Remember to check your writing using your checklist.

▶ Writing reference pp.199, 207

Introduction
Many people have problems with their workplace. We were asked to write a proposal for an ideal workplace that would address these issues. We undertook research through a survey and research on the Internet.

Background information
It is clear that many people dislike noise, preferring to work in a quiet environment, where it's impossible to hear others speaking. The phone is a particular issue here. Others like to feel that they are part of a team, and need people around them to maintain their motivation. Some dislike small offices, finding them claustrophobic. Everyone must feel comfortable, and not have concerns over issues such as meal breaks.

Suggestions for the ideal workplace of the future
The ideal workplace should have four key features.

- It should be light and airy, and have space between desks so that people feel comfortable.
- There should be ample opportunity for people to move around, and to have drinks and food at any time – not only in designated lunch and coffee breaks.
- There should be a sense of team spirit so that no-one is demotivated.
- ....

Conclusion
The ideal workplace is not a fantasy – if recommendations like these are followed through it can become reality.

1 Complete the second sentence so that it has a similar meaning to the first sentence, using the word given. Do not change the word given. You must use between three and six words, including the word given.

1 There are many things to think about before accepting a job offer. **TAKEN**
There are many things that should .... consideration before accepting a job offer.

2 It's a waste of time attending a job interview unless you really want the job. **POINT**
There .... a job interview unless you really want the job.

3 'I'm afraid that I didn't do very well in my interview,' said Mike. **ADMITTED**
Mike .... gone very well.

4 The car park is only to be used by members of staff. **EXCLUSIVE**
The car park is for .... members of staff.

5 'Fiona, I think you've been leaving work early, haven't you?' said her employer. **ACCUSED**
Fiona's employer .... work early.

6 A clear and concise CV is a must if you're applying for a job in London. **ESSENTIAL**
If you're applying for a job in London, it .... which is both clear and concise.

7 'I'm sorry that I broke your mp3 player, Brenda,' said Trevor. **APOLOGISED**
Trevor .... mp3 player.

8 Flavia regretted not going to the concert. **WISHED**
Flavia .... the concert.

2 Think of one word only which can be used appropriately in all three sentences.

1 The office staff couldn't get the new printer to .... properly.
Unfortunately, Tim's idea for a new office layout didn't .... out in the end.
Clare had to .... towards a solution to the problem over several months.

2 They asked George to take .... of the project.
There is a small .... for using the swimming pool.
Melanie was put in .... of ordering stationery for the whole office.

3 This bag comes from the company's mid-priced .... of accessories.
The mountain .... in Tibet is one of the most familiar images in the natural world.
There is a wide .... of food available in restaurants in London.

4 Under the new law, cigarettes can only be advertised at the .... of sale.
Please, hurry up and get to the .... – I'm leaving in five minutes!
It's often hard to grasp the .... Ben's trying to make – he never thinks before he speaks.

5 I was at a .... to know what to say when she told me the bad news.
The company made a huge .... of over $10 million last year.
After the accident, Graham suffered from a temporary .... of memory.

6 The boss set an upper .... for the amount of overtime anyone could do in a week.
We have no extra money – our finances are stretched to the ....
There's no .... to what you can achieve if you really try!

3 Match the sentences to reporting verbs from the box. There are two words you don't need to use.

admit   deny   advise   persuade   refuse
agree   apologise   accuse

1 'It wasn't me who upset the office manager!'
2 'If I were you, I'd say I was sorry.'
3 'You were told to write that customer a formal apology, but you didn't do it, did you?'
4 'I think it may have been my fault that the document was lost.'
5 'Thank you, but I'm afraid I haven't got time for a coffee at the moment.'
6 'I think you've got a point about that letter. I'll rewrite it.'

On the road

Speaking 1: choosing an image
(Parts 3 and 4)

1 Work with a partner. Tell him/her about something which has inspired you and why. It could be a person, an event, a piece of music, a book, etc. What do you think makes something inspirational?

2 Do this speaking task with a partner.

I'd like you to imagine that a college is running a photographic competition. The college wants to find the best inspirational image to use on a poster which will be put up around the college buildings. The college wants the poster to promote international understanding. Here are some of the photographs that have been submitted.

Talk to each other and decide which image should be chosen and why.

3 Discuss these questions.

1 What qualities make a person an inspiration to others?
2 What can we learn from international travel?
3 Does international travel have any disadvantages?
4 Should young people be encouraged to travel? Why?/Why not?

Grammar 1: review of narrative tenses

1 Choose the correct alternative in each of these sentences. Then match them to the statements a–i about use of tenses.

1 You *sit / are sitting* in my seat – could you move, please?
2 He *went out / has gone out* without speaking, and she *never saw / has never seen* him again.
3 He *travelled / was travelling* through Greece when he met his future wife.
4 The train *had already left / has already left* Switzerland when the snow started.
5 I've *finished / 'd finished* my homework – can we go out now?
6 She *read / 's read* the guidebook on Brazil last week because she's so keen to go there.
7 I'm *visiting / visit* my friend in Brazil next week.
8 I've *been staying / 've stayed* in this resort for two weeks, and it's great!
9 She *'d only lived / 'd been living* in the city for a week when she lost her passport.

We use:

a) the past continuous to say that something was in progress at a particular time or event.
b) the past perfect to show that something happened before something else.
c) the present continuous for temporary actions and situations that are currently in progress.
d) the past simple with expressions that refer to a completed period of time, e.g. *yesterday*, *in 1999*.
e) the present perfect to indicate that a finished action or event is related to the present.
f) the present continuous for future arrangements.
g) the past simple to talk about the past (unless there is a reason to use a different tense).
h) the present perfect continuous used for an unfinished action continuing into the present.
i) the past perfect continuous to show that one long event happened before another in the past.

2 Complete the text with the correct form of the verbs in brackets – present continuous, past simple, past continuous, present perfect, present perfect continuous, past perfect or past perfect continuous.

▶ Grammar reference p.197 (16)

Why did I do it?

Climbing volcanoes (1) .... (*become*) a popular tourist pastime in recent years, as it offers a tempting combination of physical exertion and personal danger. I have always wanted to try it, and when I found out that the cone of Maderas in Nicaragua (2) .... (*collapse*) inwards leaving a crater lake at the top, this seemed to be my chance. I thought that swimming in a crater lake might be fun, so I (3) .... (*persuade*) two friends, Rob and Sarah, to go with me. Unfortunately, we had done very little planning before the trip, and so the whole venture turned into a disaster. Once we (4) .... (*arrive*) at the summit we realised that a thick mist and heavy rain (5) .... (*obscure*) the view. Rob and Sarah wanted to go back down immediately, but I felt that as we (6) .... (*come*) this far it would be a waste of effort not to swim. I (7) .... (*know*) that nothing ever lives in crater lakes, which was rather spooky, and the moment I dived in to the muddy water I felt that it (8) .... (*suck*) me down into its lifeless depths. I (9) .... (*never/feel*) so terrified in my life! After I had struggled out of the water, we started back down but by then it (10) .... (*rain*) hard for such a long time that the slope was slippery and dangerous. When we finally (11) .... (*arrive*) back at the hotel, caked in mud and soaking wet, Sarah discovered that she (12) .... (*pick up*) an obscure mountain parasite and was covered in red swellings. Since then I (13) .... (*not/climb*) again, and when friends ask 'so, (14) .... (*you/climb*) any more volcanoes soon?' my answer is clear – absolutely not!

3

1 Do you think that people who do unusual and dangerous things like this are:
- adventurous?
- irresponsible?
- stupid?

Explain your opinion to a partner.

2 Prepare to tell your partner about a similar incident that you have heard of, or a time when you had a difficult or unusual experience yourself. Make notes on what you want to say, and think about the tenses you need to use. Then talk to your partner and answer any questions they may have.

3 Write your notes up as a paragraph. Check your tenses, and make sure that they are accurate.

Reading: multiple matching (Part 4)

1 Look at the headline of the article. In what ways do you think young people travelling in another country might:

- make friends with local people?
- upset local people?

2 Discuss these questions.

1 What problems might you have travelling in a country where you don't know the language?
2 What type of gifts do people from your country give when they visit people abroad?
3 What type of souvenirs do you like to bring back when you travel?

3 Read the article quickly. Which section talks mostly about:

things to take with you? buying things?
photography? speaking another language?
problems on the road?

4 You are going to read an article about young people travelling abroad. For questions 1–15, choose from the sections of the article (A–E). The sections may be chosen more than once.

In which section does the writer ...

criticise the behaviour of some travellers? **1** ☐

admit to being too stubborn in one situation? **2** ☐

remember the kindness of a particular local official? **3** ☐

express a dislike for a certain piece of equipment? **4** ☐

suggest remaining calm in the face of provocation? **5** ☐

recall being given advice about a personal matter? **6** ☐

suggest a better alternative to a financial transaction? **7** ☐

advise against having a tight schedule when travelling? **8** ☐

encourage us to find out about the needs of local people? **9** ☐

recall choosing to travel in a relatively uncomfortable way? **10** ☐

remember sharing a common interest with a group of strangers? **11** ☐

mention being given a reward for being a source of amusement? **12** ☐

suggest that some activities require the consent of local people? **13** ☐

admit to finding some difficult situations amusing to look back on? **14** ☐

acknowledge that some people may find it hard to acquire a useful skill? **15** ☐

How to be a good traveller

You should aim to make friends on your international travels and avoid upsetting anyone.

A If you want to break the ice in almost any social situation abroad, remember you're a guest in someone else's country, so you
5 should make some effort to speak the language. Obviously you can't expect to be fluent, even just getting by can be difficult if you haven't got the time or aptitude, but any attempt,
10 however embarrassing, makes an enormous difference. The first time I set foot in China, I only knew three words of Mandarin, which I'd never heard pronounced properly. In the
15 event, my first attempts at conversation proved so entertaining to my hosts that I was promptly presented with a gift. So it's worth trying to meet local people and
20 getting into conversation. Even if you end up speaking mostly in a shared second language, you can learn a lot about one another. I once travelled third class on a train from Harare to
25 Bulawayo, partly because I thought it would make the overnight journey more interesting. Since there were no spare seats, I ended up crammed between carriages. But it wasn't long
30 before the guard took pity on me, inviting me back to his cabin where he plied me with both stories and refreshments until I couldn't take any more of either.

B   The key to stress-free travel is never to give yourself a deadline to meet. As soon as you do, things inevitably start to unravel, and there's often very little you can do about it, so you have to make the most of things. I often find that the highlights I tell the most entertaining anecdotes about are times when things didn't quite go according to plan. For example, on what should have been a twelve-hour, cross-country drive to the airport in Mongolia, our jeep got stuck in a bog. Forced to camp overnight, we awoke to find a small party of local nomads on horseback, complete strangers, organising our recovery. We were eventually delayed by twenty-four hours, but it turned out to be the most memorable day of the entire trip.

C   In many countries, haggling is part of everyday life, but unless you're after something quite pricey, it's not worth taking to extremes. I once spent a fraught morning in a Nairobi market haggling over the price of a rug until I was blue in the face, but the seller wouldn't budge below his final price. It was only later that I realised I'd been giving this guy a hard time for the sake of one euro. The bottom line is, stop haggling when you stop enjoying it. Of course, even if you're as nice as pie, there are always going to be people who try to take advantage or abuse their position, and that's true of any country. If you do feel an official is being unreasonable, be polite and stand your ground. The worst thing you can do is lose your temper; the chances are that's exactly what your antagonist is after, and it'll just make them all the more determined to be difficult.

D   Travelling should always be a two-way experience. The more your hosts can learn about you and your country, the more you'll both get out of it. Ideal in this regard are postcards from home; pictures of the capital will always go down well as the scenes may already be familiar to your hosts, but pictures of where you actually live and snaps of friends and family are ideal for breaking the ice. It's amazing how many times I've been told which of my friends I should marry, for example! Gifts are also a good idea, but in addition to, not as a substitute for, getting to know people. If you do some research beforehand, you can take something that might also be useful or of interest to those you meet. In many countries, few things will ingratiate you more with your hosts, for example, than things connected with the 'beautiful game'. I was on a kayaking trip in a remote region when I first experienced this phenomenon. We were on the riverbank, surrounded by a group of excited young children, but having not a word of their language, all I could do was smile. Then one kid gave us the thumbs up sign and said 'Manchester United' in heavily-accented English. A lively exchange of players' names ensued, much to everyone's amusement.

E   But you'll want to take home some mementos too, and this usually involves photography. I'm not a fan of sneaking shots of people with long telephoto lenses unless they're just a small part of a bigger image. Many people are camera-shy and, in some cultures, suspicious of photography, thanks largely to insensitive foreigners thrusting cameras in the direction of reluctant subjects, particularly children. So if you're into portraits, make the effort to talk to your subject first. To my mind, a portrait without a name or a story has no more value than a landscape without a location. But, at the very least, get permission first. If you ask someone to do something for a photo, then it seems reasonable to recompense them for their time, but this is no substitute for giving people some of your own time.

5 Complete the collocations using one of the words from the box. Look back at the article to check your answers.

break	get	give	go	lose	make
meet	set	stand	take		

1 You have to .... the ice when you meet new people for the first time.
2 It's useful to be able to .... by in a language.
3 You have to .... an effort if you want to make friends.
4 It's difficult when you first .... foot in a country.
5 I hope someone will .... pity on me if I get lost.
6 Did everything .... according to plan?
7 It's important to .... all your deadlines.
8 Did that man .... you a hard time?
9 In an argument, it's important to .... your ground.
10 Try not to .... your temper when people are being difficult.

6 Discuss these questions.

1 How do foreign tourists and travellers behave when they visit your country?
2 Do you agree with the advice given in the article?

Vocabulary: dependent prepositions – adjectives and nouns

Adjective + preposition

1

1 Adjectives with related meaning may be followed by the same preposition. Match each set of adjectives to one of the prepositions from the box. You will need to use one preposition twice.

at	by	about	to	of	from	with

1 good   excellent   competent
2 concerned   worried   nervous
3 different   separated   apart
4 similar   related   equivalent
5 typical   characteristic   true

6 fascinated   gripped   captivated
7 accessible   open   restricted
8 pleased   happy   delighted

2 Are the prepositions usually followed by a noun, a gerund or either?

2 Discuss these questions.

1 What do you get worried about?
2 What are you competent at?
3 Who are you most similar to in your family?

Noun + preposition

3 Nouns, verbs and adjectives that share the same root may be followed by the same preposition. Complete the sentences with nouns formed from the adjectives in Exercise 1 and add an appropriate preposition.

1 Enforced .... friends can ruin relationships when people have to spend a long time apart.
2 What is the actual .... the situation? It seems to me that most people are lying about what happened!
3 Why is there such a .... trendy holiday destinations nowadays? People are obsessed with them!
4 Her extreme .... flying really restricted the amount of travelling she was able to do.

4 Some nouns, verbs or adjectives that share the same root may be followed by a different preposition. Complete the sentences with nouns formed from the adjectives in Exercise 1 and add an appropriate preposition.

1 There are often many .... European languages, which can help people pick them up easily.
2 I wish long haul travellers would show more .... the environment and fly less.
3 There are far fewer .... holiday packages than travel companies want us to believe – I think they are all the same really.
4 He really loves travelling and gets a great deal of .... seeing different places.

5 How much do you think travel will be restricted in the future? What will cause this? What would make you agree to restrict your own travel plans?

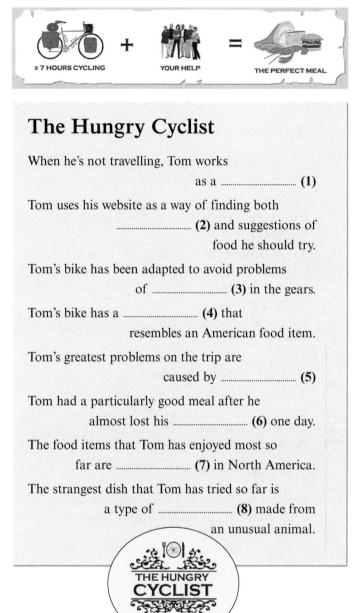

x 7 HOURS CYCLING   YOUR HELP   THE PERFECT MEAL

The Hungry Cyclist

When he's not travelling, Tom works
as a .... (1)

Tom uses his website as a way of finding both
.... (2) and suggestions of
food he should try.

Tom's bike has been adapted to avoid problems
of .... (3) in the gears.

Tom's bike has a .... (4) that
resembles an American food item.

Tom's greatest problems on the trip are
caused by .... (5)

Tom had a particularly good meal after he
almost lost his .... (6) one day.

The food items that Tom has enjoyed most so
far are .... (7) in North America.

The strangest dish that Tom has tried so far is
a type of .... (8) made from
an unusual animal.

THE HUNGRY CYCLIST

Listening: sentence completion
(Part 2)

1

1 Look at the images from Tom Kevill Davies'
website which is called 'The Hungry Cyclist'.
What sort of trip do you think he's going on?
What kind of help do you think he needs?

2 You're going to hear about Tom's trip through
the Americas. Make a list of the vocabulary
you expect to hear related to how he's
travelling. Think about:

• the equipment he'll need
• problems he might have.

2

1 Listen to the radio feature about Tom and
answer the questions.

1 Which countries has he visited so far?
2 How many kilometres will he travel in total?
3 What's the purpose of his trip?

2 Listen again and complete the sentences.

3 Look at these answers that students wrote
in the exam for the above task. Why would they
be marked wrong in the exam? What advice
would you give these students?

1 *graphhic design*	6 *dropped his gloves*
4 *bells*	7 *roadside diners*
5 *hills*	8 *chicken*

4 If Tom was cycling around your country,

• which route would you advise him to take?
• what would you advise him to eat?

Grammar 2: emphasis (cleft sentences with *what*)

1   Look at this extract from the listening text.

What Tom eventually hopes to do is to raise £100,000 for charity.

Why did the presenter choose to use this structure?

2   Look at the dialogues below. What does the structure beginning with *what* emphasise in each answer?

- a whole sentence
- the object
- the verb or event

1   A: They have to be there by six in the evening and I think it's a long journey by train.
    B: OK – what they need to find out is which train leaves before lunchtime.

2   A: He's always lucky – I bet that he was in time for the bus!
    B: Quite right – what he did was catch the bus with about five seconds to spare!

3   A: Why was he so late? I just don't understand it!
    B: I think that what happened was he arrived at the airport in good time but got held up in the queue to check in.

3

1   Rewrite the following sentences. Emphasise the bracketed part of each sentence using one of the ways shown in Exercise 2.

Example:
I want to know (how you travelled to France last year).
What   _I want to know is how you travelled to France last year_ .

1   She (learned Italian so that she could speak to people when she went to Rome on holiday).
    What she ....

2   (People who are always late) annoy me most.
    What ....

3   (He couldn't visit Iguazu when he went to Brazil the first time) and that made him determined to go back.
    What ....

4   (He went on a course to become a flight attendant) last year.
    What he ....

5   I'd really like to have (a holiday in Antarctica).
    What ....

6   (She told her boss how she felt about the restructuring of the company).
    What ....

2   Rewrite the following sentences without using a cleft structure.

Example:
What is happening nowadays is that people are travelling more.
People are travelling more nowadays.

1   What he really loves is travelling by plane.
2   What I like to do is take photographs of every place I visit.
3   What I do is use the Internet to stay in touch when I travel.
4   What I am enjoying is the chance to travel abroad for my work.
5   I was furious about the delay, so what I did was complain directly to the airline.
6   To my amazement, what the airline did was refund all my money!

3   Choose the correct alternative to complete the statement about cleft sentences.

Cleft sentences are most often found in *informal speech / formal speech / written texts.*

▶ Grammar reference p.195 (6.1)

4

1   Choose one of these topics to speak about.

1   What I really need to do to improve my English speaking is …
2   I had a surprise last week. What happened was …
3   What I value about my best friend is …
4   What I'd really like to achieve in my life is …
5   What really annoys me is …

2   Listen to a student talking about the first topic. What does she need to do? Why?

3   Prepare to speak on your chosen topic for at least a minute. Remember to begin with the cleft sentence you chose.

4   Work in groups. Take turns to talk about your topic, and answer any questions.

> **TIP!** Although cleft sentences are found in informal speech and sound very natural, don't overuse them as this can sound forced.

Speaking 2: individual long turn (Part 2)

1 Look at the three pictures, and read the task.

The pictures show people doing things while travelling. I'd like you to compare two of the pictures, and say why you think the people have chosen to do these things while travelling, and what they tell us about the people's attitude to travelling.

2 In Part 2 you will be asked to compare different pictures. When you compare you need to express things that are similar and things that are different, and you will also need to speculate about the pictures.

Read the example opposite and put the highlighted phrases in the correct part of the table. Two have been done for you as examples.

What you think/ speculating	Comparing and contrasting
it looks as if	

Qualifying what you say	Giving reasons/explaining
a lot more	

Example:

In the first picture there is a man sitting on a station platform; it seems to be early morning and what I think he's doing is waiting for a train. I don't think he's going to work because he's dressed casually so it looks as if he's just going somewhere for the day, or maybe he's meeting someone off the next train to arrive at the station. However, in contrast in the second picture there are a lot of people who are also on a station platform but some of them are dressed a lot more smartly and to me they come across as feeling bored because they do this journey every day and that's why they're trying to pass the time by reading a newspaper.

3 Listen to a student comparing pictures B and C. Add any more words or phrases they use to the table in Exercise 2.

4 Now do the task with a partner, using the pictures on page 182. Try to use the phrases from the table, and a cleft sentence.

Exam focus

Paper 3 Use of English: open cloze (Part 2)

About the exam: Paper 3, Part 2 is an open cloze passage with 15 gaps. One word goes in each gap. Most of the gaps will need grammatical words, e.g. prepositions, articles, auxiliaries, etc. rather than vocabulary related to the topic.

Suggested procedure

1 Read the complete text quickly, ignoring the gaps, to get an idea of what it's about and how it is structured.

2 Read the text before and after each gap carefully. Think about the type of word which is missing.

3 If you're unsure of any answers (e.g. which preposition to put), then guess – remember you don't lose marks for wrong answers!

4 When you've finished, read the whole text again to make sure it all makes sense with your answers in place.

1 For questions **1–15**, read the text below and think of the word which best fits each gap. Use only one word in each gap. There is an example at the beginning (**0**).

Example: | 0 | *have* |

HOLIDAY SNAPS

Have you ever noticed how most of us (**0**) __*have*__ a tendency to take too many pictures on holiday? Finding (**1**) .... in a beauty spot, we want to hold on to the experience and so (**2**) .... comes the camera. But the camera takes our attention away from the place itself with (**3**) .... result that, in effect, we stop looking. What's (**4**) ...., only rarely (**5**) .... we study this type of photograph closely afterwards. (**6**) .... if we save and print it, it becomes just (**7**) .... of many in an album of similar shots.

John Ruskin, writing when photography was (**8**) .... its infancy in the 19th century, fought bitterly (**9**) .... the trend. He argued that, (**10**) .... of taking photographs, we should all learn to draw. His view was that if you try to draw anything, (**11**) .... simple it may seem, you (**12**) .... be forced to look at it more closely. In looking at things in this way, you come to appreciate (**13**) .... they actually look like. He tells us, for example, that (**14**) .... most of us have never really studied a tree, we say things like: 'I'd love to go to India.' 'Nonsense,' says Ruskin. 'First learn to see a tree properly, then move on to your house and (**15**) .... the time you're ninety, you might be ready for a trip to India.' These are wise words for our over-travelled, but under-observant age.

2 Discuss these questions.

1 Do you agree that we should learn to draw instead of taking photographs? Why?/Why not?

2 How has the digital camera changed people's attitudes towards photography?

3 Do you think people will take more or fewer photographs in the future? Why?

Writing: competition entry (Part 2)

1 Look at the photograph.

- Why do you think it was taken?
- What does it show about travel nowadays?

2 Read the following competition announcement and for questions 1 and 2 choose the answer (A, B, C or D) which you think fits best according to the text.

Something to say about travel today?

Enter our competition for the Travel Photograph and Article of the Year! There are two categories:

- Face to Face – people or animals
- The personal approach – issues in travel.

Submit one photograph and article (220–260 words) in your chosen category. In your article you should explain what your photograph says about travel today, with supporting details. You should increase awareness of the issues while clearly stating your own point of view and engaging the reader.

1 The aim of the competition is to

- **A** inform readers about travelling around the world.
- **B** allow individuals to express their personal opinion.
- **C** give young people an opportunity to become photographers.
- **D** explain environmental issues raised by travellers.

2 The article submitted must be

- **A** informative.
- **B** interesting for people working in the travel industry.
- **C** light-hearted and amusing.
- **D** supported by proof of academic research.

3

1 Think back to the previous work you have done on articles. Look at the Writing reference on page 208 if necessary. What are the four main aims of an article that is also an entry for a competition?

- a) to engage the reader
- b) to explain a point of view
- c) to organise the article clearly and in an interesting way
- d) to present facts and figures
- e) to win a prize

2 How can you achieve these aims? Choose four ideas.

- a) plan your ideas carefully in paragraphs
- b) use rhetorical questions
- c) use direct speech
- d) use a range of interesting and varied vocabulary
- e) use connectors and link ideas well
- f) think about layout, using headings and bullet points

4

1 Look back at the photograph on page 113 and the competition announcement. Your friend wants to submit that photograph for the competition, and has to write the article to go with it but is not sure how to go about it. What advice would you give your friend?

2 Listen to someone giving advice to their friend. Was it the same as yours?

3 Listen again and note down six key things you must do when writing your article for this competition.

5 Read this article which was written in answer to the task. Answer these questions.

1 What is the aim of the introductory paragraph?
2 Has the writer included all of the necessary points from Exercise 3?
3 Has the writer included any of your ideas?
4 Does the article include varied and interesting vocabulary? Give some examples.

5 What linking words or phrases are used? Find some examples.
6 How does the writer engage the reader? Give examples.
7 Is it written in an informal or formal style? Give examples.

6 Now write your own answer to the task. You can use a different photograph as your entry if you prefer; choose one from the photographs on page 104 or page 107.

1 Think of three points you could make in your article about issues raised by the photograph. Plan your paragraphs. What will you include in your introduction? What will you say in your conclusion?

2 Refer to your grammar checklist and to the checklist in Exercise 3 to make sure you have completed the task.

▶ Writing reference p.208

Travelling around the world seems to be an attractive way to spend your time. But it's not all good news on the personal front. Have you ever thought about the negative side of travel? And I'm not talking about environmental issues, either!

First, think about the time you waste in airport concourses. Arriving early, checking in, waiting for the plane to leave – think what you could do more usefully in the time. I can think of about ten things immediately!

Then there's the time you spend away from your family. Certainly, you may be travelling with friends, for fun rather than for work – but not everyone you love will be with you. Friends of mine spent a year backpacking around the world, and when asked whether they would do it again, replied with a very definite 'no!'.

Of course, there is another side to the coin – I can't pretend it's all bad news. The opportunity to see the world, experience other cultures, have amazing adventures – these are part and parcel of travelling. But nevertheless the negative issues already raised have to be balanced with these advantages. And as the photograph shows, the personal disadvantages are very great. So all in all, is travel worth it? It's your call, but I hope that I have at least made you think!

1 Read the text below. Use the word given in capitals at the end of some of the lines to form a word that fits in the same line. There is an example at the beginning (0).

Bag Manners

A few months ago, standing in a **(0)** _seemingly_ endless check-in queue
at an airport (that perhaps should remain nameless), I couldn't help but
overhear an angry businessman loudly complaining to the **(1)** ....
behind the desk about our delay. His tone was very aggressive and
he was using very **(2)** .... language that I thought was quite
(3) .... to the situation.

The airline **(4)** .... didn't bat an eyelid, however, simply making a calm
apology as she continued with the **(5)** .... for checking in his bags, then
handing him his **(6)** .... pass with a smile.

As he walked off, still muttering obscenities, I moved forward to
take my turn. I **(7)** .... with the woman, commenting on her
(8) .... in the face of such unnecessarily ill-mannered
(9) .... She winked at me and replied: 'Don't worry, madam. That
gentleman is going to New York, but his suitcase is going to Beijing.'

The moral of the story? If you want to avoid the **(10)** .... of lost
luggage, never be rude to airport check-in staff!

SEEM	
ATTEND	
OFFEND	
APPROPRIATE	
EMPLOY	
PROCEED	
BOARD	
SYMPATHY	
PATIENT	
BEHAVE	
CONVENIENT	

2 Complete the second sentence so that it has a similar meaning to the first sentence, using the word given. Do not change the word given. You must use between three and six words, including the word given.

1 The aim of the competition is to inform readers about the region. **PROVIDE**
The competition aims ....
information about the region.

2 The people in the photograph look like experienced travellers. **IF**
The people in the photograph look
.... experience of travelling.

3 I get most annoyed when tourists don't show respect for local customs. **IS**
The thing .... when tourists don't show respect for local customs.

4 There don't seem to be quite as many tourists in the city this year. **SLIGHT**
There seems to have been .... in the number of tourists in the city this year.

3 Add a prefix to each of these words to make it negative. Then complete the sentences using the negative words.

…necessary	…convenient	…practical
…eventful	…behaviour	…considerate
…related	…respectful	

1 I thought it was .... to pack gloves for a beach holiday.
2 It was an .... flight so we arrived feeling calm.
3 I think it is .... to local people to take photographs of them without asking.
4 The timing of the flight was rather .... for us as it meant we had to wait around all day.
5 It's a nice guidebook, but its size makes it .... for walking holidays.
6 I think it was .... of Gemma not to call to say she'd be coming home a day later than planned.
7 My enjoyment of the trip was .... to the fact that I'd won it as a prize in a competition.
8 Because of their earlier ...., we decided not to take the children to the cinema.

Listening 1

1

🔘 **1** You hear two people talking about the environment and the natural world. Choose the answer (A, B or C) which fits best according to what you hear.

Extract One

1 The man thinks that awareness of the natural world and environmental issues is

   A not very important.
   B nothing to do with him.
   C irrelevant because it's too late to do anything.

Extract Two

2 The woman thinks that awareness of the natural world and environmental issues is

   A quite important.
   B something she can help with.
   C something everyone should have.

2 Whose attitude do you agree with? Why?

2

1 How aware are you of environmental issues and the natural world? Work with a partner and do the 'eco-friendly' quiz.

1 How much of your food is processed, packaged and comes from far away?
a) most of it
b) about half of it
c) very little of it

2 How often do you travel by public transport instead of using a car?
a) rarely or never
b) whenever possible
c) every time I go out

3 Compared to people in your neighbourhood, how much waste do you generate?
a) much more
b) about the same
c) much less

4 In your house or flat, do you
a) always leave electrical appliances on standby?
b) turn off lights and electrical appliances when you leave the room?
c) only turn lights and electrical appliances on when you need to use them?

5 When you buy consumer goods for yourself or others, do you
a) go for the one with the most elaborate packaging?
b) avoid any that seem to have too much packaging?
c) choose the one with the simplest packaging?

6 When you buy cosmetics or medicines, do you
a) never read the label?
b) check to make sure the product has not been tested on animals?
c) only buy products made by companies with a good environmental policy?

7 Do you think that endangered species should be
a) allowed to become extinct because it's the natural order?
b) moved into zoos and animal parks?
c) protected in their natural habitat?

Add up your score
a = 0, b = 1, c = 2
The higher your score, the more environmentally aware you are.

2 Discuss these questions.

1 What general environmental issue does each question raise?
2 What do you think your own responsibility is to these issues?
3 How much can any individual do to bring about change in these areas?
4 How important is it for people to engage with the natural world?

3 Think about other issues that could show how environmentally conscious you are and write three more questions for the quiz.

Grammar 1: countable/ uncountable nouns

1 Look at the alternatives in these sentences. Which one is possible or likely? Which one is not, or is less likely? Why?

1 Scientists are only just coming to an understanding of the true nature of *space / the space*.
2 This encyclopaedia is incredibly heavy – whatever is it made of? *An iron / Iron*?
3 I need *some advice / an advice* about how to look after my new goldfish.
4 There hasn't been *much news / many news* about the latest volcanic eruptions in Asia, so they can't have been serious.
5 I usually like to have *a coffee / coffee* before I do anything else in the morning.
6 We had *an amazing time / amazing time* on a wildlife safari last year!
7 They are doing *excellent research / an excellent research* into animal behaviour at my local zoo.
8 I just can't bear it if there's *a hair / hair* in my food – it makes me feel ill!
9 We can't decide what to do until we find out *additional information / an additional information* about the whole thing.
10 *A travel / Travel* is one of my main free-time interests.

2 Work with a partner. Are these words countable, uncountable or both? How does the meaning change if they're both?

1 coffee
2 hope
3 water
4 point
5 idea
6 power
7 authority

▶ Grammar reference p.194 (4)

3 Think of one word only which can be used appropriately in all three sentences. In this exercise, all the words are nouns. Remember to look for phrases which will help you, and think about whether you need the singular or plural form. You will need the same form in all three sentences.

1 Remember to keep your .... on the weather so that you don't get caught in the rain.

They bought the shares with an .... to making a quick profit.

Although they knew about the planned party, the boy's parents decided to turn a blind .... and let it go ahead.

2 I don't know how dangerous the jungle is – if you go, you'll have to take your ....

The .... are that the zoo will be forced to close.

Doing the course will certainly improve your .... of getting a job.

3 She's in no .... to undertake such a physically demanding trip.

He was allowed to leave the country on .... that he returned within three weeks.

Anyone suffering from a serious medical .... should think twice before undertaking strenuous physical exercise.

4 The team is now back to full .... after a number of injuries to key players last month.

It's always an advantage to be able to negotiate from a position of ....

It is easy to understand the .... of public feeling against the use of nuclear energy.

5 I have absolutely no .... what he means!

Can you give me a general .... of what your plans are?

He still makes mistakes, but I think he's got the right .... now.

6 He has shown no .... in taking part in the trek across the mountains.

I believe that it is in the public .... that the facts of the situation are made known.

There is a disturbing lack of .... in recycling in the area where I live.

> **TIP!** Underline phrases that helped you to identify the missing word and add them to your vocabulary lists.

Reading: gapped text (Part 2)

1

1 Look at this list of endangered species. How many of each are there left approximately? Match each animal to a number.

1	Giant panda	a)	48,500
2	Bengal tiger	b)	3,735
3	Orang-utan	c)	1,600
4	Asian elephant	d)	25,600 – 32,750
5	Black rhino	e)	3,000 – 4,500

2 How important do you think it is to save **all** the endangered species in the world? Are some species easier to save than others? Why?/Why not?

2 You are going to read a newspaper article. Six paragraphs have been removed from the article. Choose from the paragraphs A–G the one which fits each gap (1–6). There is one extra paragraph which you do not need to use.

A safari to save the big cats

Getting Namibia's farmers on board a large conservation project has been one of the challenges for the AfriCat Foundation.

Clive leaned out of the Land Rover's door and raised his antenna, rotating it in a semi-circle. We listened hard. The receiver hissed. 'Nothing,' he said. 'Just white noise.' We made off again down the track for a couple of kilometres, past thick clumps of bush and thorn, to pause once more. And this time we clearly heard the signal, a steady beep that announced our quarry – a radio-collared cheetah – was near.

1 [   ]

Mo, our cheetah, was on the move, but we eventually caught up with him dawdling in the long grass. He had last hunted a few days ago and was now contemplating another meal. Just seven metres away, I could sense his dismissive demeanour. So we left him to it, trotting away into the seemingly infinite *veld* of central Namibia, and headed back to our villa.

2 [   ]

Donna Hanssen, one of the owners, explained the big cats' plight in Namibia. Much of this arid country is given over to livestock and game farms. Cattle in particular require vast tracts of land and it's a generous farmer who shares his thin pastures with much game.

3 [   ]

Hanssen herself has a farming background. Her parents moved here in 1970 and struggled to run a viable cattle farm. With its rocky hills and escarpments parcelling huge tracts of land threaded by seasonal streams and rivers, their land is as ruggedly beautiful as its soil is poor. Their herds never thrived. For a while they even encouraged commercial hunting instead. AfriCat and Okonjima's evolution as a luxury wilderness lodge in the early 1990s changed all that.

4 [   ]

Since July 1993, 868 cheetahs and leopards have been rescued, 86 per cent of which were released into the wild. Their guiding principle is this: relocating and releasing a cheetah back into the wild is the only route to conservation. Even if it survives just a few years, that may be long enough for a cheetah to rear cubs and secure another generation.

5 [   ]

This ambitious project began in 2000 with the support of the Tusk Trust. Here, in a 10,000-acre enclosure now restocked with game, young cheetahs are honing their hunting skills in preparation for final release. They are fed just enough not to starve but are largely forced to fend for themselves. Generally, three months seems sufficient to sharpen their hunting instinct.

6 [   ]

Old habits die hard, though. Once the hunks of donkey meat had been given out, each animal scampered off with its own ration to consume it alone and fast, for in the wild scavengers often help themselves to cheetah kills before they've even had a chance to tuck in.

A Even at the best of times, it's not easy to make a living. What's more, in the absence of other prey, carnivores rapidly acquire a taste for livestock – so are often shot on sight. With Namibia estimated to have nearly a quarter of the world's cheetahs, the looming question was: could they cheat their seemingly inevitable decline?

B Leaving the track to head cross-country on foot, we were steered by the equipment as surely as ants to honey. 'Watch those aardvark holes,' urged our guide, for not only can they twist ankles but it is not unknown for warthogs or leopards to occupy them. Neither likes a two-legged surprise on its doorstep.

C We drove for hours on tracks that ranged from graded to barely defined. Small, flat-topped hills, or kopjes, stood like sentries on immense plains with tantalising horizons. The light was brilliant, the space bewitching. Occasionally the forward trackers radioed directions or updates to our guides. The process resembled an elaborate, grown-up version of hide-and-seek.

D One afternoon, we visited the vast Welfare enclosure. Its cheetahs are unsuitable for release, usually because of injury or habituation to man, and will forever need feeding. They now associate vehicles with food and within minutes several bounded across the plain towards us.

E That apparent simplicity is deceptive. Many rescued animals are orphaned cubs, inexperienced in hunting. Mo, the cheetah we had tracked earlier, exemplifies one solution – rehabilitation.

F This formed part of the Okonjima guest farm, run by the AfriCat Foundation, which aims to safeguard the well-being of Namibia's large carnivores, principally cheetahs and leopards. What began as a welfare mission has expanded into education and, most importantly, the conservation of these exquisite animals – exquisite, that is, unless you happen to be a farmer.

G Today, they try and work with farmers, encouraging them not to shoot predators on sight and offering to remove the animals instead. Altruism, you might say, has emerged from pragmatism. Yet there is little doubting the passion driving the Foundation.

3 Discuss these questions.

1 Whose responsibility is it to save endangered species?
2 Should money be spent on other things (such as climate change) instead? Why and what?

4 Match the verbs 1–8 to words a–h to make a common collocation. Look back at the article to check your answers.

1 to hone	a) a taste for something
2 to fend	b) an ankle
3 to acquire	c) into the wild
4 to be shot	d) your skills in something
5 to rear	e) a living
6 to make	f) young
7 to be released	g) on sight
8 to twist	h) for oneself

Exam focus

Paper 4 Listening: multiple choice (Part 3)

About the exam: Paper 4, Part 3 is a 3–4 minute interview or discussion involving two or three speakers. It is usually a media broadcast in which a subject is discussed in depth. There are six multiple-choice questions which follow the order of the text, mostly focusing on the speakers' attitudes and opinions. The questions deal with the main ideas in the text, but won't use the same words. Remember, they are testing your understanding of longer pieces of text, not just individual words or phrases.

Suggested procedure

1 You have a minute to read the questions before the recording begins. Read them quickly, underlining the main words in the question stem and options.

2 Each question focuses on one piece of text and they come in order. Think about how the text will be divided into six parts – how will you know when to move on to the next question?

3 The first time you listen, concentrate on the question stem. Can you hear the answer to the question without looking at the options? Is there an option that matches the answer you have heard?

4 Listen again and check that the option you have chosen is correct and the others are wrong.

5 If you're not sure, guess. You've probably understood more than you think, and no marks are deducted for wrong answers.

1 You will hear an interview with Jake Willers, a naturalist who is also the presenter of a wildlife programme called *Insects from Hell*. For questions **1–6**, choose the answer (**A**, **B**, **C** or **D**) which fits best according to what you hear.

1 What attracts Jake to the type of animals known as arthropods?

A the scope that exists for future research
B the family tradition of study in this area
C the amount of data that has been collected
D the number of individuals found in each species

2 What does Jake suggest about Hollywood films about insects?

A They have titles that don't reflect their content.
B They tend to put people off his own programmes.
C They lead people to take the animals less seriously.
D They do not necessarily feature the most dangerous species.

3 Jake thinks he was chosen to present the TV series because

A he was already well-known as a presenter.
B he was willing to be filmed in unpleasant places.
C he came across as relaxed and natural on screen.
D he had experience of explaining things to children.

4 What does Jake say about the content of the programmes?

A He likes to write his own script in advance.
B He insists that any information given is accurate.
C He accepts that it is primarily intended as entertainment.
D He puts forward ideas for possible locations and activities.

5 Jake feels that the incident with a baby elephant he describes shows

A how crucial it is to have expert guidance.
B how all animals can behave unpredictably.
C how brave you need to be in his line of work.
D how the best bits of action cannot be planned.

6 In terms of his future plans, Jake suggests that

A he hopes to travel even more extensively.
B he intends to continue with both of his jobs.
C he regrets having become a television personality.
D he would like to gain some broader work experience.

2 What sort of person do you think Jake is? Would you be able to work with things like insects?

If you could meet him, what questions would you ask Jake about his work?

£200,000 Dog

JOB: crime scene investigation dog

PAY: free accommodation and food; earned £200,000 last year

CAREER: joined South Yorkshire Police at 12 weeks – few months training

HOBBIES: chasing her tail, eating

£129,000 Man

JOB: Chief Constable

PAY: £129,000 per year

CAREER: joined police in 1979; promoted to Superintendent in 1995; promoted to Chief Constable in 1999

HOBBIES: rock climbing, mountain walking

Use of English: open cloze (Part 2)

1

1 Look at the information above about a police dog and a police chief and answer the questions.

1 Why do you think the police dog earns more?
2 What special skills might the dog have?

2 Read the text opposite quickly to see if you were right. Ignore the gaps for the moment.

2   Read the text and think of the word which best fits each gap. Use only one word in each gap. There is an example at the beginning (0).

Sniffer dog earns more than Police Chief

Keela the police dog is something (0) __of__ a star. Her special talent is (1) .... able to locate tiny pieces of evidence that can later be confirmed by forensic tests. It is an ability which has (2) .... her in the forefront of detective work across Britain. Indeed Keela, a 16-month-old springer spaniel, has become (3) .... an asset to South Yorkshire Police that she ended (4) .... earning more last year than the region's Chief Constable.

Thought to be the (5) .... one of her kind, Keela is (6) .... is called a 'scene-of-crime' police dog, and her secret (7) .... her sense of smell. She has been trained to detect microscopic traces of blood on weapons, no matter (8) .... thoroughly they have been cleaned; even on clothing washed several times in biological powder.

Keela, (9) .... parents were also police dogs, joined the force at twelve weeks old and was quickly identified (10) .... having the perfect temperament for this kind of work. In situations (11) .... other dogs might bark and (12) .... excited on finding something, Keela has the ability to stay completely still and pinpoint a precise area with her nose.

Her unique talents mean that Keela is much (13) .... demand by police forces across the country, and she is hired out to them at £530 a day, plus expenses. (14) .... figure is ten times that (15) .... an ordinary police dog might earn, giving her owners an income of around £200,000 per year.

3   Find words or phrases in the text which mean:

1 something of great value to someone
2 to have the right character for something
3 to locate something exactly
4 special skills which others don't have
5 very popular or sought after

Grammar 2: introductory *It*

It as preparatory subject

Spoken sentences are often begun with a preparatory *it* because this allows the speaker to place more emphasis on the most important part of what he or she wants to say. It also sounds very natural.

Example:

The heavy rain made driving difficult.

It was the heavy rain that made driving difficult

It emphasises *the heavy rain*.

1

1   What is *it* emphasising or referring to in each pair of sentences? Underline the information.

1   a) It was John who came out with me, not James.
    b) It was Saturday that we went out, not Sunday.

2   a) It's interesting how important pets are to many people.
    b) It's amazing what some people will do for their pets.

3   a) It's important to be aware of environmental issues.
    b) It's not unusual to find environmental issues on the front page of newspapers nowadays.

2   Look at the pairs of sentences again. Which pair is emphasising:

1   an infinitive expression?
2   a clause beginning with a *wh-* word?
3   what comes first in the sentence?

2   The following sentences are all grammatically correct, but would sound more natural if they began with *it*. Change each one, keeping the meaning as close as possible to the original. Then practise saying the sentence to a partner.

Example:

That she should be told about it was essential.
It was essential that she should be told about it.
Just to catch sight of them in the wild was a privilege.
It was a privilege just to catch sight of them in the wild.

1   How easy it is for natural habitats to disappear is frightening.
    It ....

2   That most people feel indifferent to the fate of some species of animals is unlikely.
    It ....

3   For us to have seen a condor in the wild was thrilling.
    It ....

4   When you return my book doesn't really matter.
    It ....

5   That the conference will take place next month was confirmed yesterday.
    It ....

— **Watch Out!** ◄

All sentences in English need a subject. When there is not an obvious one, use *there* in front of nouns or noun phrases and *it* in front of adjectives and noun clauses to provide a subject.

Which sentences are correct?

a) Is hot today, don't you think?
b) It is hot today, don't you think?
c) There's a man in the garden!
d) It's a man in the garden!

▶ Grammar reference p.196 (9.1)

It as preparatory object

It can be used before the object of a verb, and in this case it is called a preparatory object.
It can follow the patterns below.

Subject/verb/it/infinitive or clause

I/find/it/hard *to* believe how many endangered species there are.
They/made/it/clear *that* they were fond of animals.
I/hate, love, like/it/*when* they sing that song.

3   *It* is missing in each of these sentences. Put *it* in the correct place.

1   She thought was strange that he hadn't contacted her.
2   His headache made difficult for him to concentrate.
3   She thought had been a mistake not to sign the contract immediately.
4   I found exciting that I was asked to take part.
5   His behaviour made impossible for me to continue to work on his project.
6   I hate when he shouts like that.
7   I love when they have fireworks at a party.

▶ Grammar reference p.196 (9.2)

It + reporting verb

It is common with reporting verbs or with set phrases when the writer wants to appear to be objective.

Example:
It is thought that water once existed on Mars.

4 Rewrite these sentences using the correct form of the word in brackets.

1 Many people believe that global warming is caused by human activity. (*think*)
2 The evidence seems to show that world temperatures are rising. (*appear*)
3 Most people know that we should recyle wherever possible. (*common*)
4 The evidence suggests that there are many species on the verge of extinction. (*seem*)

5 Work with a partner. Some of these sentences contain a mistake with *it*. Find the mistakes and correct them.

1 I cannot bear it to see people being cruel to animals.
2 She loves it when people give her presents.
3 I find it interesting to hear you talk about your experience in the jungle.
4 He made obvious to everyone that he was not going to get involved in the project.
5 I'll leave it to you to choose it the film we watch.
6 I knew it that they were unhappy about the plan.
7 They owe it to us to be honest about their feelings.
8 It was James who gave me a lift last week.

Other patterns with *it*

There are some set expressions with *it*.

6 Work with a partner. Complete these sentences with your own ideas. Then explain your sentences to your partner.

It's really vital that … because …
It's exciting when … as …
It's really worth … since …
It's often said that … but I think …
I take it that … as …

Speaking: sounding interested

1

1 Listen to two people talking about zoos and answer the questions.

1 Which one sounds the most involved in what they are saying?
2 Which one doesn't sound very interested?
3 How did you decide?
4 What effect does the attitude of the speaker have on the listener?

2 Which of the following statements are true?

To involve a partner in a conversation:

- it is always necessary to disagree with them
- it is a good idea to ask them for their opinion
- it isn't a good idea to use question tags
- it is important to answer using more than one or two words
- intonation is important to give a good impression
- you should talk a lot.

2 Which of the following phrases are engaging? Which are off-putting? Try saying them to a partner and see what they think.

That's really interesting – tell me more.
Do you think so?
No, I don't really agree – but what I think is …
I suppose so.
I totally agree – and what's more …
A good point – it's absolutely true that …

3 Discuss the following question with a partner:
Do you think that zoos have a place in modern society?

1 Begin the conversation by expressing your view in a bored way.
2 Then change to be more interested.
3 Finally change to sound interested, engaged and involved.

4 Discuss these questions. Try to sound interested, and to engage your partner in the conversation.

1 Does it really matter if some animals become extinct?
2 How can ordinary people help endangered animals?
3 Do we have a responsibility to future generations? What?
4 What can we learn from studying animals?

Vocabulary: phrasal verbs and compound nouns

Phrasal verbs with *up* and *down*

1

1 Look at these short texts containing phrasal verbs with *up* or *down*. Complete each gap using the correct form of a verb from the boxes.

keep   make   catch

1 I went on a tour of the wildlife park but I couldn't .... up with the group – in fact, I got so far behind that I was a bit worried I might get lost! I tried to .... up with them, but whenever I thought I had .... up enough ground they moved away before I actually reached them. Finally, the guide saw me, and stopped.

calm   cut   narrow

2
Man: The planet is in danger! We all have to
          .... down on carbon emissions and recycle
          more!! We have to do it now!
Woman: .... down, James – don't panic so much!
          I'm sure it's not as serious as you think – and
          anyway what can we really do about it?
Man: It's no wonder the planet's in trouble if
          everyone takes that attitude! There's plenty
          we can do – experts have .... it down to a
          few key things – like recycling. That's why I
          get so depressed thinking about it – we can
          all make a difference!

freshen   tidy   do

3 Sorry I won't be joining you tonight, Carlo – I have friends coming at the weekend, so I've got to .... up the flat to get ready for them – I've left things all over the floor! The whole place needs .... up, though really I should .... it up completely – redecorate everywhere. Never mind – it'll have to do for now and they probably won't mind too much!

liven   speed   speak

4
Woman: Pete – this is a terrible connection – I
        can't really hear you. Could you ....
        up a bit?
Man: Can you hear me now? I'm trying to tell
        you that I'm going to be late – my train
        is stuck outside Birmingham and unless
        it .... up a bit, I won't make it
        before nine.
Woman: Don't worry – the party will only just be
        .... up by then! We'll save some
        food for you – just get here as soon as
        you can.

die   close   settle   track

5 Following fierce protests from animal rights campaigners, the local zoo has been .... down while allegations of cruelty to the animals are investigated. Police have managed to .... down video evidence which will be presented at a court hearing next week. They have appealed for protesters to .... down, and keep away from the court at this time, to allow the strong feelings already fuelled by the demonstrations to .... down.

2 Now match each text to the general meaning of *up* or *down* common to all the phrasal verbs in that text.

A indicates a difference in size or intensity
B indicates that something is being improved or prepared
C indicates thoroughness or completeness, and usually of ending or change
D indicates that someone is moving closer to someone else
E indicates an increase in quantity or intensity

2 Complete the following sentences with the correct missing particle: *up* or *down*.

1 Old glass is often melted .... for recycling.
2 It's too hot to go out now – let's wait until later when it might have cooled .... a bit.
3 Before he could sell his old car he had to touch .... the scratches to improve its appearance.
4 James sidled .... to Jane and whispered to her.
5 The building had been burning steadily for an hour when suddenly the flames flared .... and it started to collapse.
6 Don't creep .... on me like that! You made me jump!
7 The zoo's debts were mounting .... so the owners began looking for official sponsors.
8 The original article was too graphic in its detail so the editor watered it .... before publication.

Compound nouns formed from verbs

3 Which two of these sentences are possible?

1 The rain downpoured in the afternoon.
2 The rain poured down in the afternoon.
3 There was a downpour in the afternoon.
4 There was a pourdown in the afternoon.

4 Complete the following sentences with a compound noun made from the word in capitals and a particle from the box.

up	down	out	back	away

1 The relationship between the two groups had suffered a complete .... **BREAK**
2 She suffered a bad stomach .... after eating some contaminated food. **SET**
3 I like getting .... on my homework – it's useful even if not always good! **FEED**
4 I've got far too much stuff in my flat – I need to have a complete .... **CLEAR**
5 I can't be bothered to cook tonight – let's get a .... **TAKE**
6 The project suffered a severe .... when the main sponsor pulled out. **SET**
7 There was a great .... for the rock concert, including the country's number one singer. **LINE**
8 The company's finances suffered a real .... after the chairman resigned. **TURN**
9 The school leaver waited anxiously to hear the .... of his first job interview. **COME**
10 Some people can change their attitude and develop a whole new .... on life. **LOOK**

Writing: report (Part 1)

1 Look at the following Part 1 task.

Your school is planning to run a special event called World Awareness Day. The principal has asked you to write a report on the best way to approach this and what to include, based on questionnaires completed by students.

Read the extracts from the questionnaires, and the suggested timetable for the day. Write a report for the principal outlining the situation and making recommendations for what should be included and when, giving reasons.

Write your **report** in 180–220 words.

> Films about endangered animals – make people see the issues! Maybe lectures?

> Sponsored clean-up of school – make people see amount of rubbish around

> Fines for litter – money used for recycling bins in school. Event will have a long-lasting effect!

> Waste of time. Let's have a football game instead!

> Bring friends from outside school – spread the message!

> Good idea – special lunch? – bread and fruit – healthy – no meat

> Sponsor an animal – cute one like a polar bear – that'd be fun!

Timetable:	
9–10	lessons
10–12	activities?
12–1	lunch
1–4	activities?

2   Now look at the three plans that were written by students to answer the task. Which plan do you think is best? Why?

Plan A

> 1 Survey questions and answers
> 2 Analysis of answers
> 3 Problems uncovered by survey
> 4 Suggestions for the day

Plan B

> 1 Reason for writing
> 2 Survey results
> 3 Recommendations for the day
> 4 Conclusion

Plan C

> 1 Introduction
> 2 Information about environmental issues
> 3 Survey results
> 4 Suggestions for the day

3   Here is some advice about writing a report in Paper 2, Part 1. Do you think the advice should be 'do' or 'don't'?

1 .... begin by stating the purpose of the report
2 .... summarise given information succinctly
3 .... use adjectives and adverbs for effect
4 .... use bullet points where appropriate
5 .... include all the words from the input texts
6 .... divide the report into sections with headings if appropriate
7 .... develop ideas in task input with your own details
8 .... use an impersonal semi-formal/formal style
9 .... give your own opinion throughout
10 .... use appropriate linking words
11 .... use all the information from the input

4

1 Read the first part of a sample answer below. Which plan does it follow?

2 How has the writer dealt with the input?

- included everything in the order given
- used the same words
- grouped input ideas into logical groups

> This report will assess suggestions made by students for a World Awareness Day in the school, and make recommendations for what should be included in the day.
>
> Survey results
> Suggestions were collated from questionnaires completed by 80 per cent of students. Most were keen to support the day, although some felt that it would be useless and preferred a sporting activity such as a football match. Suggestions were divided into recommendations for the day, and ideas that would have an effect in the long-term. The former included a vegetarian lunch, films and lectures so that people could be informed, and clearing up litter in the school grounds. Among the most popular long-term ideas were providing recycling bins for the school, bringing in people from other schools even though this would have a knock-on effect on the whole community, and also sponsoring an endangered animal.
>
> Recommendations
> The proposed timetable has two slots for activities. Recommendations for using the allocated times are:

5

1 Work with a partner. Discuss how to deal with the recommendations, and how they should be grouped in the time slots. Think about:

- how many recommendations you should make, given the time constraints
- whether any suggestions are not useful for the day
- what activities could happen at the same time
- when lectures would be most acceptable and effective
- when outside work should be done.

2 Discuss the approach to take in the report. Should you use bullet points or text? Where should you include your own opinion?

3 Now complete the task with your own ideas.

4 Exchange your work with a partner. Give feedback using the advice from Exercise 3.

6   Look at the task on page 192. Write your own answer to the task, using the approach above as a model.

▶ Writing reference pp.199, 207

Use of English: multiple-choice cloze (Part 1)

1 For questions **1–12**, read the text below and decide which answer
(**A, B, C** or **D**) best fits each gap. There is an example at the beginning (**0**).

Happy to be average

At a dinner party I was at recently, conversation was (**0**) .....**A**..... fever pitch. A group
of very boring parents were (**1**) .... about just how exceptional their children were.
'Little Rosie was walking almost before she was born,' said one. 'That's nothing! Little
Bobby was using conditional tenses at thirteen months and was even (**2**) .... his
mother,' said another.

Then came the (**3**) .... of a woman who had, until then, chosen to (**4**) ....
silent. What (**5**) .... was her child bringing into the world? The table hushed as she
spoke. 'Well, Theo's entirely average,' she said. 'But I love him.'

How brave she was to value the average, thereby elevating it to the extraordinary. The
ironic thing, (**6**) .... , was that the rest of the dinner guests then started to compete
all over again, saying that actually their child was (**7**) .... more average than hers
because, etc., etc. It made me (**8**) .... that being confident enough to say you are
entirely average (**9**) .... that you're actually anything but.

The world is full of superlatives. We have become (**10**) .... to everything being
new, brilliant, fabulous, the latest or the best ever. So much so that we too (**11**) ....
talking like the advertisers who are always telling us that things are glamorous, fairy-
tale, glittering and wonderful. I'm sure that I'm not (**12**) .... in feeling very tired
of it all.

0	**A** reaching	**B** raising	**C** getting	**D** making
1	**A** applauding	**B** praising	**C** boasting	**D** complimenting
2	**A** altering	**B** correcting	**C** amending	**D** revising
3	**A** attempt	**B** go	**C** turn	**D** try
4	**A** remain	**B** repose	**C** rest	**D** resist
5	**A** gifts	**B** donations	**C** presents	**D** contributions
6	**A** therefore	**B** even though	**C** nonetheless	**D** of course
7	**A** effectively	**B** considerably	**C** eventually	**D** constructively
8	**A** perceive	**B** imagine	**C** realise	**D** suppose
9	**A** means	**B** tells	**C** speaks	**D** points
10	**A** acknowledged	**B** accepted	**C** accustomed	**D** acquainted
11	**A** fall back	**B** come down	**C** get round	**D** end up
12	**A** individual	**B** unique	**C** single	**D** lonely

Use of English: open cloze (Part 2)

2   For questions **13–27**, read the text below and think of the word which best fits each gap. Use only one word in each gap. There is an example at the beginning (**0**).

Save the rhinos

The Save the Rhino Trust (SRT) is located (**0**) ...*in*.... the northwest of Namibia, far away from the country's farming heartland. Its cause is a black rhino subspecies commonly known (**13**) .... the 'desert-adapted' rhino, a hefty beast that trots up hillsides to escape (**14**) .... worst of the heat, drinks only every third (**15**) .... fourth day and eats plants (**16**) .... sap is poisonous to man. These fellows are nothing if (**17**) .... survivors.

By the early 1980s, poachers had nearly wiped them (**18**) .... Some hunters even shot them from helicopters – (**19**) .... much for notions of sportsmanship. (**20**) .... their lowest point, there were perhaps 55 individuals left – but a recent census estimated about 130. That might seem a spectacular turnaround (**21**) .... it needs to be viewed against an overall fall in Africa's black rhino population of around 90 per cent (**22**) .... 1960.

In search of these elusive animals, I had come to the Palmwag concession – a former farm (**23**) .... the land had originally been tamed by (**24**) .... rid of all the rhino. Now, there is a magnificent area of wilderness (**25**) .... aside for considerate tourism, game drives and the SRT base. This year's particularly wet rainy season meant the rhino were harder to find. There was (**26**) .... a lot of water around that (**27**) .... of keeping close to perennial springs, the rhino were wandering far and wide, enjoying a spell of rich and plenty. We were forced to do the same.

Use of English: word formation (Part 3)

3   For questions **28–37**, read the text below. Use the word given in capitals at the end of some of the lines to form a word that fits in the gap **in the same line**. There is an example at the beginning (**0**).

Working at a theme park

Working as a Personal (**0**) *Assistant* (PA) at a theme park can be	**ASSIST**
a lot of fun. It can offer a varied role and a friendly teamwork	
atmosphere, (**28**) .... to Suzy Baines who has worked at one	**ACCORD**
of the largest in England for fifteen years. Suzy is now PA to	
the theme park's Head of (**29**) .... As she says, in her job,	**MARKET**
no two days are the same.	
'I can't imagine working anywhere else – it really is so much	
fun. Apart from PA duties, I organise (**30**) .... and the	**CONFER**
(**31**) .... our staff make at them, and take the minutes in	**PRESENT**
meetings. The staff here are a (**32**) .... bunch, and so I get	**CREATE**
involved in the planning of new attractions. But my main job	
is to act as a (**33**) .... I produce a weekly news-sheet for	**COMMUNICATE**
staff to keep them up-to-date with all the latest (**34**)	**DEVELOP**
We have around 550 permanent staff and a further 1,300 work	
here on a (**35**) .... basis during the summer months.	**SEASON**
The people here are all like family and everybody (**36**)	**GENUINE**
cares about everybody else. But if you're having a (**37**)	**FRUSTRATE**
day and things are getting on top of you, there's no better cure	
than leaving everything and going for a ride on a rollercoaster!'	

Use of English: gapped sentences (Part 4)

4 For questions **38–42**, think of **one** word only which can be used appropriately in all three sentences. Here is an example (**0**).

Example:

0 Naomi is a very approachable woman and people find her ..*easy*.. to talk to.

My grandmother thinks that I have a very ..*easy*.. life compared to her experience of being a teenager.

It's ..*easy*.. to see why so many people support the local team who have done so well in recent seasons.

38 Tom and Angela were disappointed not to receive a .... of cutlery as wedding present.

The college is drawing up a .... of rules regarding the use of the computer facilities in the library.

Elsa has been collecting *Star Wars* figurines for 12 years, and needs one more rare figure to complete the ....

39 As sales continued to decline, Patrick had no .... but to close down the business.

At the new shopping centre, customers will find a wide .... of goods on display.

Although Sally Green would have been Paul's .... for the job, other members of the interview panel had different ideas.

40 So did you .... any conclusions once you'd completed your research into the issue?

People don't need to learn how to .... these days as most designs can be created on a computer.

To decide who had won first prize, the organisers of the competition decided to .... the names out of a hat.

41 Tom's story about the dog was rather boring and failed to .... the group's attention.

We didn't take the car on holiday as the boot wasn't large enough to .... all our luggage.

Clarice went on to .... a number of responsible positions in the company before her retirement in 2005.

42 My clothes feel very .... since I lost weight.

I had to pay for the cup of coffee with a £20 note because I didn't have any .... change.

The little girl had had a .... tooth for some weeks, and on Friday evening it finally came out.

Use of English: key word transformations (Part 5)

5 For questions **43–50**, complete the second sentence so that it has a similar meaning to the first sentence, using the word given. **Do not change the word given.** You must use between **three** and **six** words including the word given. Here is an example (**0**).

Example:

0 The two friends were sitting on their own looking at a computer screen. **FRONT**

The two friends were sitting by ..*themselves in front of*.. a computer screen.

43 I think it would've been nice to have had an older sister. **WISH**

I .... an older sister.

44 The car really needs cleaning. **TIME**

It's high .... cleaned.

45 I was just about to send you an email with all the information. **POINT**

I was .... you an email with all the information.

46 Raymond is obsessed with buying football memorabilia on the Internet. **BECOME**

Buying football memorabilia on the Internet .... for Raymond.

47 'Having children changed my life,' said Molly. **WHICH**

Molly said that it .... her life.

48 Lots of people think that global warming has been exaggerated by the media. **WIDELY**

Global warming is .... exaggerated by the media.

49 The sun was so strong that walking across the sand dunes became exhausting. **STRENGTH**

It was .... made walking across the sand dunes so exhausting.

50 'I reckon you should turn left here,' said the old man we'd asked for directions. **ADVISED**

The old man we'd asked for directions .... a left turn there.

UNIT
11 Always on my mind

Grammar 1: modal verbs 2

1

1 Read through the text below. Which person is describing:

a) the earliest memory?
b) an impossible incident?
c) an event that could have had serious results?
d) a family celebration?

EARLIEST MEMORIES

Julie

I remember sitting on my grandmother's lap for a birthday, I think it was mine because they told me I could blow out the candles and I kind of knew the concept of it but didn't know quite how to do it. I remember crying when one of my cousins eventually had to blow out the candles. Anyway, when I told my mother this, she said I couldn't have remembered it because it was only my second birthday, but I'm sure I do.

Helen

I was on holiday at the seaside. I went down to the edge of the sea to play, then when I looked back I couldn't see my family. So I wandered along the beach looking for them. I walked and walked for a long time, but I don't remember feeling scared or anything. Then an old couple found me and took me back to their home and gave me something to eat. Then eventually they called the police – which they ought to have done in the first place, of course – and my parents came to collect me. They must have been incredibly worried – I'd been lost for four hours.

Ian

One of my earliest memories, from when I was about four, is seeing a speedboat race across a moonlit sky. Honest, it's there in my mind's eye and I can even remember thinking 'That's weird' at the time. I suppose it can't have happened. People say it might have been a dream, but I'm sure I remember it.

Gary

My eighty-year-old grandmother once told me that she could quite clearly remember being born! She described the traumatic experience of suddenly being surrounded by bright light and loud voices 'like someone turning the volume right up on the television'. She also remembered that later on she felt calm and settled and said that this may have been as the nurse gave her to her mother to hold in her arms.

2 Underline ten examples of modal verbs in the past form in the text. Match them to the following uses:

Possibility: ....
....
....
....
Logical deduction: ....
Obligation/necessity: ....
Advice (weak obligation): ....
Permission: ....
Ability: ....
....

▶ Grammar reference p.196 (10)

2 Complete the sentences using a past modal verb from Exercise 1. Sometimes two answers are possible.

1 I think my earliest memory is when my little brother was born, and I cried because I wanted a little sister – but I'm not sure if I actually remember it, I .... / .... remembered hearing my parents tell the story.

2 I was playing with someone in the garden – it .... / .... been my sister, because she's five years younger than me.

3 My father says when he was little he had to ask if he .... leave the table after meals, and he wasn't allowed to unless he'd finished all his food.

4 I got into trouble with my grandfather once because he gave me some money and I lost it – he said I .... been more careful.

5 I remember I jumped into a swimming pool once when I was just six, and I .... swim, but fortunately it was just the shallow end so I was OK.

6 My mother says that when I was tiny she went shopping with me in my pushchair and left me outside a shop and didn't remember until she got home – she .... run all the way back!

Vocabulary 1

Expressions with *take*

1

1 Complete the short dialogues by matching each sentence to a response below.

1 It was a long time before he could take it all in and understand what people were telling him.
2 The class took to the new teacher the moment she walked into the classroom.
3 You can't take anyone else on – the budget just won't stand it.
4 You cope so well – you always take everything in your stride.
5 Sometimes it's easy to take advantage of people, especially when they are rather naïve.
6 I think the boss really takes me for granted sometimes – he never thanks me for the work I do.
7 The show was amazing – it really took my breath away.
8 Running the department single-handed is hard work – it's taken a lot out of you and you need to watch your health.
9 If you feel bad about what she said, then take it up with her – don't let it go.
10 When he told me about the job I took it as an offer, but in fact he was just talking in general terms and I'd got the wrong end of the stick.

a) That's true, but it's just a case of doing what's right and not asking too much of them.
b) I realise that – I'll be careful not to overdo it and get ill.
c) I think everyone felt the same – she's so charismatic and easy to like.
d) Well, perhaps they just weren't explaining the situation clearly enough.
e) I know – we can't really afford to pay the staff we've got already.
f) So you misunderstood what he was saying – that's a shame!
g) Thanks – I do try not to make things more difficult than they are.
h) You should tell him how you feel – it's not nice to feel unappreciated at work.
i) I know – I've never seen anything like it. It was fantastic!
j) You're right – I'll speak to her about it in the morning.

2 Now tell a partner what you think the highlighted expressions mean.

Expressions with *mind* and *brain(s)*

2

1 Complete the sentences using the correct form of expressions from the box.

speak (your) mind
take (your) mind off something
out of (your) mind
read someone's mind
put (your) mind at rest
~~change (your) mind~~
make up (your) mind
have something on the brain
pick (someone's) brains
rack (your) brains

Example:
She never sticks to what she says – she's always
  changing her mind .

1 I wish he would decide what he wants to do – he can never ....
2 I've got an essay to write on psychology, and you know a lot about it – can I .... for some ideas?
3 You seem to have a lot of problems – why don't you come to the cinema to stop you thinking too much – it will .... your difficulties for a while.
4 That's a crazy thing to suggest – I think you must be .... to think it would work!
5 I downloaded that tune last week and now I can't stop singing it – I've ....
6 You've thought of exactly the same idea as I did – you must have ....!
7 If you are worried about the situation, then you'll have to tell someone – don't be afraid to .... and tell them how you feel.
8 If you go and speak to a doctor, then he can reassure you about your concerns – he can ....
9 He had no idea what to do, and spent a long time .... trying to think of a solution.

2 Now tell a partner what you think the expressions in the box mean.

3 Tell a partner about a time:

• something took your breath away
• something took a lot out of you
• you changed your mind
• you racked your brains about something
• you spoke your mind
• you read someone's mind.

Exam focus

Paper 1 Reading: multiple choice (Part 3)

About the exam: In Paper 1, Part 3, you read a
long text and then answer seven four-option
multiple-choice questions which test your
detailed understanding of the main ideas in the
text, as well as the attitude and opinion of the
writer. The questions follow the order of the text
and may focus on the meaning of whole
paragraphs, on points of detail or the use of
particular expressions.

Suggested procedure

1 Read the task rubric, heading and any sub-
headings to see the type of text you are going
to read and something about the topic.

2 Skim the text quickly to get a general idea of
what it is about and how it is organised. Think
about the main topic of each paragraph.

3 Look at each question stem, but not at the
options for the moment. Mark the part of the
text where you expect to find the answer to
each of the questions.

4 Now read the text carefully. When you reach a
part you have marked, look at the question
stem and the options and decide which of
them is correct.

1 You are going to read a magazine article
about memory. For questions **1–7**, choose the
answer (**A, B, C** or **D**) which you think fits best
according to the text.

1 What does the writer imply about the singer Tori
Amos?

A She is not alone in suffering from unexpected
lapses of memory.

B She could give no explanation for her sudden
loss of memory.

C She is more than usually prone to short-term
memory loss.

D She may have forgotten her lines as the result of
an illness.

2 The writer mentions two of her friends in the
context of short-term memory loss in order to

A show how different people react to it.

B illustrate how prevalent it currently is.

C demonstrate how embarrassing it can be.

D underline how it affects people in different
ways.

3 In the third paragraph, the writer suggests that

A there are ways of improving someone's memory.

B people will need their memories less in the
future.

C technology has increased our potential memory
load.

D our brains are good at prioritising what to
remember.

4 The writer quotes Dr Larry Jacoby to help explain
why in social situations

A people often fail to remember the details of
long anecdotes.

B people tend not to pay close attention to what
others are saying.

C people don't realise when others are not really
listening to them.

D people may forget who it is they have told a
particular story to before.

5 In the fifth paragraph, the writer

A acknowledges the truth behind a popular belief.

B admits that she makes little effort to recall
certain details.

C accepts that her short-term memory is bound to
deteriorate.

D agrees with the suggestion that memory loss
may be avoidable.

6 The phrase 'to this end' (line 78) refers to

A preventing short-term memory loss.

B understanding ourselves better.

C remembering things in detail.

D improving social skills.

7 What does the writer suggest about the event
called *Stop the Clock*?

A Much of it was about memory rather than the
perception of time.

B It did not really address important issues to do
with memory.

C Part of it was of particular relevance to her
professionally.

D It was hard to give the discussions her full
concentration.

2 Do you have a good memory? What things
do you find easy or difficult to remember? Why?

Where is my mind?

At a recent concert in Los Angeles, the singer Tori Amos was midway through her hit song *Winter* when, suddenly, inexplicably, she forgot the lyrics. Rather than warbling on about fires burning and flowers
5 competing for the sun as her eager fans were expecting, she stopped in her tracks and started singing about how tired she was feeling. Amos, it seems, had become the latest victim of the short-term memory-loss epidemic.

It's a particularly modern affliction. We are fast
10 becoming the amnesia generation, plunged by the ever-increasing pace of our lives into a fog of retold anecdotes, lost information and missed appointments. I was driving through London in a friend's car recently, when the
15 heavens suddenly opened. 'Oh dear!' my friend screamed, helplessly cranking various buttons and levers. 'I can't remember how the windscreen wipers work.' Another friend managed to
20 cruise through town for a full forty-five minutes before realising that all those people were not, in fact, waving and pointing at her new haircut, but at the briefcase that she had left balanced
25 on the roof of her car.

All the evidence is that our memories aren't what they used to be. Indeed, in a recent report, the think tank Demos predicts that we could become a society of memory haves and have-nots, with
30 only those who can afford to pay for costly brain-enhancement treatments getting the best opportunities in life, from exam passes to the boardroom. But are our memories getting worse, or is it just that we don't care enough to remember? We are bombarded with so much
35 more information than previous generations. In days gone by, you might have known only thirty people in your entire lifetime. Now, you probably talk to thirty new people in a single day. That's a lot more to remember. And technology hasn't helped. We no longer dial numbers, we
40 just press a key. We don't need to remember birthdays or anniversaries or the times of important meetings when we have software to beep at us, and our brains have adapted accordingly.

But some experts think there is another reason why we forget the details of social conversations. Often, we 45 don't remember things because we're not listening. Instead, we're tuning in to our inner dialogue, the one that's going 'Does this shirt look OK?' or, even more distracting, 'What am I going to say next?' Another hazard of social-memory loss is unwittingly retelling the 50 same anecdote to the same audience on different occasions. There is, apparently, a reason for this. 'Two processes are at work when we tell an anecdote,' says Dr Larry Jacoby at the University of St Louis. 'The first is the sheer familiarity of the tale, built 55 up over many tellings. This makes it all too likely to swim into our consciousness. The second is the recall of whether you have told this group this story before. As long as that works, you will not 60 bore them with it again. But recall depends on well-functioning frontal lobes.'

It used to be widely thought that short-term memory worsened with age, 65 while long-term memory got sharper. This would certainly explain why I can remember the songs my mother played when I was growing up, but cannot recall the name of our new neighbour. Alas, the memory 70 experts aren't prepared to let us off so easily. 'Memory is a muscle. Use it or lose it,' advises expert Robert Allen, for example, and he would seem to have a point.

Of course, memory is not just about remembering names or where we put the keys. It is about who we are. 75 If we can't even remember the details of what we said and to whom, then how can we possibly hope to make sense of our lives? To this end, London's Southbank Centre recently staged *Stop the Clock*, a month-long event devoted to the perception of time. During the event, the 80 Dutch thinker and memory guru Douwe Draaisma led a discussion looking at why we remember certain things and not others, and the impact of memory on writers. It was very thought provoking, apparently and I had fully intended to go. But when it came to it, I was so 85 preoccupied with other things that it slipped my mind.

3

1 Match the following verbs to a word or phrase to form a common expression used in the text.

to stop	to slip	to press	to build up
to swim	to dial	to tell	to let

familiarity with something   a number
someone off easily   in her tracks   my mind
into our consciousness   a key   anecdotes

2 Which of the expressions means: a) to forget b) to get to know something?

Use of English 1: multiple-choice cloze (Part 1)

1

1 Discuss these questions.

1 How easy do you find it to concentrate:
• when you're doing homework?
• when you're watching a film?
• when you've got something on your mind?
2 How long can you concentrate for?

3 Talk about things that:
• help you to concentrate
• prevent you from concentrating.

2 Read the text quickly to compare your ideas with those of the writer. Ignore the gaps for the moment.

2 Read the text again and decide which answer (A, B, C or D) best fits each gap. There is an example at the beginning (0).

How to concentrate

Concentration is good in exams, bad in orange juice. Concentration happens when you **(0)** __A__ to focus on one thing to the **(1)** .... of all others, and concentrating on that one thing **(2)** .... you to stop worrying about a lot of other things. Sometimes, of course, your mind concentrates when you don't want it to. Maybe you can't get something out of your head, such as a problem you have to **(3)** .... up to, or an embarrassing situation you've been in. That's why collecting things as a hobby is popular; it **(4)** .... your mind off other things. Indeed, some people seem to prefer looking after and cataloguing their collections to actually doing anything with them, because this is when the **(5)** ...., single-minded concentration happens.

The natural span for concentration is 45 minutes. That's why half an hour for a television programme seems too short **(6)** .... an hour seems too long. But many people's lives are **(7)** .... of concentration. Modern culture is served up in small, **(8)** .... digestible chunks that require only a short **(9)** .... span – although young people can concentrate on computer games for days at a **(10)** ....

Sticking out the tongue can aid concentration. This is because you can't **(11)** .... yourself with talking at the same time and other people won't **(12)** .... to interrupt your thoughts, because you look like an idiot!

Copyright Guardian News & Media Ltd 2006

0	**A** manage	**B** achieve	**C** succeed	**D** accomplish
1	**A** removal	**B** exclusion	**C** omission	**D** rejection
2	**A** lets	**B** means	**C** makes	**D** allows
3	**A** face	**B** confront	**C** tackle	**D** meet
4	**A** brings	**B** puts	**C** holds	**D** takes
5	**A** arresting	**B** gripping	**C** absorbing	**D** enthralling
6	**A** otherwise	**B** whilst	**C** whereby	**D** thus
7	**A** absent	**B** devoid	**C** lacking	**D** deficient
8	**A** gently	**B** plainly	**C** surely	**D** easily
9	**A** attention	**B** application	**C** consideration	**D** contemplation
10	**A** length	**B** stroke	**C** time	**D** sequence
11	**A** sidestep	**B** distract	**C** sidetrack	**D** disturb
12	**A** risk	**B** chance	**C** dare	**D** brave

Grammar 2: emphasis with inversion

1

1 Tick the sentence which is more emphatic in each of the following pairs. Mark the words that have been inverted with arrows.

Example:

a) I had only just sat down to eat when the phone rang.

b) Hardly had I sat down to eat when the phone rang. ✓

1 a) Seldom have I come across such a strange story.
b) I have seldom come across such a strange story.

2 a) You must not leave your bag unattended at any time.
b) At no time must you leave your bag unattended.

3 a) I didn't realise how hot it was until I went into the garden.
b) Not until I went into the garden did I realise how hot it was.

4 a) You mustn't go back into the building after midnight no matter what happens.
b) Under no circumstances must you go back into the building after midnight.

5 a) Not only did I hate the book, but I hated the film of the book too!
b) I hated the book and I hated the film of the book too!

2 Complete the rule.

When words and phrases like *not only*, *under no circumstances*, ..., ..., ... and .... begin a sentence the .... and subject are inverted.

┌─ Watch Out! *no sooner/hardly* **◄──**

Choose the correct alternative in each sentence. Then complete the rules below.

a) No sooner had he left the room *than / when* they started talking about him.

b) Hardly had he left the room *than / when* they started talking about him.

1 Use .... when you start a sentence with *no sooner*.

2 Use .... when you start a sentence with *hardly*.

▶ Grammar reference, p.195 (6.2)

2 Rewrite these sentences using the adverbial in brackets at the beginning and make all the other changes necessary to give greater emphasis to each one.

1 I had just sat down to read the newspaper when the telephone rang. (*Hardly*)

2 Less than a second after she stood up to speak the fire alarm went off. (*No sooner*)

3 He forgets people's names and also finds it hard to remember place names. (*Not only*)

4 You should never let anyone into your house unless you have seen their ID. (*Under no circumstances*)

5 She never doubted that he was telling the truth. (*At no time*)

6 I started to write the letter and then realised that I had lost their address. (*Only after*)

3 Rewrite these sentences using standard word order to make them less emphatic.

1 Rarely do you find a household without a computer these days.

2 Hardly had she started to have a shower when the postman knocked at the door.

3 Only after I had left for the airport did I remember that my passport was still in my desk in the study.

4 Not only did he trust her, he never doubted her loyalty to him.

5 At no time in recent history have we seen such rapid progress in medical science.

4 Complete the second sentence so that it has a similar meaning to the first sentence, using the word given. Do not change the word given. You must use between three and six words, including the word given.

1 Jane realised what she'd forgotten to do as soon as she arrived. **SOONER**
No .... she realised what she'd forgotten to do.

2 The use of mobile phones is absolutely forbidden inside the laboratory. **MUST**
Under .... used inside the laboratory.

3 It's not often that you find someone with such a good memory. **COME**
Seldom .... someone with such a good memory.

4 It was the first time that I'd tried mental activities to help me concentrate. **BEFORE**
Never .... mental activities to help me concentrate.

Speaking 1: individual long turn
(Part 2)

1

1 Work with a partner. Read the following exam task. How many parts are there to the task?

> Look at the pictures. They show people concentrating in different situations. I'd like you to compare two of the pictures, and say why it is important for the people to concentrate in these situations and how easy it might be for them to concentrate.

2 Take turns to choose two pictures, and then do the task. Remember to talk about the second part of the task (highlighted), and practise timing yourselves so that you feel how long a minute actually is.

2 Which situation do you think is the most difficult to concentrate in?

Vocabulary 2

Phrasal verbs with *think*

1 Choose the best preposition to complete the phrasal verbs in each of these sentences.

1 His suggestion does make sense – at least it's something to think *about / on*.
2 I can't think *of / about* anything better to do in this situation.
3 Their proposal needs to be carefully thought *out / of* before they put it to the committee formally.
4 I can't make up my mind immediately – I need more time to think things *over / up*.
5 The whole day was a complete disaster – whoever planned it didn't think things *out / through* carefully enough.
6 The student was standing outside the classroom trying to think *over / up* a good excuse for being late.

Expressions with *think*

2 Read the text below, and replace the highlighted phrases with the correct form of an expression from the box. You may need to make other changes to the sentence.

think the world of   think outside the box
think positively   think on (your) feet
think better of (something)   think straight

James was finding it hard to concentrate. He knew that he had to work on his essay, but he was finding it hard to (1) organise his thoughts clearly because his mind was in such turmoil. It was hard to forget that his best friend, who (2) was the most important person in his life, was at that very moment struggling to pass his entry test for university. James had already advised Neil to (3) approach the whole thing expecting to succeed, but he knew that Neil was very nervous even though he had done a lot of work in preparation for the written test. James also knew that Neil would have to pass an interview as well as a written test, and that he couldn't prepare anything for this – he would have to (4) react to whatever the interviewers asked him. It would be important for Neil to make a good impression, but then he had always been good at presenting original ideas – he was good at (5) approaching topics or problems from new and unusual angles. Eventually James gave up on trying to work and decided he would call Neil. Then he (6) changed his mind – what would he say if Neil had not got in?

3 Tell a partner about a time you needed to
- think outside the box
- think on your feet.

Use of English 2: gapped sentences (Part 4)

Think of one word which can be used appropriately in all three sentences.

1 During the concert, Tori suffered an unexpected .... of memory for a few minutes.

The owners do not accept any responsibility for .... or damage to vehicles parked in this car park.

When Jason set up his own business he expected to make a .... for the first few months.

2 Chloe realised that it was pointless arguing with her boss any further because they were clearly not of the same .... on the issue.

The good thing about having such a close friend is that I can almost read his ...., and never have to ask him what he thinks.

The fact that he'd offended Tania had been on Terry's .... for some time.

3 Looking at Barry's assignment, you get a real .... of the pride he takes in his work.

There is no .... in washing the car before the journey, it'll only need doing again once we get there.

Fortunately, Louis had the .... to check the brakes before he rode off on the bike he'd borrowed.

4 Fiona had a free afternoon, so was able to give the problem her full ....

The new research has been the subject of considerable media .... recently.

I think we should bring the problem to the .... of the local council.

5 Sarah had to admit that 'mind gym' was a .... she'd never come across before.

The local politician is hoping to be re-elected for a second .... of office.

I think that in the short ...., we should concentrate on keeping the service running.

Listening: sentence completion
(Part 2)

1 Discuss these questions.

1 What makes people laugh?
2 How do you feel after having a good laugh about something?
3 Is it easier to laugh with other people? Why?
4 Is laughter always a sign of happiness?

2 Look at the task in Exercise 3.

1 Before you listen, think about:

- the type of words that are missing in each gap
- the type of information you are listening for in each answer.

2 Can you predict what some of the missing words might be?

3 You will hear a radio presenter called Tom Membury introducing a programme on the subject of laughter yoga and its founder Dr Kataria. Complete the sentences.

Laughter Yoga

Tom compares laughter to .... **(1)** in terms of its emotional benefits.

Tom uses the word .... **(2)** to describe how laughter affects an audience.

Dr Kataria first got the idea of laughter therapy from a .... **(3)**

Dr Kataria stopped using jokes in his sessions as some people found them .... **(4)**

Dr Kataria found that laughter is good for us even when .... **(5)** is not the stimulus.

Dr Kataria claims that medical conditions such as .... and .... **(6)** may be prevented by laughter.

Tom mentions an event called .... **(7)** at which Dr Kataria often appears.

Tom played a game involving pretend .... **(8)** at the laughter yoga session he attended.

---

4 Were your predictions for questions 1, 5 and 6 correct?

Would you enjoy a laughter therapy session? What sort of people do you think go to them?

Writing: article (Part 2)

1 In Paper 2, Part 2, you may have to write an article. Even though they may be on different topics, good articles share some common characteristics.

1 Work with a partner. Think about any magazine articles you have read recently and suggest possible characteristics of a good article.

2 Now read the following article which comes from a general interest magazine, and see if any of your points are included.

1 What is it that makes you feel happy? Is it what happens to you, or is it how you feel about it? And have you ever considered the question anyway?

2 According to psychologists, it's not events (good or bad) that determine our feeling of well-being, but how we think and react to them. Very successful people can be miserable if they have a constant sense of having just missed out on something – conversely, people who appear to have less can feel incredibly happy and fortunate because they value what they have. It's the old 'is the glass half empty or half full?' question, and your answer is crucial.

3 Match a purpose below to each paragraph. There is one purpose you do not need to use.

a) Provide background information
b) Introduce the main idea
c) Give examples and further details
d) Engage the reader in the topic
e) Summarise discussion and draw conclusions

4 Choose the best title for the article.

a) Good and bad feelings
b) Coming to terms with envy
c) Go for gold, but be happy with less

2 Here are some suggestions that might make any article interesting. How many of these are included in the article you have just read?

1 attention-grabbing title
2 intriguing and thought-provoking opening paragraph

3 But how do we get to be 'glass half-full' people? One suggestion is not to compare yourself with others, especially those who seem to have more. Another old saying – 'the grass is always greener on the other side of the fence' – is very true, but of course that green grass may be all an illusion. We don't really know whether the other person is happy at all – we just imagine they are, and so feel bad in comparison. But developing a positive outlook on life is very important. People who look on the bright side see possibilities in everything – they never imagine doors closing, only opening. It's an enviable state of mind, and it's a pity they don't sell it in the local supermarket. If they did, then I for one would buy buckets of it! But that's not going to happen, so perhaps the answer when we come second in a race, or see our neighbour converting his house in a way that we could never afford, is not to envy, but to aspire.

4 What we should do to be happy is not to look at what might have been but at what still could be. And then just go for it! But the deal is that we have to accept whatever consequences there are philosophically and without regret – and be happy about it.

3 rhetorical questions addressed directly to the reader
4 speaking directly to the reader, using 'you'
5 using grammatical structures to give emphasis
6 giving interesting or surprising facts or information
7 using a range of interesting vocabulary, often colourful
8 backing up ideas with specific details and concrete examples
9 including direct speech
10 having an interesting and 'punchy' final paragraph or conclusion

3 The writer has used a lot of interesting and varied vocabulary, including expressions.

1 What do you think the following sayings or expressions in the article mean?

a) Is the glass half empty or half full?
b) The grass is always greener on the other side of the fence.
c) They never imagine doors closing, only opening.

2 Find words or expressions in the article that mean the same as:

1 on the other hand (para 2)
2 vital, very important (para 2)
3 something we think is true but is not (para 3)
4 a good attitude towards life (para 3)
5 people who are optimistic (para 3)
6 an attitude that we would all like to have (para 3)
7 take a chance and do your best (para 4)

4 Look at the two tasks on page 189. Choose the article you want to write and work with another student who has chosen the same task.

5 Plan your article with your partner, and then write it.

1 Decide how you are going to organise your article. How many paragraphs? What will be the general purpose and topic of each one?
2 Look at the points included in Exercise 2. Which ones will you include in your article? They may not all be appropriate.
3 Write your article.
4 Exchange your article with your partner. Make notes of ways in which they could improve their article, and discuss them together.
5 Read the model answer on page 208. Check that you are following the 'Dos and Don'ts' suggested.
6 Write your final article, using your own grammar checklist to make sure that it is accurate.

▶ **Writing reference p.208**

Speaking 2

1 Work with a partner and discuss the following questions.

1 Why can't you tickle yourself?
First, tickle your partner's hand by wiggling your fingers softly in the centre of their palm. Check if they find it ticklish. Now make exactly the same movements on your own palm. What is the difference?

2 Can you always identify what colour something is?
Ask your partner to hold out sideways at arms length two pieces of different coloured card, while you focus on their nose. Make sure you don't see the pieces of card beforehand. What colour are they?

Student A look at page 189 for the answer to question 1.
Student B look at page 190 for the answer to question 2.

Then explain the reasons to each other.

2 Work with a partner. Look at the cubes and describe what you see. Do you see the cubes protruding out of the page or intruding into the page? Do you see the same thing? Does what you see stay the same, or does it change?

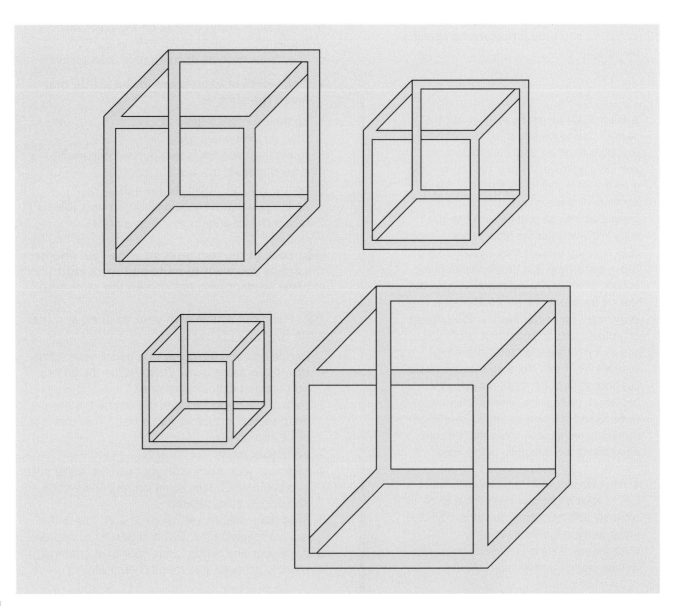

1

1 Read the text below. Use the word given in capitals at the end of some of the lines to form a word that fits in the same line. There is an example at the beginning (0).

A workout for the brain

The brain workout is a **(0)** _fitness_ trend which requires neither a yoga mat nor a pair of trainers. **(1)** .... have shown that new nerve cells appear in the brain throughout life, and so mental exercise can be **(2)** .... in ensuring that the brain functions efficiently. As a result, both clinical research **(3)** .... and private companies are exploring what are known as 'brain enhancement techniques' which seek to **(4)** .... the enormous capabilities of the human brain. What's more, the exercise analogy has proved a popular one with software **(5)** .... offering such things as 'neurobics' and a number of 'mind gym' courses now being offered **(6)** ....
Apparently, people have different brainwave patterns for different activities. For example, the beta brainwave helps us to make decisions, whilst the theta brainwave helps us to relax and remember things. Sometimes one brainwave can become **(7)** ...., for example people with high stress levels can get stuck in a high beta state.
The mind gym sessions help such people to regain **(8)** .... between these brainwaves.
Training focuses on techniques such as speed reading, memory **(9)** .... and improved powers of concentration. Small sensors placed on the client's head allow brainwaves to be viewed on a computer screen. Sportspeople and business executives, high **(10)** .... individuals who cannot allow their minds to wander for a second, have been amongst the main clients so far.

FIT
SEARCH

BENEFIT
ESTABLISH

MAXIMUM

PACK

COMMERCE

DOMINATE

MOBILE

CALL

PERFORM

2 Look back at your answers and find:
- a verb made from a noun
- an adjective made from a verb
- a word to which you added both a prefix and a suffix.

3 Look at these answers which students wrote. Why would they not get the mark in the exam? What advice would you give these students?

1: _research_
3: _establishment_
8: _immobility_

2 Replace the highlighted phrases with a phrasal verb or expression with _think_.

1 I just don't know what to do – I'm so confused, I can't get my ideas in order.
2 The whole project failed, because the planning was so bad – we just hadn't considered all the knock-on effects properly.
3 My aunt is fantastic – she's such fun, and I love her to bits.
4 It's very difficult to invent a good excuse quickly for something you've done wrong.
5 Employers like it if you can approach problems in a different way.

A matter of time

The Futuro House

Designed in 1968 by Finnish architect Matti Suuronen, the Futuro house was a classic flying saucer shape — an ellipsoid shell constructed in fibreglass and reinforced plastic, with ellipse-shaped
5 windows, door handles, light fittings and even ellipse-shaped power sockets. In theory its design was 'based on pure mathematics', but in fact this seems highly dubious — the project supervisor remembers Suuronen having a much more intuitive approach.
10 There were no detailed drawings for the prototype, and he would 'drop by the plant' and make suggestions such as 'take away a bit here, add a bit there'.

The initial commission was for a ski cabin, which
15 could be helicoptered into rough terrain, but manufacturer Polykem hoped that mass production worldwide would follow, and that the basic shell could be adapted for both domestic and commercial use. All looked to be going well until the 1973 oil
20 crisis more than tripled production costs; but for this we might all now have one.

As it is, there are thought to be at least 30 surviving Futuros, including one in Japan, one in the USA and four in Finland. But meanwhile the Futuro
25 has been reinvented as an art icon, and found its way back into the glamorous world of parties and spectacle when the prototype was used to house a headline-grabbing installation art project. What is intriguing about the Futuro is that, forty years on, we
30 still see this object as futuristic, giving weight to the somewhat questionable theory that it was actually an example of post-modernism before its time.

Reading 1: multiple choice (Part 1)

1 Do you like modern things, or are you interested in things from the past?

2

1 Work with a partner. Look at the picture above and discuss these questions:

1 When do you think this object was designed?
2 What do you think it is used for?
3 Does it make you think of the past, the present or the future?
4 What type of people would you associate with this object?

2 Read the first text to see if your ideas were right. Did anything surprise you?

3 You are going to read three texts which are all connected in some way with the idea of time. Choose the answer (A, B, C or D) which you think fits best according to the text.

1 In the first paragraph, the writer suggests that when developing the Futuro, Matti Suuronen

  A was keen to keep the design a secret.
  B had a rather poor grasp of mathematics.
  C was unwilling to trust his project manager.
  D tended to be more interested in style than precision.

2 What does the writer find strange about attitudes towards the Futuro today?

  A People still think that it looks like a futuristic object.
  B People fail to see that the design was ahead of its time.
  C People see it as a work of art rather than something practical.
  D People in various parts of the world are keen to preserve them.

Watercolours of a history waiting to happen

Years ago David Mandell began to record his sinister dreams. He painted their images, then embellished them with footnotes to add to the details of what he had 'seen'. On 11 September 1996 he dreamed the
5 destruction of two towers. Beside the towers, in Mandell's painting, was outlined the head of the Statue of Liberty. Around the towers the painting depicted billows of smoke. Five years later to the day something remarkably akin to Mandell's ghastly premonition
10 actually happened. This we know, for tucked into a corner of his painting, easy to miss, there was the silhouette of an aircraft.

The salient questions begin with the obvious: are Mandell's dreams a spate of coincidence? Is he a seer
15 able to glimpse future events in his dreams or is he merely a sad old fake? His other dreams included premonitions of other disasters and momentous events – perhaps most remarkable was his picture of the gas attack on the underground in Tokyo. Beside the image,
20 Mandell's notes named the Japanese capital as the venue of the outrage.

The programme scrupulously sought to establish whether or not Mandell was receiving apocalyptic warnings. Each key painting had been photographed by
25 staff at his local bank, in front of a calendar-clock clearly displaying the date by which the painting had been made. Every painting predated the incident it foretold. The shots were examined by a forensics expert who certified them genuine. Mandell passed a lie-detector
30 test, then allowed himself to be hypnotised. One expert thought he was mirroring the laws of probability – but the evidence suggested, given the relatively small number of dreams recorded and his high 'hit-rate', that Mandell was mirroring the laws of improbability.

Golsoncott

When I was hanging around the nearby lanes as an adolescent, waiting for life to begin, I saw Golsoncott as a place where
5 nothing ever happened. I thought of it fondly, but reckoned that it was elsewhere that things went on and that in due course one would go forth to elsewhere, with all that that implied. And so I did, but in due course
10 also Golsoncott became a retreat, a haven when rather too much was happening, the stable element in an unreliable world. You could know that it would always be the same, year by year. Absence of event was now the treasured aspect.

15   During the 70 years of the family's occupation of the house no-one was born there, though three people died: my grandfather in 1941, my grandmother 34 years later, and finally my aunt Rachel. Events of a significant kind. To a 15-year-
20 old, things happening means a few ups and downs in daily life, and Golsoncott was indeed fairly immune to that. One calm rural day slid blandly into the next, with only the weather serving up any potent kind of change. And even that interference
25 with prescribed routine was sternly resisted: family ethos was that you ignored weather and simply did what you had intended to do. You went for a walk in the rain; that was what raincoats were for.

3 What do we learn about David Mandell's paintings from the review?

A They have yet to undergo scientific analysis.

B They are hard to understand without his written notes.

C They may have been painted after the events they depict.

D They seem to predict the location as well as the type of event.

4 In the third paragraph, it is suggested that

A the programme had made exaggerated claims about the dreams.

B the expert had been unable to give an adequate explanation for the dreams.

C there was insufficient evidence to make any sort of assessment of the dreams.

D the programme makers had uncovered the answer to the mystery of the dreams.

5 In the first paragraph, the writer is explaining

A why she felt trapped at Golsoncott.

B why she decided to leave Golsoncott.

C how her attitude to Golsoncott changed.

D how she came to regret leaving Golsoncott.

6 Which phrase from the second paragraph reinforces the idea introduced by the phrase 'with all that that implied' in line 8?

A ups and downs in daily life (line 20)

B fairly immune to that (line 21)

C slid blandly into the next (line 22)

D sternly resisted (line 25)

4   Do you think that what happens to a person in the past can influence their future?

Which of the three texts made you think about the relationship between the past and the future most? Why?

Vocabulary: idiomatic language/collocations

1

1 Look back at the three texts on pages 142 and 143. Find words or phrases that mean the same as:

1 difficult to trust (text 1)
2 when something is made in large quantities (text 1)
3 something that represents an important idea in art (text 1)
4 adding importance or value to an argument or idea (text 1)
5 seeing something briefly (text 2)
6 doing something thoroughly to high standards (text 2)
7 a record of the number of instances of something (text 2)
8 moving around slowly without any purpose, doing very little (text 3)
9 eventually (text 3)
10 good times and bad times (text 3)
11 a philosophy for living (text 3)

2 Now complete the sentences using the correct form of one of the expressions.

1 The idea that anyone can predict the future accurately is very suspect – in fact, I think it's

....

2 The evidence .... the argument that there was a town on the site in times gone by.
3 Cars nowadays are .... which has reduced manufacturing costs and made them more affordable than they were in the past.
4 His dreams seemed to give him a brief .... into the future.
5 I seem to spend a lot of my time just .... waiting for other people – it's very frustrating!
6 Life is full of ...., highs and lows – that's what makes it challenging.

2

1 Look at the following extract from text 1. What does the highlighted phrase mean?

... it was actually an example of post-modernism before its time.

2 Complete the sentences with a collocation with *time* from the box.

| in no time   waste of time   at the time |
| pressed for time   for the time being |
| running out of time   time after time |
| in time   kill time |

1 I think that studying History in school is useless – it's a complete ....
2 I decided to go on holiday to India last year. It seemed like a good idea ...., but I didn't realise that I had chosen the hurricane season!
3 I'm studying hard, so I've told my friends that .... I'm not going out at weekends.
4 Sue is so quick – she learned how to use the new software ....
5 I'm sorry, I can't stop now – I'm really .... I'll catch you later.
6 Peter has been delayed, so I'm going to get a coffee to .... until he gets here.
7 The train was held up by signalling problems, but luckily I arrived just .... to catch the plane.
8 We must reach a decision by 8 o'clock and it's 7.45 now – we're rapidly ....
9 I've told you .... not to do that, but you just keep doing it!

3 Work with a partner. Take turns to describe a situation to illustrate one of the phrases from Exercise 2. Your partner should say which phrase you are illustrating.

Example:
A: *I had to wait for the bus for ages, so I bought a magazine to read.*
B: *You were killing time.*

Grammar 1: passives 1

1

1 Read the title of the article on page 145. What do you think the article will be about? Skim it quickly to check your ideas. Have you ever heard of a job like this?

2 Read the article again. Rewrite the numbered sentences using the passive form.

Example:
(1) ... in which older people from diverse ethnic backgrounds are encouraged to share and record their memories

THE MEMORY BANKER

Meena Khata loves her job, because she can travel the world and immerse herself in different cultures. But she does this without ever leaving her office in London.

It is here that she runs a project (1) <u>which encourages older people from diverse ethnic backgrounds to share and record their memories</u> in order to bring alive a past that (2) <u>people might otherwise lose</u>. Age Exchange is a unique organisation that uses story-telling, drama, art and dance to build bridges between generations. (3) <u>Someone set up Age Exchange in 1983</u> as a reminiscence theatre company, but demand grew and in 1987 (4) <u>they opened the Reminiscence Centre</u>. Meena is one of only eight full-time workers with the project, and (5) <u>the director has assigned many vital jobs such as running the shop, museum and tea-room to volunteers.</u>

Meena plans to record people aged 50 and over talking about their childhood, family, homes and memories of their country of origin. Among questions (6) <u>she will ask them</u> are why they came to Britain, and what their first impressions were. Creative activities such as drama and dance provide trigger material that unlocks their memories. Participants create memory boxes containing images and objects that illustrate their stories.

(7) <u>We should not ignore this opportunity to capture living history.</u> There is a danger that once the older generation has gone, their stories will disappear, and (8) <u>will close a rich vein of living history for future generations.</u>

3 The numbered sentences in the article would be better in the passive form, for one of three reasons. Match each reason to the sentences.

a) The agent is unknown or obvious.

b) The focus of the sentence is on the event and not the agent.

c) The agent is people or things in general.

Passive infinitives

> If the subject is not the agent, we can use a passive infinitive.

Example:
> The stock is *to be checked* every Friday so that levels can be maintained.
> The report was thought *to have been leaked* to the press by a secretary.

2 Complete the second sentence so that it has a similar meaning to the first sentence, using the word given and a passive infinitive. Do not change the word given. Use between three and six words, including the word given.

1 The original plan was to finish the project by the autumn.
HAVE
In the original plan, the project .... by the autumn.

2 I won't have any repetition of this bad behaviour at any time. **REPEATED**
I don't want this .... at any time.

3 She wants everyone to realise that she is an intellectual. **SEEN**
She wants .... an intellectual.

4 Everyone believes that they have moved away from the area. **HAVE**
They are .... from the area.

5 People say that he has recovered from the accident quite quickly. **SAID**
He .... from the accident quite quickly.

6 No-one can do anything about the situation. **NOTHING**
There .... about the situation.

▶ Grammar reference p.196 (12)

3 Discuss these questions.

1 Read the last sentence of the article again. Do you agree with the writer about the danger in the last paragraph, or do you feel that it is not important?

2 Which is more important to have recorded: people's stories and memories or facts and dates of important events?

3 What personal things would you like to be saved from your early years? Why?

4 Have you ever seen anything displayed in a museum that was used by someone in your family? If yes, how did it make you feel? If not, how would it make you feel if you did?

5 What aspect of the town where you live would you like to be preserved for the future? Why?

Reading 2

1

1 Work in groups of three.

Student A read the book synopsis on page 189.
Student B read the book synopsis on page 190.
Student C read the book synopsis on page 192.

2 Tell one another about what you have read. What idea do they all share?

3 Would you like to read any of the books? Which one and why? If not, why not?

Do you believe that time travel is possible or is it just fiction? Why?/Why not?

2 Read the text in Exam focus Exercise 1. Does the writer believe that time travel might exist? How are his ideas similar or different to yours? Which of the three books you discussed in Exercise 1 is mentioned?

Exam focus

Paper 3 Use of English: word formation (Part 3)

About the exam: In Paper 3, Part 3, you read a short text from which ten words have been removed. The gapped words are listed to the right of the text, but not in the form that is needed in the context of the text. You need to change the words, usually adding prefixes and suffixes, to match the sense of the text.

Suggested procedure

1 Read the text quickly to get a general idea of what it is about and how it is organised. Don't answer any of the questions until you've read the whole text.

2 Look at each gap in turn and think about the sentence. What type of word is missing; an adjective, noun, verb, etc.? If it is a noun, is the word singular or plural? If it is an adjective, is it positive or negative? If it is a verb, which tense will it be in?

3 When you have answered all the questions, read the text carefully again. Does it make complete sense with all the words you have created?

1 For questions **1–10**, read the text below. Use the word given at the end of some of the lines to form a word that fits in the gap in the same line. There is an example at the beginning (0).

Example: | **0** | *physicists* |

The enigma of time travel

Is it possible to travel backwards and forwards through time?

For decades the world's top (0) ..*physicists*.. have been trying to   **PHYSICS**
answer this question. But so far, nobody has come up with any
(1) .... proof that travelling through time is actually impossible,   **CONVINCE**
although all sorts of (2) .... to the idea have been raised.   **OBJECT**
For example, some say that time travel might lead to what they
call 'temporal paradoxes', like going back in a time machine and
(3) .... meeting your own mother before she gave birth to you.   **ACCIDENT**
It sounds like the plot of a classic science-fiction film, doesn't it?
And it's a sign of just how (4) .... the concept of time travel is to   **APPEAL**
serious scientists that it was left to a (5) .... to come up with the   **NOVEL**
idea in the first place. That honour goes to H.G. Wells, in his 1895
classic *The Time Machine*. Was Wells dabbling in a field that he
didn't understand? Was it all just a bit of literary (6) ....?   **SPECULATE**
Maybe not: Einstein's theory of (7) .... does not disallow the   **RELATIVE**
(8) .... of time travel. And modern scientists looking for what's   **EXIST**
called the 'Theory of Everything' are (9) .... to rule out the   **WILL**
idea completely. So who knows, the idea of travelling through time
may not be as (10) .... as many people think.   **RIDICULE**

2 Discuss these questions.

1 If you could travel back in time, which period of history would you like to travel to? Why?

2 Would you prefer to travel to the future? Why?/Why not?

Grammar 2: the future in the past

1 We can use the *past continuous* to talk about plans in the past that were in the future at the moment of speaking or writing, e.g. *We were meeting at 6 o' clock, but Joe called and changed it to 6.30.*

2 We can use *was going to* when we talk about plans in the past that we still haven't fulfilled, e.g. *I was going to post the letter, but I forgot.*

3 We can use *was thinking of + -ing* for future plans that are not definite, e.g. *I was thinking of tidying the house this weekend.*

1 Match these sentences to one of the uses above. In which one is the plan not fulfilled?

a) I posted Sally's parcel for her. It wasn't a problem as I was going to the post office that afternoon anyway.

b) I was having my hair cut that afternoon, but I cancelled the appointment when I heard the news.

c) I was thinking of phoning you anyway this afternoon.

▶ Grammar reference p.198 (16.4)

2 Complete these mini-dialogues using the correct form of the verb in brackets.

1 A: Look – the cinema is closed next week for refurbishment.
   B: Oh, that's annoying – I .... (*see*) the new blockbuster sometime soon.

2 A: Hello, Peter – what a coincidence that you've phoned right now!
   B: Why?
   A: Well, I had just picked up the phone and .... (*call*) you!

3 A: This morning I was told that Jane .... (*come*) tonight, but I can't see her here.
   B: Well, we invited her but she phoned this afternoon and said she .... (*work*) late and had to cancel.

4 A: Hi, Sue – I'd like to talk to you about the new project. Is this a convenient time?
   B: Actually, I .... (*just go*) for lunch. Why don't you come – we can talk over a sandwich.

5 A: We .... (*go*) on an organised tour of Rome last month, but we both got flu and had to pull out at the last minute.
   B: What a shame!

3 There are other ways of expressing the future seen from the past. Choose the best form of the verb in each of these sentences.

1 Our broadband connection wasn't working, and we hoped that the technician *wouldn't take / won't take / didn't take* long to reach us!

2 When the train broke down between stations, we had no idea that we *should be / would be / will be* stuck there for five hours!

3 The project manager hoped that the project *will have been / would have been / had been* up and running by January, but it wasn't.

4 As he walked towards her she realised that he *is about to / was about to / has been about to* speak to her.

5 On the itinerary, we *were to arrive / were about to arrive / would arrive* at the station at nine, but the train was late and we missed our connection.

4 There is a mistake in each highlighted word or expression in the text. Correct the mistakes.

Digging up (and burying) London's past

Archaeologist Duncan Hawkins redrew the maps of Roman London three years ago after discovering an Ancient Roman palace four metres below street level. At the time he called it the most exciting discovery to be made in London for years, even though he always suspected he (1) were going to find something in the area because of references in other documents. The actual discovery was made because a builder (2) would erect an apartment block in the area, and had to undertake an archaeological survey first as a precondition. This survey exposed the site. Once they had started to dig, archaeologists knew it was crucial that they completed their research within six months because the building work (3) is scheduled to go ahead at that time. What about the site now? It is buried below the block of flats! How does Hawkins feel about this? His position is clear. Archaeology has a dual role – to preserve the past, and disseminate information to increase our understanding of the past. Without the opportunity to do the dig, he (4) would still look for confirmation of the site among contemporary documents. He always intended to bury the palace carefully, so that other archaeologists (5) will be able to find it when further building took place, however far into the future that (6) were.

5 Tell a partner about a time when you

• were hoping to do something but couldn't

• would have done something if you could

• were about to do something which fell through.

Listening: multiple matching
(Part 4)

1   Discuss these questions.

1   Do you often play computer games?
2   Why do people enjoy playing the games?
3   Which are the most popular genres? Why?

2   Make a list of the good and bad features of computer games you have played. Think about:

- the setting
- the plot
- interactivity
- graphics, etc.

3   You will hear five people talking about a computer game they played recently. Remember that you must complete both tasks as you listen. You will hear the recording twice.

TASK ONE

For questions 1–5, choose from the list A–H what each person says is the best feature of their game.

A It's fast moving.

B It's easy for beginners.

C It has well-known characters.

D It has good puzzles.

E It's designed by experts.

F It has realistic graphics.

G It has an unusual setting.

H It has a strong plot.

Speaker 1   **1**
Speaker 2   **2**
Speaker 3   **3**
Speaker 4   **4**
Speaker 5   **5**

TASK TWO

For questions 6–10, choose from the list A–H each person's main criticism of their game.

A It's too similar to its predecessors.

B The graphics are disappointing.

C The audio is poor quality.

D There are technical problems.

E It becomes too complex.

F It involves a further payment.

G The characters don't speak.

H It gets boring after a while.

Speaker 1   **6**
Speaker 2   **7**
Speaker 3   **8**
Speaker 4   **9**
Speaker 5   **10**

Speaking: two-way conversation
(Part 3)

1   In Part 3 of the Speaking test you have to complete a task with your partner.

Think about the best way to do this. Which one of the following pieces of advice is not correct? What is wrong with it?

- Try to make a decision about the task immediately.
- It doesn't matter if you don't talk about every picture, as long as you use good language.
- Talk about each picture in turn, before reaching a decision.
- Don't worry about the timing – the interlocutor will stop you at the end of the time.

2   In this part of the test, you should interact with your partner and show evidence of turn taking. With a partner, think of some ways you can ask each other's opinion, or take turns to speak, e.g. *Do you agree with me? Is that what you think?*

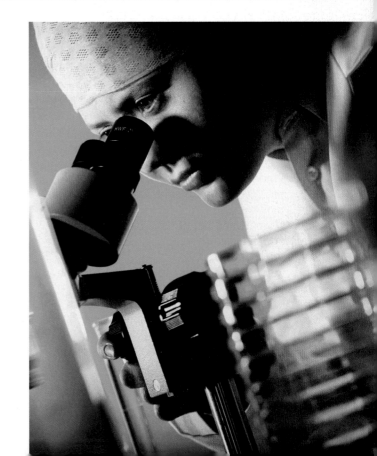

3 Look at the following task. Do the task with your partner, trying to follow the advice in Exercise 1 and using as many different ways of taking turns with your partner as you can.

Here are some things that have had a great impact on the way we live today.
Talk to each other about what life would have been like if these things had never been discovered or invented. Then decide which one has had the least impact on life today.

4 Look at the photos. Discuss these questions.

1 Which thing do you think will continue to have the greatest impact in the future?

2 Which thing do you wish had not been discovered or invented? Why?
3 What invention can you think of that was predicted incorrectly?
4 How important do you think it is to continue to make technological and scientific advances?
5 What invention would you like to work on? Why?
6 What can we learn about any society from the things that it values?

5 Share your ideas on the questions in Exercise 4 with the rest of the class. Were their answers similar to yours? Make a note of any useful ideas that you didn't think of.

Use of English: open cloze
(Part 2)

1 Discuss these questions.

1 Why do people generally like science-fiction books and films? Do you enjoy them? Think of some well-known novels, films, TV programmes, etc.
2 What do you think science-fiction can tell us about:
- life today?
- the past?
- the future?
3 What do you know about the TV series *Star Trek*?
   Do you think programmes like this are ever scientifically accurate?

2 Read the text to see what the writer thinks about the scientific predictions in *Star Trek* and compare your ideas. Ignore the gaps for the moment. Does anything surprise you?

3 Read the text again and think of the word which best fits each gap. Use only one word in each gap. There is an example at the beginning (0).

4 Can you think of any other science-fiction programmes, books or films which have:

- successfully predicted future events?
- remained convincingly futuristic despite developments in technology?

Star Trek: the future as predicted in the past

Even **(0)** *though* the fantasy television series *Star Trek* has been around for over 40 years, it may still have some clues to offer about our own future. Many scientists are avid fans, and ever **(1)** .... the show started in the 1960s, it has been praised **(2)** .... a source of inspiration and visionary ideas. **(3)** .... to one of the programme's scientific advisers, we've caught **(4)** .... with and gone beyond many of the things featured **(5)** .... the original series. So how much of the programme has become science fact, **(6)** .... how much is still science fiction?

(7) .... things as tricorders, communicators and interactive computers are **(8)** .... longer fantasy. Magnetic resonance imaging, mobile phones and the Internet appeared in real life long **(9)** .... the 23rd century, **(10)** .... is when the show had predicted that such technology **(11)** .... be available. Even dermal regenerators, used in the fictional 24th century to heal wounds instantly, anticipated today's use of lasers to heal tissue and repair eye damage.

The transporter is probably the most memorable feature of *Star Trek*, but could it become **(12)** .... reality? Physicists **(13)** .... the idea of teleportation seriously and there have been various attempts to 'transport' objects from **(14)** .... place to another. Sadly, however, **(15)** .... *Scientific American* magazine is to be believed, 'the teleportation of large objects or humans remains a fantasy'.

Writing: essay (Part 2)

1 In the exam you may have to write an essay in which you present an argument. You should

- use a semi-formal style
- make sure that you organise your argument clearly
- link your ideas appropriately
- remember that the purpose is to explain your point of view or persuade the reader to agree with you.

You can organise an essay in different ways. You can:

a) present both sides of the argument one by one and then say which one you agree with:

> 1 Introduction stating situation
> 2 Two or three points supporting one side of the argument
> 3 Two or three points supporting the other side of the argument
> 4 Conclusion stating your opinion

b) present arguments for and against specific points and then say which one you agree with:

> 1 Introduction stating situation
> 2 Point 1 - arguments for and against
> 3 Point 2 - arguments for and against
> 4 Point 3 - arguments for and against
> 5 Conclusion stating your opinion

c) present only one side of the argument, backing up your ideas with details:

> 1 Introduction stating situation and your opinion
> 2 Points for + supporting detail
> 3 Points against + supporting detail
> 4 Conclusion confirming your opinion

2 Think about the purpose of an essay, an article and a report. Complete the table using words and phrases from the box.

> uses colourful language
> uses semi-formal language
> uses objective language, often with the passive
> presents a clear argument in linked paragraphs
> can use bullet points
> uses paragraphs for effect
> makes recommendations based on facts
> entertains
> persuades through discussion
> known reader (x 2)
> general reader

	essay	article	report
language			
purpose			
organisation		*uses paragraphs for effect*	
target reader	*known reader*		

3 Look at the following task. Decide:

- whether you agree or disagree with the statement
- how you want to organise your essay
- what details you want to include.

> You have had a class discussion on the value of studying the past, and whether it is important to help us prepare for the future. Now your teacher has asked you to write an essay giving your opinions on the following statement:
> *There is little point in preserving buildings and stories from the past – we should look to the future, not live in the past.*
>
> Write your **essay** in 220–260 words.

4

1 The essay below was written in answer to the task. Read it and answer these questions.

1 What organisation has the writer used?
2 Is the style semi-formal or informal?
3 What is the purpose of the rhetorical question at the end of the introduction?

Some people say that it is a waste of time to preserve history, and that the past is gone and should be forgotten. But is this really true?

On the one hand, there is a strong argument for looking forwards, not backwards. Life is for living and for taking risks, and we can never fully appreciate what living conditions were like 500 years ago. So what is the point in preserving old buildings, and learning about them? Money could be better spent on other things.

On the other hand, although it is true that we can't change the past, it is where we came from. So if we can understand it, and how people lived, then we can also understand more about ourselves. And surely we have a responsibility to future generations, so that they too can understand their background?

It seems to me that knowing where we came from gives us a sense of identity and understanding of ourselves. For this reason, I feel that there is a lot of point in preserving old buildings and stories from the past, and that the statement is wrong. Obviously we should not live in the past, but we should remember it.

2 Complete the following outline of the essay in note form.

Introduction: _statement of topic_

Second para:

Point 1 ....

Third para:

Point 1 ....

Conclusion: ....

3 Highlight four linking words or phrases in the essay. Which one introduces:

- the first idea?
- a contrasting idea?
- an opinion?
- a reason?

4 What is the effect of using these words?

- surely (para 3)
- too (para 3)
- obviously (para 4)

5 Look at the essay again. Underline:

- a phrase which introduces a general statement rather than the writer's opinion
- a rhetorical question
- the sentence in the conclusion that links back to the introduction.

5 The essay is too short (200 words). Work with a partner and think of one extra detail that you could add to each of the middle paragraphs. Then add your points to the essay. Make sure that you link them in using appropriate linking words.

6 Now look at the following task . Write your own answer, using one of the approaches suggested. Remember to plan your ideas and to link your paragraphs and ideas within paragraphs.

You have had a class discussion on why it is important to preserve the past. Now your teacher has asked you to write an essay giving your opinions on the following statement:
We should spend more money on preserving our past – it is too important to lose.

Write your **essay** in 220–260 words.

▶ Writing reference p.210

1 Think of one word only which can be used appropriately in all three sentences.

1 The date for the opening of the new museum has been .... for next September.

A research project has been .... the task of investigating whether time travel already exists.

Beverley had .... out at dawn, determined to find the archaeological site before lunchtime.

2 On his trip across the USA, Brett didn't make it to San Francisco because he ran out of ....

With the benefit of hindsight we can see that the invention was years ahead of its ....

It's not that Phoebe was wrong, she just didn't choose a good .... to bring up the subject.

3 Contributions to the international charity appeal have .... one million dollars.

Eric .... over, picked up the photograph and realised he was looking at himself as a small boy.

In the 1970s, Britain only had three TV channels and popular programmes often .... an audience of over 20 million.

4 There's no .... in doing further research into time travel as it's clearly never going to be possible.

On entering the old castle, you get a real .... of history and how life must have been in the past.

Penny was so absorbed in the sci-fi novel that she had lost all .... of time passing.

5 The college principal said that he .... to bring the catering facilities up to date.

We decided to ask the lecturer exactly what he .... when he used the word 'teleportation'.

Of all the awards that the actress won during her career, the Oscar .... the most to her.

2 Choose the correct alternative in each of these sentences.

1 Tom said he *had / would have* every intention of finishing his research project before the end of term.
2 When it was first televised, nobody *could predict / could have predicted* how successful *Star Trek* was going to be.
3 Many of the predictions which David *made / could make* have come true.
4 As a schoolboy, Jeremy *wanted to / was wanting to* become a professional footballer.
5 Some people dream about famous events long before they *happen / would happen*.

3 Complete the second sentence so that it has a similar meaning to the first sentence, using the word given. Do not change the word given. You must use between three and six words, including the word given. Here is an example (0).

0 The architect wanted nobody to know about his new idea. **KEEP**

The architect wanted ...*to keep his new idea a*... secret.

1 Our visitors experienced a two-hour delay on the motorway. **HELD**
Our visitors were .... two hours on the motorway.

2 Someone ought to have let the police know about the incident at once. **REPORTED**
The incident should .... the police at once.

3 Sally originally intended to travel by air rather than by train. **WAS**
Sally's .... travel by air rather than by train.

4 If we want to bid in the auction, we must do it soon. **OUT**
Time .... if we want to bid in the auction.

5 At least thirty Futuro houses may still be in existence. **THOUGHT**
At least thirty Futuro houses .... exist.

6 Sally didn't know it, but her attitude would soon change. **ABOUT**
Sally didn't know it, but there .... change in her attitude.

7 John's hair really needs cutting. **TIME**
It's .... hair cut.

8 Tommy's plane should have landed at 15.00, but there's no sign of it yet. **SCHEDULED**
Tommy's plane .... at 15.00, but there's no sign of it yet.

13 A way with words

Reading: multiple matching (Part 4)

1 Discuss these questions.

1 Do you like reading about celebrities? Why? What is so fascinating about them?
2 Do you think there is too much written about celebrities in the media generally nowadays?

2 Read the article on page 155 quickly to see if your ideas are the same as the writer's and find:

- the names of two publishers
- the names of three ghost writers
- the names of two celebrities.

3 Which section talks about:

1 the attitude of new celebrities?
2 the results of an unexpected success?
3 how a ghost writer works?
4 how a deal was struck?
5 what a celebrity autobiography contains?

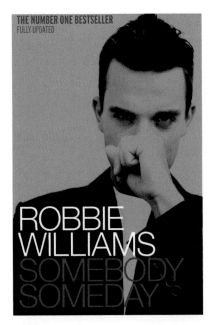

THE NUMBER ONE BESTSELLER
FULLY UPDATED

ROBBIE WILLIAMS
SOMEBODY SOMEDAY

4 You are going to read an article about ghost writers, the people who actually write many celebrity autobiographies. For questions 1–15, choose from the sections (A–E). The sections may be chosen more than once.

In which section of the article is each of the following mentioned?

a ghost writer whose work is said to have influenced other writers **[1]**

one publisher's modest expectations for a celebrity autobiography **[2]**

the attitude of aspiring celebrities to the media **[3]**

the need to fulfil people's expectations regarding the celebrity **[4]**

the changing status of ghost writers in the profession **[5]** **[6]**

the lack of prestige celebrity autobiographies once had in the industry **[7]** **[8]**

the reason why celebrities feel a need to produce an autobiography **[9]**

the need to keep on good terms with the celebrity **[10]**

the range of companies now publishing celebrity autobiographies **[11]**

the type of consumer that celebrity autobiographies appeal to **[12]**

the lack of recognition ghost writers can expect in return for their efforts **[13]**

the indifference of one celebrity to a book's success **[14]**

a ghost writer who had problems getting close to the celebrity concerned **[15]**

5 Match the words and phrases from the article to their closest synonyms.

1 to be looked down upon (A)   a) of low social status
2 clued-up (A)   b) money earned from sales of a book
3 must-have (A)   c) show disgust for
4 to turn up one's nose (B)   d) become friends
5 downmarket (B)   e) considered inferior to
6 royalties (B)   f) aspiring
7 to turn down (B)   g) essential
8 to tap (C)   h) become more confidential
9 shirty (D)   i) well-informed
10 would-be (E)   j) refuse
11 to open up (E)   k) exploit
12 to bond (E)   l) showing irritation

The Ghost Writers

The celebrity autobiography is the publishing phenomenon of our age.
But who actually writes them?

A   New-style celebrity autobiographies have two things in common: they are available in all manner of retail outlets, and none of them was actually written by the person whose name appears on the cover. Ghost writers, who used to be rather looked down upon in the industry, are well on the way to becoming the dominant literary figures of our time. According to Lucie Cave, who wrote the autobiography of a *Big Brother* winner: 'All of these people who emerge from shows like *Big Brother* know just how much they can sell their first interview for. They're far more clued-up than ever before.' The celebrity autobiography is a natural extension of that. It's become the must-have accessory for anyone who's reached a certain level of fame. Obviously these people can't write their books themselves, so they need someone to do it for them.

B   And yet only a few years ago, publishers regularly turned up their noses at celebrity autobiographies on the grounds that they were either too downmarket or wouldn't sell. But now they're all in on the act, from the loftiest to the lowliest. So what happened to cause such a massive shift in attitude? To answer that question we need to follow a trail that leads back to the British celebrity model Jordan. In November 2003 some very unlikely looking people came to see the publisher John Blake at his London office. Blake's company specialises in the 'stack-'em-high' showbiz end of the market. 'A succession of what looked like wideboys turned up, all of them covered in gold chains,' he recalls. 'They said: "Do you want to do Jordan's book? We want a million pounds up front and none of this nonsense about royalties."' Amused but far from tempted, Blake declined, assuming that would be that. But still Jordan's 'people' continued calling him up periodically. Eventually, after every other publisher had turned the book down, Blake signed Jordan and her ghost-writer, Rebecca Farnworth, for a comparatively low fee of £10,000. 'I can't say we had a great deal of faith in the book,' he recalls.

C   *Being Jordan* came out on a Thursday in May. By Saturday it had sold 100,000 copies, beating other celebrity autobiographies such as Bill Clinton's *My Life* hands down and outselling that week's number-one novel by ten-to-one. 'It was amazing,' Blake remembers. Everyone concerned was overjoyed – everyone, that is, except for Jordan herself, who took the whole thing in her stride. 'I don't think she actually read the book. For her it was just like doing another calendar or a magazine shoot.' It was at this point that the rest of the book trade belatedly roused itself from its stupor and took notice. 'There had definitely been a lot of snobbery about these sorts of books before,' says Ben Dunn, editorial director at Fourth Estate. 'But what was extraordinary was that the people buying the Jordan book weren't traditional book-buyers. You had a situation where people were tossing paperbacks into their supermarket trolleys along with packets of biscuits. Suddenly, there were whole new marketing possibilities waiting to be tapped.'

D   When the market exploded, so the ghost-writers' profile within the book trade – and in several cases their bank balances – exploded with it. The man widely credited with taking greatest advantage of a changing climate is the veteran journalist Hunter Davies, the author of some forty books, including footballer Wayne Rooney's autobiography *My Story So Far*. 'The most important thing of all in ghosting,' says Davies, 'is getting the voice right. However, you're not necessarily trying to get their real voice, but rather the voice that people perceive as belonging to them. For instance, with Wayne, we all knew that he's only young and had virtually no education, so I had to keep it relatively simple. The result, while hardly introspective, did afford readers a glimpse of life inside Wayne's head.' Another very successful ghost-writer says: 'You're not their friend, but you must have an equality of relationship that makes it appear that you are. Nor are you their personal assistant, although if they ask you to do anything for them, you'll do it, because any use of the word "no" could result in them getting shirty.'

E   The new celebrity autobiographies may not be high art, but the most successful ones deliver an alluring mix of scandal, confession, hardship and glamour. Mark McCrum is one of a new breed of ghost writers. When he wrote Robbie Williams' *Somebody Someday* – and in the process redefined for the profession what a ghosted autobiography could be – he was one of several would-be ghosts who were interviewed for the job. As he says: 'I found it very difficult at first – it was always rather formal, a bit like interviewing royalty. Then, right at the end, he opened up about his life and I really felt that I'd bonded with him.' But whatever else ghost writers might be in it for, it's not the glory. If they're lucky, they might get a credit, although this is likely to be buried away in such tiny print that you'd be lucky to find it without a magnifying glass.

Vocabulary 1: adverbials expressing attitude

1

1 How do we express our feelings and ideas clearly? Look at the statements below. One word in each sentence tells you how the person is feeling. Underline the word, and decide which person is indicating that:

a) they have heard that something is true though they are not sure.

b) something is easily noticed or understood.

c) they think that there is no doubt about something.

d) they are speaking for only themselves.

e) they are giving the most important information.

f) they are speaking directly and honestly.

g) what they are saying is in fact their true opinion, or contrasting what has been said before.

1 Frankly, I think that books written by celebrities are usually overrated.

2 Actually, on second thoughts I don't really want to go out tonight.

3 Well, basically it's just a matter of filling in a form and they do the rest for you.

4 I wasn't at the conference myself, but apparently it was a success.

5 Many people enjoy going to the cinema but personally I prefer the theatre.

6 He was so upset – clearly not inviting him to the party was a mistake.

7 We don't have much money, so obviously knowing the total cost of the trip is very important.

2 Two of the words are almost interchangeable. Which are they?

2 Work with a partner. Decide which of the alternatives in the following sentences is most likely, and why.

1 The young man was reading avidly and was *actually / personally / obviously* enjoying the book.

2 Well, *basically / apparently / personally* all that happened was that I was told to concentrate more in class!

3 I've known Carlo for years – *obviously / actually / personally* he's my oldest friend.

4 It's a difficult situation all round, and *frankly / apparently / clearly* I wish you hadn't said what you did.

5 Unfortunately I couldn't be at the meeting, but *clearly / apparently / frankly* from what I've heard it was useful and productive.

6 Going on what happened afterwards, it was *clearly / frankly / personally* the wrong decision.

7 *Apparently / Obviously / Actually* no-one is suggesting that it was your fault – you weren't even there!

8 It's easy to find out everything you need to know about the project. *Apparently / Clearly / Basically* all you have to do is go on to the Internet and download the information pack.

3 Look at the following statements.

I'm amazed that reading hasn't died out all together by now – what's the point of it nowadays? Technology has taken over and we just don't need it.

In historical terms, reading and writing have only been accessible to everyone quite recently, but it has changed the world. Where would we be without them?

Work with a partner. Choose a statement each and think of four arguments to support it. Then discuss them with your partner. Use adverbials where appropriate to show how you feel.

Grammar 1: participle clauses

Participle clauses are quite formal and appear more in writing than in speaking. They are formed by replacing something in a sentence with a present participle (*-ing*) or a past participle.

Example:
'You see, I'd arrived for work late so many times in the past that it wasn't a surprise when the boss told me off!'
Having arrived late for work on numerous occasions, Jack was given an official reprimand by his superior.

Clauses including a participle can be used to replace a relative pronoun and a verb, and to replace words which give reasons, show results or indicate time.

To replace a relative pronoun and a verb

1 Look at these sentences and answer the questions below.

1 a) People who play sport regularly are generally healthier than those who don't.
   b) People playing sport regularly are generally healthier than those who don't.

2 a) Children who are brought up to read books cope well at school.
   b) Children brought up to read books cope well at school.

1 Which sentence in each pair uses a relative clause? Which one uses a participle clause?

2 Which pair of sentences (1 or 2) has an active meaning? Which one has a passive meaning? Complete the rule.
A participle clause with an active meaning uses a
.... participle.
A participle clause with a passive meaning uses a
.... participle.

2 Using participle clauses occasionally gives you the opportunity to use a range of structures. Rewrite the extracts from different written documents below, replacing the relative clauses with participle clauses.

Example:
Students who finish first should leave the exam room quietly.
Students finishing first should leave the exam room quietly.

1 The witnesses saw a fire which was burning in the distance.
2 Not all the people who were registered for the conference actually attended.
3 The piece of wood that was holding the window open had fallen out, and this allowed the burglar to enter the house.
4 Your priority when you are making a career move should be the salary.
5 We obtained a copy of the government report which was published last week.
6 Anyone who wants to join should register on the website.
7 He was working at a desk which was piled high with papers, and clearly his working conditions were poor.

To replace words which give reasons, show results or indicate time

3 Look at these sentences. Which word in the first sentence in each pair indicates reason, result or time? What has replaced it in the second sentence? Complete the rules below.

1 a) Since we had paid so much for the holiday, we were upset that the hotel was so bad.
   b) Having paid so much for the holiday, we were upset that the hotel was so bad.

2 a) Once she had finished her homework, she decided to go out.
   b) Having finished her homework, she decided to go out.
3 a) She had been told that she could apply for the course, so she sent in a form.
   b) Having been told that she could apply for the course, she sent in a form.

Words such as ...., ... and .... can be replaced by a participle clause.
When the sentence is in the past, the participle clause can be formed by .... + past participle.

4 Rewrite the sentences using participle clauses, and removing the linking words or expressions. Make sure that you use the correct tense.

Example:
Because I was brought up in Spain, I speak both Spanish and English.
Having been brought up in Spain, I speak both Spanish and English.
We have two small children and as a result we don't go out much in the evenings.
Having two small children, we don't go out much in the evenings

1 We arrived very late, so we decided to get a taxi from the airport.
2 I saw what the food was like in the hotel, so I went to a restaurant to eat.
3 Once they had announced their proposals, the management expected the workforce to support their new pay structure.
4 I looked forward to the party for weeks, and so I was upset when it was cancelled.
5 When he had finished his lunch, he rushed out of the house to catch the train.
6 I ordered a steak, and consequently I was annoyed when the waiter brought me fish.

▶ Grammar reference p.196 (11)

5

1 Read the text below. Which argument do you think the writer supports?

2 Rewrite the text using participle clauses to replace the numbered sections and making any other changes necessary.

The hardest thing we do?

How do we all develop language? The linguist Noam Chomsky believed that (1) <u>we are born with an innate knowledge of grammar with the result that</u> we don't need anyone to teach us the grammar of our native language; (2) <u>once they have started to speak</u>, children automatically speak grammatically. There is support for this theory from studies of child language (3) <u>which show</u> that children use the correct word order without ever having been taught what that order is.

In contrast, the psychologist B.F. Skinner believed that children must be taught language, (4) <u>because what they should do is copy models</u>. They imitate everything they hear around them (5) <u>and in this way they learn the rules</u> of their native language. But an interesting argument against this is that the amount of time it would take for a child to imitate everything they heard would actually exceed the age of the Earth!

3 Discuss these questions.

1 Which theory do you like the sound of?
2 Do you think it is easier to learn a language when you are young or when you are older?
3 What aspect of learning a language do you find most difficult?

Speaking: discussion (Parts 3 and 4)

1 Work with a partner and complete the following task. Look at the pictures on page 183. Remember to express your own opinions and to ask your partner what they think.

Here are some pictures showing different occupations in which further study is often undertaken. First, talk to each other about how important it might be to continue to study in these occupations. Then decide in which occupation further study is most difficult to do.

2 Discuss these questions.

1 Some people say that studying is a waste of time, and getting experience is more important. What do you think?
2 What are the advantages and disadvantages of studying alone and studying with a teacher? Do you think that it is different when you are learning a language from learning anything else?
3 How far do you agree that studying at school is more important than studying as an adult?
4 What do you think are the most important subjects to include for young people nowadays? How important is it to learn other languages?
5 How important are communication skills?
6 How do you think technology will influence education in the future?

Exam focus

Paper 3 Use of English: multiple-choice cloze (Part 1)

About the exam: Paper 3, Part 1 is a short cloze passage from which twelve words have been removed. For each gap, you must choose which of the four words in the multiple-choice question fits the gap best. These questions test your understanding of fixed phrases, collocations, linking words and expressions and complementation (e.g. dependent prepositions, gerund and infinitive, etc.), as well as your lexical knowledge.

Suggested procedure

1 Read the text quickly to get a general idea of what it is about and how it is organised. Don't answer any of the questions until you've read the whole text.
2 Look at each gap in turn and think about the sentence. Can you predict the missing word before you look at the options?
3 Look to see if the word you predicted is one of the four options. If it isn't, look for reasons why the options don't fit the gap. For example, the wrong preposition may follow, the meaning may not be exactly right, etc.
4 If you're not sure of an answer, guess – you don't lose any marks if you get an answer wrong.
5 When you've answered all the questions, read the whole text again to make sure all your answers make sense in the context of the whole passage.

1   For questions **1–12**, read the text below and decide which answer (**A**, **B**, **C** or **D**) best fits each gap. There is an example at the beginning (**0**).

Example:

0   **A**   come   **B**   made   **C**   caught   **D**   met

0	A	B	C	D
	▬	▭	▭	▭

An unusually successful lesson

A school in Scotland has (**0**) ......*A*...... up with an unusual way to improve its pupils' health and well-being, (**1**) .... at the same time helping them to become better learners. The six-year-old children have started doing a type of massage that was developed in Sweden. In the classes, each child chooses a partner and takes it in (**2**) .... to receive a massage of their back, neck and shoulders. Not only do the children (**3**) .... the activity fun, but this kind of massage also (**4**) .... muscle tension.

To (**5**) .... interest to the activity, the teachers have linked it to a story about a small boy who wants to play in the snow, but first must put on his glasses – the (**6**) .... of the glasses is traced on the children's shoulders. Then he helps his mum with the baking – this involves kneading the shoulders, and finally he goes out for a walk and has to (**7**) .... the snow off his coat on his return. The story is told slowly, each movement being repeated three times.

When the massage classes started, the children used to chatter and (**8**) .... about, but now they are quiet, their faces pictures of (**9**) .... concentration. And the activity (**10**) .... them in other ways too; they are noticeably calmer and more (**11**) .... of each other in the playground as well as being more relaxed and (**12**) .... to learn in the classroom.

1	**A** whilst	**B** otherwise	**C** whereas	**D** instead
2	**A** rota	**B** turns	**C** order	**D** sequences
3	**A** perceive	**B** find	**C** regard	**D** discover
4	**A** supports	**B** comforts	**C** relieves	**D** softens
5	**A** add	**B** earn	**C** gain	**D** increase
6	**A** figure	**B** form	**C** profile	**D** shape
7	**A** brush	**B** mop	**C** sweep	**D** dust
8	**A** joke	**B** mess	**C** laugh	**D** kid
9	**A** stressful	**B** heavy	**C** intense	**D** strong
10	**A** promotes	**B** enhances	**C** favours	**D** benefits
11	**A** friendly	**B** tolerant	**C** co-operative	**D** helpful
12	**A** enthusiastic	**B** keen	**C** optimistic	**D** fond

2   Do you think the massage classes are a good idea?

What other non-academic activities do you think could help children's concentration?

Vocabulary 2: communication – idioms

1   Look at the highlighted expressions in the following sentences. Use the context to work out what they mean. Then check your ideas in a dictionary such as the *Longman Exams Dictionary*.

1   Her manner of speech was, to say the least, rather original.
2   I hate parties where people just stand around and make small talk with people they've never met before and may never meet again.
3   My younger sister was very naughty today – she got a real talking to from our father!
4   I dislike listening to politicians when they just talk and talk and never get to the point.
5   I just couldn't make head nor tail of what the lecturer was saying – he used so many obscure words that I've never heard of!
6   I hate going out with work colleagues when all they do is talk shop – we all have a life outside the office, but they seem to ignore that!
7   I thought I'd made it clear but she got hold of the wrong end of the stick – I asked her to come on Saturday but she turned up on Sunday!
8   It's difficult to have a real conversation with him because he doesn't seem to understand turn-taking – he talks and I can't get a word in edgeways.
9   I think we've been talking at cross-purposes – I was talking about my sister, not my sister-in-law, so you have misunderstood.
10   It's difficult to work for someone who thinks they're better than you, especially when they talk down to you all the time.
11   My sister is very straight with everyone – she always speaks her mind, even if it offends people.
12   I think that we have to pull down the barriers, so to speak, between people so that we can all get on well.

WELL, OF COURSE, AS I WAS SAYING TO MARJORIE ONLY YESTERDAY, WHAT YOU HAVE TO BEAR IN MIND WHEN YOU'RE DEALING WITH THIS SORT OF THING IS THAT MOST LARGE CORPORATIONS THESE DAYS ARE ENTIRELY COMMITTED TO FULLY ROLLING OUT THE LEGISLATION...

BUT

2   Work with a partner. Think of a situation to illustrate one of the expressions from Exercise 1. Your partner should guess the expression you are illustrating.

Example:

A: *I was talking to my sister but she wouldn't listen and was going on about her own problems, so that it was impossible for me to say anything!*
B: *You mean you couldn't get a word in edgeways!*

3   Some phrases with *say* are useful in speaking. Match the functions 1–6 to the phrases a–f. Then write a two-line dialogue using the phrases. Practise saying it with a partner.

Example:

A: *I think that it's going to snow tomorrow.*
B: *Well, as it's 30 degrees today it seems very unlikely, wouldn't you say?*

1   to show that you don't know the answer to something
2   to ask someone else's opinion when you want to influence them
3   to ask someone else's opinion
4   to show agreement
5   to indicate that something is true in spite of what you have just said
6   to indicate that something is generally uncertain

a) I would say that the plan should work.
b) Sorry, I couldn't say.
c) Reading anything is a good thing. Having said that, I think it's important that books are well-written.
d) It seems very unlikely, wouldn't you say?
e) What would you say?
f) Who can say?

4   Discuss these questions. Try to use the expressions from Exercise 3 in your discussion.

1   How do you feel when people talk shop? Do you ever do it?
2   Are you good at making small talk? How important do you think it is? Think of situations when it might be an important skill to have.
3   When was the last time you got the wrong end of the stick? Describe what happened.
4   What can you do when someone talks down to you? How easy is it to deal with this situation?
5   Is it always a good thing when people speak their mind? What problems might it cause?
6   When it is difficult to get a word in edgeways, do you feel frustrated? How important do you think turn taking is in relationships?

Grammar 2: passives 2

1 Where do you think the passive is used most often? Why do you think this is? Match a source and reason to each of the following extracts.

1 Man bitten by dog
2 The house was originally built in 1854, and was extended in 1895 when the west wing was added.
3 The recommendation of the board is that the policy should be implemented.
4 The man was charged with robbery, and remanded in custody for three weeks.
5 It is hoped that the project will address the underlying issues and a reasonable solution will be reached.

Sources

press release   guidebook
newspaper headline   report
criminal record

Reasons

charge more important than the person making it
information more important than agent
no agent – object more important than subject
object or event more important than subject
needs to sound objective and impersonal

2 Read the article. Some examples of the passive have been highlighted. Match each of the uses of the passive a–d to one of the examples.

a) Using the passive means we can avoid an awkward change of subject in the middle of a sentence.
b) We often use the passive with verbs such as *think*, *believe*, *know*, *say* to give a general opinion.
c) Using the passive can make a statement sound more impersonal and less connected to the speaker.
d) We use the passive when the active form would require the use of an indefinite or vague pronoun, e.g. *someone*, *they*, *people*.

Children to be offered lessons round the clock
A truancy-hit school will lengthen its hours and add online teaching to entice bored pupils

CHILDREN attending a school criticised for its poor truancy record are being offered 24-hour teaching. As part of the two-year pilot project, they are provided with online teaching throughout the night, and classrooms are kept open from 7 a.m. to 10 p.m.

When a spokesman for the school (1) was asked about the project, she provided a written statement explaining that it was an attempt to meet the needs of children normally forced to fit in with education conventions. The statement pointed out that children must want to come into school, and most play truant because they are not engaged by the lessons. (2) It was believed that those who don't respond to the classroom might be stimulated by online learning and e-mentoring, and as a result the rates of (3) truancy would be significantly reduced during the life of the project.

The initiative has been generally welcomed as an example of creative thinking 'outside the box', and deserves to be given a fair chance, although (4) its findings will be closely monitored by educational authorities in the months to come.

---

3 Look at the words in italics in the following sentences. Is it possible to make this part of the sentence passive? If yes, make the transformation. If not, why not?

1 *Someone will be able to answer all your questions* very soon.
2 *They say that* archaeologists will soon be able to explain how the pyramids were constructed.
3 *Students have been asking* for some more revision on the Roman period of history.
4 *Everybody believes that* the government has raised taxes too much.
5 I had a great surprise today when *the people at the Inland Revenue sent me a cheque* for overpaid tax!
6 *You must clean up your room* before you do anything else!
7 The college *is going to send more than 20 students abroad to study*.
8 Someone *got a fantastically high score in the test*, but I don't know who it was!

4 Work with a partner. Look at the following situation. Discuss what you think the school should do, and then write a statement for release to the local press describing your solution. Use the passive as much as possible.

A local school is finding it difficult to motivate students to take part in extra-curricular and sporting activities, and fears that students will become unfit and unhealthy.

▶ Grammar reference p.196 (12)

Listening: multiple choice
(Part 1)

1 Discuss these questions.

1 What are the qualities of a good teacher?
2 How should the performance of a teacher be judged?
a) through exam results?
b) through student feedback?
c) by assessing his/her impact on students' lives and development?
3 Should education prepare young people for life or for work?

2 You will hear three different extracts. Choose the answer (A, B or C) which fits best according to what you hear.

Extract One

You hear part of a radio programme entitled *My Favourite Teacher*, in which a woman called Jill is remembering her schooldays.

1 Jill feels that Miss Cope's greatest quality was her ability
   A to keep control of the class.
   B to keep the class motivated.
   C to keep her students entertained.

2 Jill tells the story about the difficult student in order to underline Miss Cope's
   A inconsistent attitude to discipline.
   B impatience with certain kinds of behaviour.
   C professionalism in the face of provocation.

Extract Two

You overhear two young people talking about a course the girl did.

3 What was it a course in?
   A jewellery making
   B fashion design
   C fine art

4 They agree that the course tutors should have
   A introduced students to people who could help them in their careers.
   B helped students to organise public showings of their creative work.
   C made arrangements for students to gain some work experience.

Extract Three

You hear part of a televised debate about technology and education.

5 What is Dr Ashby doing in this speech?
   A putting forward a new theory
   B questioning the results of recent research
   C revealing the weaknesses in a common perception

6 Dr Ashby mentions television and mobile phones to illustrate
   A how technology can interfere with students' ability to learn study skills.
   B how young people are the first to see the potential of new technology.
   C how predictions about the effects of new technology came true.

3 Do you agree with Dr Ashby's point of view?

4 What other aspects of new technology can be useful in children's:

a) learning of specific skills?
b) general education for life?

5 Look at these words and expressions from Dr Ashby's talk. Listen again and decide if she used them in a positive or a negative way.

individualistic   self-centred   hype
get to grips with

Vocabulary 3: similes (*like/as*)

Similes are often used in speech or writing to make something more interesting to listen to, or to make a point seem stronger or more memorable.

Similes with *like*

Example:
He never settled anywhere for long – he moved around all the time.
He never settled anywhere for long – he lived like a rolling stone.

1   Work with a partner. What do you think the highlighted similes with *like* mean? Write down your ideas, and then check in a dictionary.

1   I'd advise you to keep out of the boss's way today. He's like a bear with a sore head.
2   When I went camping with friends last year, it was so peaceful – in spite of the uncomfortable ground I slept like a log.
3   I really didn't enjoy the party – it wasn't my scene. I felt like a fish out of water.
4   He feels so strongly about some issues, like the value of books – telling him books are a thing of the past is like a red rag to a bull.
5   He doesn't think before he speaks – he just says the first thing that comes into his mind – he's like a bull in a china shop.

Similes with *as ... as*

Other similes link an adjective and a noun to create a stronger effect.

Example:
He was very angry and went red in the face.
He was so angry his face was as red as a beetroot.

2   Match the simile halves. Are they the same in your language? Use each one in a sentence to bring out its meaning.

1 as strong	a) as a sheet
2 as light	b) as an ox
3 as white	c) as a feather
4 as quick	d) as a cucumber
5 as cool	e) as a flash

3   Use similes from Exercises 1 and 2 to describe these people.

1   John just sits around on his own – he never takes part in any office activities. ....

2   How can Sally do presentations without looking at all nervous? I'd be terrified! ....
3   Is Sue all right? She looks really pale – should we suggest she sees a doctor? ....
4   A: You look very relaxed, Carlo – did you sleep well in the hotel last night?
    B: Very well – the bed was so comfortable I slept
    ....
5   The boss just never thinks before he says anything – he really puts people's backs up sometimes.
    ....

Writing: proposal (Part 2)

1   In Paper 2, Part 2, you may be asked to write a proposal. You will be given a task and a context, but you will need to use your own ideas in the proposal.

Which of the following statements are <u>not</u> true of a proposal?

- It is written in an informal style.
- It gives facts.
- It uses a range of interesting vocabulary.
- It is possible to use headings and bullet points.
- It makes suggestions or recommendations.

2

1   Read the following writing task.

Your college wants to improve its results in foreign language exams. Your class has conducted a survey to identify the reasons for the current situation, and you have been asked to write a proposal making recommendations (with reasons) to improve it.

Write your proposal in 220–260 words.

2   Which organisation would be best for the proposal?

A	B
Introduction	Introduction
Main issues identified	Recommendations
Recommendations with reasons	Reasons for recommendations
Conclusion	Conclusion

3   Discuss with a partner your ideas for

- possible reasons for the situation
- recommendations for improving it.

3   Read the proposal below, which was written in answer to the task. Compare the ideas in the proposal with your own. Which organisation has the writer used? Fill in the missing headings. What recommendations does the writer make, and what reasons does he give?

> **TIP!** If you choose to use bullet points in a report or a proposal, make sure that you still use a range of language. Don't be tempted to use notes or simple structures.

Introduction

The survey conducted among students identified two main problems with language teaching in the college. This proposal outlines these problems and makes recommendations for solutions.

(1) ....

One of the biggest problems identified in the survey is motivation – students don't get the chance to use the foreign language outside the classroom, and so it is hard for them to be interested in it. The second problem is conected to this, which is that students find it dificult to talk to each other in another language because it feels unatural.

(2) ....

• A wide selection of DVDs should be made available in the college library for students to borow, and which can be listened to in the language being studied. This would provide motivation, giving students a real reason to listen to the language they are learning.

• There could be one day a week set aside when the whole class only speaks in the second language. If everyone takes part, then it should not feel strange and would become second nature in time. It could be lots of fun as well.

• A monthly prize could be awarded by the college to the student who has made the most progres, written the best esay or spoken the most in the second language. This would provide competition, which is well-known to be motivating.

Conclusion

All three recomendations made here would need to be fully suported by the management of the college. However, I feel that if they were to be implemented, there would be a real improvement in the situation.

4

1   Highlight five uses of the passive. Which parts of the proposal are they in? Why? Why is it important that these sections seem objective and impersonal?

2   The writer has used a range of structures. Find two participle clauses and underline them.

3   The writer has used two expressions that are too informal for a proposal. Find them and rewrite them in a more formal way.

4   The writer has made eight careless spelling mistakes. Find and correct them. What kind of mistakes were they? Do you make this kind of spelling mistake yourself? Make a note of any mistakes that you do make, and learn the correct spelling.

5

1   Read the two tasks below.

> The number of students taking part in sporting activities at your college is falling. Your class has conducted a survey to identify the reasons for this, and you have been asked to write a proposal making recommendations (with reasons) to improve the situation.
>
> Write your **proposal** in 220–260 words.

> Your college is planning to implement a programme developing communication skills for the workplace. Your class has conducted a survey to identify what students would like this programme to include, and you have been asked to write a proposal making recommendations (with reasons) on how the programme should be organised.
>
> Write your **proposal** in 220–260 words.

2   Choose one task, and discuss your ideas with a partner. Then write your proposal using the sample answer as a model. Make sure that you use an impersonal style, use the passive where appropriate and use a range of structures, especially if you include bullet points. Check your spelling once you have finished.

▶ Writing reference p.207

1 Read the text below and think of the word which best fits each gap. Use only one word in each gap. There is an example at the beginning (0).

First words

The SONY Computer Science Laboratory in Paris is a cosmopolitan place (0) *where* an international team of researchers converses in English, French and Japanese. But the air is also (1) .... of more exotic voices uttering strange words (2) .... as 'wabaku' and half-recognisable phrases like 'pushred wablueko'. These are Luc Steel's talking robots. Even the most accomplished linguist will have problems (3) .... polite conversation with them, because they don't speak any language we know. Instead they invent their (4) ....

For decades, scientists have argued about (5) .... it was that our ancestors came to evolve something (6) .... complex and elegant as language. What sort of brain would they have needed? Linguist Noam Chomsky believed that some kind of linguistic rules must be encoded in our genes and brains. (7) .... opponents argue that picking (8) .... language is simply a matter of learning, and that given enough examples we can extract meaning, rules and order from (9) .... we hear, through a sort of subconscious statistical analysis.

But Steel's research points (10) .... a third way. Time and time (11) .... he has heard new languages evolve in computers that are not programmed (12) .... with the equivalent of an innate linguistic sense or with statistical powers. Instead, for each new language, rules are gradually invented, negotiated, built upon and spread (13) .... pairs of robots talking to, and learning from, one another. In (14) .... words, language is a complex adaptive system, a living thing which organises (15) .... and spreads like a virus.

2 Complete the second sentence so that it has a similar meaning to the first sentence, using the word given. Do not change the word given. You must use between three and six words including the word given.

1 They are doing translations of that book in various European languages. **VARIETY**
  That book is .... of European languages.

2 More people are speaking the Welsh language now than they did 50 years ago. **WIDELY**
  The Welsh language .... than it was 50 years ago.

3 People now think that language developed through negotiation. **THOUGHT**
  Language .... through negotiation.

4 Children ought to learn computer skills before they start school. **TAUGHT**
  Computer skills .... pre-school children.

5 Someone asked the police spokesperson to explain why the star had been arrested. **GIVE**
  The police spokesperson .... explanation for the star's arrest.

6 Nobody pays much attention when elderly people complain about falling educational standards. **NOTICE**
  Little .... who complain about falling educational standards.

3 There is a mistake in each of these sentences. Correct the mistakes.

1 He never thinks before he says anything – he's like a horse in a china shop.
2 I've never seen him so angry – his face was as red as a rose.
3 He trains in the gym every day – he's as strong as an elephant.
4 I just didn't feel comfortable working there – I felt like a fish out of sea.
5 I don't know how I thought of the idea – it came to me in a bang!
6 I'm sorry, but I don't know what to tell to you.

UNIT
14 It's how you tell it

Reading 1: multiple choice (Part 1)

1 Discuss these questions.

1 Do you enjoy stories?
  Do you like:
  • listening to stories?
  • reading stories?
  • following stories in films or TV programmes?
  • telling stories?

2 What makes a good story: the characters, the plot or the ideas?

2 Think about an interesting story you heard/read/saw recently. What made it interesting? Was it:

• the content?
• where you heard it?
• the way it was told?

Tell your partner either the story (if it's brief!) or a quick summary of the story.

3 You are going to read three extracts which are all concerned in some way with stories. Choose the answer (A, B, C or D) which you think fits best according to the text.

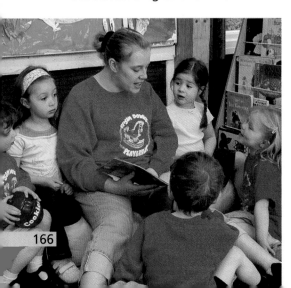

Sign in | Help   Search reviews

The Neverending Story

An excellent story, one that can be read again and again

REVIEWER: Amazon.co.uk Reviewer

It is unfortunate that a movie was made out of this book, because it really takes something away from it! This is a wonderful, original story – a boy named Bastian steals a book called *The Neverending Story* from a bookshop and hides himself in the schoolhouse attic to read it. The book he has stolen is about the magical world of Fantastica, a world that is interconnected with its ruler (the Childlike Empress); but she is dying, and Fantastica is dying with her. As he reads on, Bastian gets slowly more and more drawn into the book, until the two worlds begin to overlap ...

The style of the book is clever and elegant. It is easy to distinguish the parts set in Fantastica from the parts set in the schoolhouse, for the parts in the schoolhouse are written in italics. The ideas are original (I love the idea of the 'nothing' that engulfs Fantastica – you can't even see it properly because there is nothing to see) and nothing else I have ever read rivals it for ingenuity. Though the book is not particularly long, so much happens in it that by the time you reach the end you feel as if you have been reading it for years. The broad outline of the plot that I gave only covers the first part of the book. I can't write any more because I don't want to spoil it. The book's also humorous and gives the reader a few things to think about, though not in an obvious way – the morals are there to be picked up if you happen to notice them. This is an absolute classic, and I would unhesitatingly recommend it to anybody who loves a really good fantasy novel.

1 The reviewer says that this book is superior to others she has read because
  A the ideas it presents are so clever.
  B the style of writing is so original.
  C the plot is so dense and involving.
  D the characters are so appealing.

2 What does the reviewer feel about the more thought-provoking aspects of the book?
  A They are best ignored.
  B They are quite subtly presented.
  C They are weakened by the use of humour.
  D They are too moralistic to be taken seriously.

EXTRACT FROM THE NOVEL *THE ISLAND*

Alexis had only one clue to her mother's past: a faded wedding picture which had stood on Sophia's bedside table for as long as Alexis could remember, the ornate silver frame worn thin with polishing. In early childhood when Alexis used her parents' big, bumpy bed as a trampoline, the image of the smiling but rather stiffly posed couple in the picture had floated up and down in front of her. Sometimes she asked her mother questions about the beautiful lady in lace and the chiselled platinum-haired man. What were their names? Why did he have grey hair? Where were they now? Sofia had given the briefest of answers; that they were Aunt Maria and Uncle Nikolaos, and they had lived in Crete and that they were both now dead. This information had satisfied Alexis then – but now she needed to know more. It was the status of this picture – the only framed photograph in the entire house that intrigued her as much as anything. The couple had clearly been significant in her mother's childhood and yet Sophia always seemed reluctant to talk about them. It was much more than reluctance; in fact it was stubborn refusal. As Alexis grew into adolescence she had learned to respect her mother's desire for privacy – it was as keen as her own teenage instinct to lock herself away and avoid communication. But she had grown beyond all that now.

3 Why did Alexis find the wedding photograph in her mother's bedroom so interesting?

A It reminded her of her childhood.

B It was clearly a most treasured object.

C She didn't believe what her mother said about it.

D She remembered feeling frustrated by her mother's attitude.

4 From the last sentence of the extract, we understand that Alexis

A was no longer curious about the people in the photograph.

B regretted not being more communicative as a teenager.

C had come to understand her mother's feelings better.

D had decided to ask again about the photograph.

More than words can say

Hollywood has always mined comic books for ready-made characters with instant audience recognition. Some of the resultant films were good – think of *Superman* and the spiritual darkness of *Batman* – most less so. Some directors are mining graphic novels to better effect. Quentin Tarantino used *anime*, the two-dimensional animation style derived from Japanese *manga* comic books, for scenes in his film *Kill Bill*. Back on the printed page, however, the graphic novel form is evolving. Authors and artists now use the literary form as witness to recent events, for polemics, for coming-of-age stories and for tender tales of family life.

Graphic novels often demand three readings: once for the text, once for the drawings and once to bring the two together. Authors play with the possibilities, using the graphics to tell a different tale to the text. In *Jimmy Corrigan: the Smartest Kid on Earth* by Chris Ware, an estranged father and son are pictured in a diner scene reminiscent of Edward Hopper's painting *Nighthawks*. It is only later, when they realise that they have had their car stolen, that the reader turns back to see the thief clearly outlined by the light from the diner window. Ware varies his frame sizes too, adjusting the emphasis of each and, on some pages, creating a collage of images that illuminate the story. Other authors use whole pages to create the dramatic impact of a film close-up.

5 In the first paragraph, the writer is suggesting that

A films based on comic book characters were generally unsuccessful.

B film adaptations are influencing the development of graphic novels.

C films are harder to adapt from graphic novels than from comic books.

D films based on graphic novels rather than comic books are more realistic.

6 The graphic novel *Jimmy Corrigan* is mentioned as providing an example of

A an irritating experience for readers.

B a scene that would work well in a film.

C an imaginative use of an evolving format.

D a plot that relies more on the artwork than the words.

4 **Discuss these questions.**

1 If you had to choose, which of the three novels would you prefer to read? *The Neverending Story*, *The Island* or *Jimmy Corrigan*? Why?

2 Have you ever read a graphic novel?

3 How do you think novels will change in the future?

Use of English: open cloze (Part 2)

1 Discuss these questions.

1 How do you enjoy spending evenings with friends? Do you ever go to live performances such as a live concert or a drama in the theatre?

2 If you go to a live concert, what kind of music do you listen to?

3 If you go to the theatre, what do you like to see?

4 Have you ever been to a live show where poetry was read aloud? Do you think you would enjoy it? Why?/Why not?

2

1 Look at the title of the text below. What do you think it will say about how popular culture started?

2 Read the first three sentences to find out.

3

1 Now read the text and think of the word which best fits each gap. Use only one word in each gap. There is an example at the beginning (0).

2 Compare your answers with a partner and justify your ideas.

4

1 Read the complete text again and answer these questions. Did anything surprise you in the text?

1 How did people originally keep a record of poems?

2 What happened when people began to write poetry and stories down?

3 How popular is performance poetry today?

2 Discuss these questions.

1 Do you think you like poetry? Why?/Why not?

2 Which words sum up poetry for you?

a) interesting   d) boring

b) funny   e) irrelevant

c) difficult   f) old fashioned

3 What makes poetry different from text for you? Choose some of the following ideas.

rhyme	rhythm	strange words
lots of adjectives	difficult ideas	

The birth of popular culture

When we think of popular culture these days, (0) *what* spring to mind are pop music, and television programmes (1) .... as soap operas. Few of us would think of poetry as a form of popular culture, although a type of poetry (2) .... well be the common ancestor of much contemporary music and drama. Performance poetry is probably the oldest form of public entertainment (3) .... is. Gathered around their fires, people in pre-literate societies (4) .... listen to learned men (5) .... could recite from memory their tribe's history and traditions, often in the form of verse. Some of these ancient poems, passed (6) .... by word-of-mouth, still exist as fragments in great literary works; parts of the Greek myths and the Icelandic epics fall (7) .... this category.

When writing replaced memory (8) .... the means of recording events, however, poetry changed too. The idea of drama grew out (9) .... performance poetry, and gradually became (10) .... separate artform. Meanwhile, in rural and travelling societies, performance poetry developed into the folk songs (11) .... later fused with Afro-American traditions to become modern popular music.

(12) .... poetry itself has never died out, few people read it or attend poetry performances these days. And (13) ...., poetry still occasionally enjoys bursts of wider popularity, often connected with revolutions in popular culture, (14) .... the Punk or Reggae poets of the late twentieth century, and contemporary rap artists. Through these people, performance poetry occasionally forces (15) .... way back into the public consciousness – perhaps tapping into a folk memory of how popular culture all started.

5

1 The lines in the following poem are in the wrong order. Work with a partner and create a poem of your own, using the lines in any order. You can leave out lines if you like, but you must not change them. Remember to give your poem a title.

This is just to say
The icebox
And which
And so cold
That were in
I have eaten
For breakfast
So sweet
Saving
Forgive me
The plums
You were probably
They were delicious

2 Read your complete poem aloud to the class. Use intonation and rhythm to make it interesting. Ask the other students what they thought of your poem.

3 Now listen to the actual poem. Was your version the same or different? Which do you prefer? Why?

Vocabulary 1: books and stories

1 Complete the sentences using words from the box. You may need to change the form of the word.

> paperback   blurb   volume   copy
> best-seller   whodunit   edition   thriller

1 There are four .... of the latest version of the dictionary – it's huge!
2 I like to have two .... of my favourite book – one to read when I travel and one to keep at home.
3 Her first novel did not sell well, but her next was a .... and was sold to Hollywood.
4 His first book is still selling well, but it is now 20 years old so he has updated it and the new .... will be published next year.
5 I enjoy all kinds of books but my favourite kind of story is a .... – I love trying to guess who the murderer is before I get to the last page!
6 The kind of book I take on holiday is one that I find exciting – a .... like those written by John Grisham, that have crime and spies and so on.
7 I only buy books when they come out in .... because they're cheaper than the hardback version and lighter to carry around.
8 Before I buy a book I always flip through it to get an idea of the story and also read the .... on the back which gives me a short summary.

2 There are different ways of reading. Match the ways to the descriptions.

> wading through   dipping into
> browsing   skimming

1 I spend a lot of time looking through books in shops. I tend to read different blurbs and a couple of pages from each book before I choose the one I want to spend my money on.
2 Even if I find a book hard to read, I'll still struggle on to the end because I can't bear the thought of not knowing what happens! ....
3 I love travel books – I don't read them from cover to cover like a novel, but I tend to flip through them and find locations that I imagine I'm visiting.
....
4 When I read a text in an exam I usually read it quickly first to get a general idea of what it's about before reading it in detail.

Exam focus
Paper 5 Speaking (Parts 1–4)

About the exam: Paper 5 takes 15 minutes for a pair of candidates. There are two examiners, but only one (the interlocutor) speaks to the candidates. The assessor just listens.
You are assessed on:

- the accuracy and range of grammar and vocabulary that you use
- discourse management, e.g. the way you organise your ideas and whether they are relevant to the task you are doing
- pronunciation
- your ability to interact with your partner and with the interlocutor.

There is also a general mark given for your overall performance in the whole of the test. Although it is important that you interact with your partner, you will only be assessed on your own performance and you will not be compared with your partner.

There are four parts to the test:
Part 1 The interlocutor asks you questions about yourself and your opinions.
Part 2 You each speak for one minute alone and without interruption. You are each given a set of three photographs and asked to comment on two of them. You are also asked a brief question after your partner has spoken about their photographs.
Part 3 You work with your partner to complete a task based on pictures.
Part 4 You answer questions from the interlocutor connected with the topic of the Part 3 task.

Suggested procedure

1 Listen carefully to the instructions the interlocutor gives you for each part of the test.
2 Be positive. Speak clearly and answer questions fully, although remember that you only have to give a brief answer to the question following your partner's photographs.
3 If there is anything you don't understand, ask the interlocutor.
4 Try to use a range of language when completing the different tasks, and don't worry if you make a mistake. Accuracy is only part of the assessment criteria.

5 In Part 3, remember that one of the skills in discussion is turn-taking; co-operate with your partner and ask them for their opinion. This is a shared task!
6 Don't worry if the interlocutor stops you before you have finished speaking – that just means that you have run out of time!

Work in groups of four. Decide who will be Candidate A and who will be Candidate B, and who will be the interlocutor. The fourth student should listen and think about how well the two candidates are performing.

The student who is the interlocutor should look at the script on page 187.

Candidate A look at your photographs on page 184.
Candidate B look at your photographs on page 184.

The interlocutor should read the script and time the activities while the other two students are doing the tasks. When you have finished, discuss together:

- anything that was difficult
- ways in which performance could be improved.

Listening: multiple choice
(Part 1)

1   Look at the task on page 171. The three extracts are on different topics. Discuss these questions.

1 How many people will you hear in each extract?
2 Where does each extract come from?
3 What is the topic of each extract?
4 Look at the multiple-choice questions. How much do you know about the extract before you listen?

TIP! In the exam you have time to read the questions before each extract is played. Use all the information on the page to help you imagine the situation and think about what you will hear.

2 You will hear three different extracts. Choose the answer (A, B or C) which fits best according to what you hear. There are two questions for each extract.

Extract One

You hear the beginning of a radio discussion about celebrities.

1 According to Sally, what can psychologists now do?

   A help people who are obsessed with celebrities
   B assess how serious an obsession with a celebrity might be
   C show people how to use their obsession in a more productive way

2 What does Sally suggest about the majority of people classed as suffering from CWS?

   A There is nothing so unusual in their behaviour.
   B They are actually doing something quite creative.
   C They are in danger of becoming obsessive about their hero.

Extract Two

You hear part of a talk given to a group of parents by Derek Palmerston, an expert in education.

3 In this part of his talk, Derek is

   A criticising certain types of behaviour.
   B arguing in favour of a new approach.
   C questioning certain assumptions.

4 In the rest of his talk, Derek intends to

   A provide evidence to support a new idea.
   B compare two ways of dealing with a situation.
   C give a detailed account of the research he's mentioned.

Extract Three

You hear two friends discussing a film.

5 What is the man's opinion of the film?

   A It didn't live up to his expectations.
   B It was a waste of time going to see it.
   C It is a film that he would recommend seeing.

6 What do the two friends agree about?

   A how well the characters were developed
   B how well the battle scenes were directed
   C how good the main actor's performance was

3 Discuss these questions.

1 Would you be interested in reading stories about celebrities written by their fans?
2 Do you think it is possible to study whilst listening to music?
3 What do you think makes a good film?

Vocabulary 2: synonyms

One of the things that makes a story interesting is the variety and range of language the writer uses. Being aware of synonyms and paraphrase will also help you in the CAE exam.

1 The vocabulary in the following text is rather boring. Work with a partner, and replace each highlighted word with a synonym. Use a dictionary or thesaurus if necessary.

Janet (1) asked Carlo to take her back to the hotel. She felt (2) nervous now that she knew that the killer was still free. It was all because she had information that could convict him, and she now (3) knew that he (4) knew – so (5) as a result her life was in danger.
Once she arrived in her hotel room she sat down on the bed, (6) thinking what to do next. She didn't (7) know. She (8) was surprised when the telephone rang suddenly. She picked up the receiver, her hand shaking. The voice at the other end was strangely familiar.

2 What do you think happens next? Write a short paragraph to complete the story. Try to make it as interesting as possible. Then compare your ideas with another student.

3

1 Listen to a student reading her paragraph. Is it very different from yours? Notice any interesting vocabulary, e.g.

   • what was her heart doing?
   • how much was she shaking?
   • how did the man get into the room?

2 Record any new words in your vocabulary notebook, taking care to note its exact meaning and any contexts in which it can be used.

Writing: the set book (Part 2 question 5)

About the exam: In Paper 2, Part 2, Question 5, you can choose to answer a question on one of the set books. You may be asked to write an essay, an article, a report or a review. You can follow the general guidelines for each task type, but the details will come from the set book you choose.

You don't have to answer Question 5, but if you do, you need to know the book well enough to be able to answer the question by referring to the story or the characters.

Suggested procedure

1 Read the book all the way through, and enjoy it! Get a general idea of the story and the characters, and think about any parts you really enjoyed. Talk about it to your friends, and see what they thought about it.

2 Read the book again, this time more carefully. Make notes for yourself under the following headings:

- Plot: main events and the order that they happen in the story
- An important decision, event, letter, meeting, etc. that has an effect on the plot
- Characters: what they are like, how and why they are important in the story
- Places: quick descriptions of setting and locations
- Your own reaction: your feelings about the book, with reasons for why you feel like this.

> **TIP!** You don't have to be positive about everything in the book – it's all right to dislike parts of it as long as you have good reasons and can explain your ideas!

1

1 Work with a partner. Choose one of the set texts, or a different book that you have both read. Make a list of some questions that could be asked about the book.

2 Read the following questions. Are they the same as yours? Add yours to the list, and then discuss them all. Make sure that you think of examples from the book to support your ideas.

1 What makes the book interesting or exciting? Describe a memorable or exciting moment to your partner.
2 Choose the most interesting character and describe him/her. Is this also your favourite character?
3 Is the title a good one? Why?/Why not?
4 Would the book make a good film? Why?/ Why not?
5 Would you recommend this book to a friend? Why?/Why not?

2

1 Look at the two tasks on page 191. In the exam the questions would be on the specific set text and not general.

2 Read this answer, which was written in answer to task a). Notice how the writer has given an idea of the plot, and used examples from the book to support his views.

The last book I read that I really enjoyed reading was 'The Pelican Brief' by John Grisham. Why did I enjoy it so much? It is a real page turner, a whodunit with many unusual aspects, and a brush with romance.

The story is full of twists. Late one night Abe Rosenberg, the Supreme Court's liberal judge, is gunned down in his own home. The same night, the court's youngest and most conservative judge is strangled. What linked the two men and why were they killed? Darby Shaw thinks she knows the answer. She is a talented law student who begins her own investigation into the murder of two Supreme Court Judges, during which she stumbles across an obscure case that links the murders to a rich businesman. As if that wasn't bad enough she then finds a connection with the President of the United States. Her dilema is clear – who can she tell and who can she trust? It turns out that she can trust no-one and has to strugle to survive long enough for the truth to be told.

'The Pelican Brief' is a fun and quick read, but due to its episodic nature it does feel a little rushed in places. I found the final third a little confusing, and had to read it carefully to see what was going on; this means that I have a small resavation in recommending it wholeheartedly. However, it is fast-moving and exciting, and all in all it is well worth a try!

3 Work with a partner and answer the questions.

1 What kind of book is *The Pelican Brief*?
2 Is the style of the review semi-formal or informal? Find some examples to prove your idea.
3 The writer has made four spelling mistakes. Find and correct them.
4 Find words or phrases that mean:
   a) an interesting book (para 1)
   b) a complicated story (para 2)
   c) come across by chance (para 2)
   d) a book that is easy to read (para 3).

3

1 **Work with a partner. Think of a book that you could either write a review of for task a) or write an essay on for task b). Decide:**

- what style you will use
- what evidence you will use from the book to support your ideas
- how you will organise your answer.

2 **Write your answer. Show your partner and check each other's work for:**

- spelling
- punctuation
- grammatical accuracy.

Grammar: mistakes to avoid

Spelling

It is important to get spelling right in the exam, as you will not get the mark in Paper 3, Part 2 or in Paper 4, Part 2 if you spell the word incorrectly. Keep a note of your own mistakes and try to look out for them in your writing, then you can avoid them. NB Both British and American spelling is acceptable.

Mistakes often occur in words that have:

- double consonants, e.g. *different*, *necessary*. It is also easy to add consonants when you are not sure if they are doubled or not, e.g. *exaggerated*
- silent letters (letters that you don't pronounce when you say the word), e.g. *know*, *right*, *though*
- letters which may sound like other letters, or are difficult to guess from the pronunciation, e.g. *grammar*, *magazine*
- prefixes and suffixes, e.g. *respons**ible**, **mis**taken*
- plurals.

Other problems can occur in words that:

- sound like other words (homophones), e.g. *here/hear*, *weather/whether*
- have problems with letter order, e.g. *receive*, *believe*.

TIP! Learn the two rules below.
i comes before *e* except after *c*, e.g. *friend*, *ceiling*
is is a verb, *ice* is a noun; so *advise* = verb, *advice* = noun

1 Choose the correct spelling of the words in each of these sentences.

1 What is your key *recommendation / reccommendation* for the project?
2 I *believe / beleive* that they are going to bring out a film of the book.
3 I thought that film was *incredably / incredibly dissapointing / disappointing*.
4 I'm studying performing art – I love the course *becuase / because* it includes *movment / movement* through dance.
5 I had a real *argument / arguement* with my friend about the merits of the book.
6 It's *their / there* party so the *choise / choice* of food is up to them.
7 I *practise / practice* dancing every day, which keeps me *supple / suppel* and fit.
8 I just don't feel *comfortable / comfortible* with the idea of asking him to pay – he can't really *afford / aford* it and we could cover his costs *ourselves / ourselfs*.
9 *What / Waht* do you think about the idea of *watching / waching* television tonight instead of going out?
10 I think children *benefit / benefit* greatly from learning other *languages / langages* when they are young.
11 One of the popular courses at university nowadays is *psychology / phsycology* and many employers seem to think that it's *usful / useful* for the workplace.

2 Work with a partner. Think of five words that you have difficulty spelling. Dictate them to your partner and see if they can get them right.

Punctuation

Common mistakes with punctuation are:

- commas
- apostrophes
- hyphens
- exclamation marks
- question marks
- semi-colons, colons.

3 Discuss with a partner:

- what you find difficult about using any of the punctuation above
- any ideas for remembering how to use each one.

Watch Out! *apostrophe*

An apostrophe indicates something is missing, or possession, and is not used when the word is just a plural.

Which one is correct in the pairs of sentences? What is missing? Which one is just a plural?

1 a) It's raining.
   b) Its raining.
2 a) You're coat is hanging in the hall.
   b) Your coat is hanging in the hall.
3 a) Video's for sale
   b) Videos for sale

---

4 There are two mistakes in each of these sentences. There may be a mistake where there is punctuation used incorrectly, punctuation that should not be there or punctuation that has been omitted. Find the mistakes and correct them.

1 I do like going to the cinema; however I really didnt enjoy the last film I saw.
2 My favourite English meal is fish and chip's, although I also like roast beef?
3 Im meeting my friends at the theatre because theyr'e probably going to arrive quite late.
4 My five year old nephew loves reading – its really good that he does.
5 It was your' idea to go out last night so its not my fault that you are tired this morning!
6 People say that young people don't read much nowadays so how often do you read a book
7 I find it very strange the way english people eat potatoe's with every meal!
8 I could'nt answer the last question in the test so I asked the teacher afterward's.
9 The review's of the film were really good, so I was very disappointed that I couldnt go.
10 Let's go to the show tonight instead of saturday because, I'm really looking forward to it and I can't wait!

5

1 Work with a partner. Think of any difficulties that you have with any form of punctuation. Write a sentence and show it to your partner to check if you have got it right.

2 This extract from an informal letter has no punctuation. Work with a partner and insert the correct punctuation.

> this book grabbed me from the first page whenever I had to put it down I couldnt stop thinking about it its not unlike a sherlock holmes novel but set in new york and not England the storys full of twists and turns these kept me guessing the whole time the authors attention to detail brings the city vividly to life overall it was a thrilling exciting read and Im sure youre going to love it

Writing: Paper 2 overview

1 In Paper 2 Writing you have to do two tasks and you have one hour and a half to complete the whole paper. There are two parts, and each question carries equal marks.

Part 1 is compulsory and you may be asked to produce an article, a report, a proposal or a letter (180–220 words).

In Part 2 you choose one task from four (220–260 words).

Questions 2–4 may include:

- a newspaper or magazine article
- a contribution to a longer piece such as a leaflet or brochure
- a semi-formal or informal letter
- a report
- a proposal
- a review
- a competition entry
- an information sheet
- an essay
- a reference.

Question 5 is based on set texts, and you may have to write an essay, a review, an article or a report.

2 Work with another student. Decide which of the items in Exercise 1 you generally find easier to write. Discuss why.

3 Look at the following task and read the answer on page 190.

You see the following announcement of a competition in an international magazine.

HOLIDAY OF A LIFETIME

We are offering you the chance to win one of a range of exotic holidays, all expenses paid for two weeks, for you and a friend. Just write to us, describing the most exciting holiday you have ever had. Winning entries will be published.

Send entries to: The Editor, Today Magazine, PO. Box 743, London.

Write your **competition entry** in 220–260 words.

4 Read the task and the answer again. Decide if the answer would be classed as a band 3 (satisfactory) or band 5 (very good) on the CAE Paper 2 marking scale given below.

Band 5 For a Band 5 to be awarded, the candidate's writing has a very positive effect on the target reader. The content is relevant* and the topic is fully developed. Information and ideas are skilfully organised through a range of cohesive devices, which are used to good effect. A wide range of complex structures and vocabulary is used effectively. Errors are minimal, and inaccuracies which do occur have no impact on communication. Register and format are consistently appropriate to the purpose of the task and the audience.

Band 3 For a Band 3 to be awarded, the candidate's writing has a satisfactory effect on the target reader. The content is relevant* with some development of the topic. Information and ideas are generally organised logically, though cohesive devices may not always be used appropriately. A satisfactory range of structures and vocabulary is used, though word choice may lack precision. Errors which do occur do not cause difficulty for the reader. Register and format are reasonably appropriate to the purpose of the task and the audience.

5 Look at the Examiner Comments on the answer on page 192. Then improve the answer by addressing the comments.

6 Now choose one of the following writing tasks (or the task in Exercise 3). Your answer should follow the instructions given. Write 220–260 words.

1 Your local council is concerned about traffic problems where you live. You have been asked to write a short report on the state of public transport in your area with recommendations on how to encourage the local population to use public transport more and their cars less.

Write the report.

2 A magazine for students of English as a Foreign Language has asked for articles on sensible ways of preparing for English language exams. You decide to submit an article. Suggest strategies for organising revision in the weeks before the exam and provide specific ideas as to how students should use their time in the week before the exam.

Write your article.

3 You have been asked to contribute an information sheet for school leavers who are hoping to go to college. Include information about how to choose a course, what to think about when choosing a place to study and how to prepare yourself for living away from home.

Write the text for the sheet.

1 When you select the task to answer in Part 2, remember to:

a) choose a text type which you feel confident about, and that you feel you can write well. Ask yourself if you have written this kind of text before, if you can organise your material appropriately and if you are sure about the appropriate style.

b) make sure you have clear ideas of what you will include as the content. Do you know the key topic vocabulary you will need?

c) plan your paragraphs before you start to write a full text.

d) include all the points asked for in the task.

2 Discuss your choice of task with another student. Explain why you think this is the best choice for you.

3 Now write your answer. Remember not to take longer than 45 minutes and remember to check your work.

7   Now look at all the writing assessment bands on page 211 in the Writing reference. Give your work to another student so they can suggest which band they think your answer might come in. Discuss with your partner which areas of your answer could be improved.

8   If necessary, rewrite your answer. Try and improve it so that it would come in a higher band.

Reading 2: planning to take an exam?

1

1 Doing well in an exam is not only a matter of learning. Look at the headings a–f, and discuss with a partner what kind of advice you think would be included in each one.

a) Making the most of past papers
b) Being aware of your particular issues
c) Looking after your body
d) Getting into the swing of it
e) Getting things into your head
f) Keeping yourself going

2 Now read the text and match each heading to the appropriate paragraph (A–F). Fill in the gaps in the paragraphs with either *Do* or *Don't*.

2   Which piece of advice do you think is the most useful? Can you think of any other piece of advice that might be useful for other students to have?

(A) ....

You should have a grammar checklist in which you have noted down your usual mistakes. (1) .... go through this often to make sure that you are aware of what your own mistakes are, so that you will be less likely to make them in the exam.
(2) .... forget to go through some of your old written work to check that you have included all your usual mistakes, and notice helpful comments that your teacher has written.

(B) ....

It's important to get exercise, because it relaxes you and stimulates your brain. (3) .... plan a study routine that doesn't include time for sport or exercise.
   Sitting at a desk all day is not good for you. (4) .... have frequent breaks and change positions often. You should stretch regularly, and try to relax– it's very easy to become stiff and tense across the shoulders without realising it.

(C) ....

Try to watch DVDs in English, and read anything you can find in English. (5) .... look up every word – enjoy the rhythm of the language!
   In the weeks leading up to the exam, (6) .... try to immerse yourself in English. Persuade your friends to speak to you in English, and encourage them to correct your mistakes.

(D) ....

It is important that you are totally familiar with the format of the exam and what is expected of you. (7) .... practise in the correct time for each paper.

(8) .... let exam practice take over your language learning – the exam will test what you know, so make sure that you go back and look at all the language work you have done during the course, not just at the exam tasks.

(E) ....

(9) .... eat too much chocolate or sugary foods – these will give you a quick sugar boost but it will not last – it is better to eat bananas, raw vegetables and wholemeal bread which will give you energy over a longer period.

(10) .... control your blood sugar levels, and make sure you have regular meals to maintain your energy levels.

(F) ....

The words and phrases in the language boxes of the writing reference section of this course book are useful. (11) .... learn the phrases by heart, and try to use them appropriately when you are doing the Writing paper.

When you go through your vocabulary notes, make sure that you learn words in phrases and (12) .... learn them individually. (13) .... make a note of different forms of the words as this will help you with the cloze passages and with the word building in the Use of English paper.

Certificate in Advanced English quiz

How well do you know the CAE exam?
See how many of these questions you can answer and then check to see if you were right.

1   How many papers are there in the CAE exam? What is each one called?

2   How long does each paper last?

3   How many marks is each paper worth?

4   Do you have to get a pass mark in all the papers?

5   Can you make notes on the question paper?

6   Are you allowed to use a dictionary?

7   When should you write in pen and when in pencil?

8   In what order should you do the tasks in Paper 1?

9   How long do you get to answer each part in Papers 1, 3 and 4?

10 How many questions do you answer in Paper 2?

11 What happens if you write too many words in Paper 2?

12 How many parts are there in Paper 3? What is each part called?

13 Can you give alternative answers if you're not sure?

14 Does your spelling always have to be correct?

15 How many times do you hear each listening text?

16 How long do you have to copy your answers on to the marksheet at the end of the listening paper?

17 Are all parts of the speaking paper assessed?

18 Are you in competition with your partner in the speaking paper?

19 How long is it before you get your result?

20 What information do you get on a) the results slip b) your certificate?

Paper 5 Speaking tasks

Unit 3 Speaking: language of possibility and speculation

Exercise 4, p.37

Unit 4 Speaking: Parts 3 and 4

Exercise 1.5, p.43

Unit 5 Speaking: agreeing and adding information (Parts 3 and 4)
Exercise 2, p.59

Unit 6 Exam focus: Paper 5 Speaking: collaborative task/ discussion (Parts 3 and 4)

Exercises 1 and 2, p.71

- How do these things reflect changes in family life?
- Which picture best shows the biggest impact on family life?

Unit 7 Speaking 1: two-way conversation (Part 3)
Exercise 2, p.81

Unit 6 Exam focus: Paper 5 Speaking: collaborative task/discussion (Parts 3 and 4)

Exercise 2, p.71

Student A (interlocutor)

Part 3 (collaborative task)

Say to Students B and C: 'Now I'd like you to talk about something together for about three minutes. Here are some pictures showing different things that can have an impact on family life. First, talk to each other about the positive and negative impact on family life reflected in these pictures. Then decide which picture best shows the biggest impact on family life today. All right?'

After about three minutes, say 'Thank you' and stop the discussion.

Part 4 (discussion)

Ask Students B and C some of these questions, in any order. Stop them after about five minutes. You may not need to use all the questions if the students have a lot to say.

1 What do you think is the best age for young people to leave home and live by themselves?
2 What makes it easy or difficult to get on well with siblings?
3 Do you think that parenting should be taught in schools? Why?/Why not?
4 How easy is it for children to understand their parents? What can help them to do this?
5 How important is it for parents to establish rules for their children?

Unit 9 Speaking 2: individual long turn (Part 2)

Exercise 4, p.111

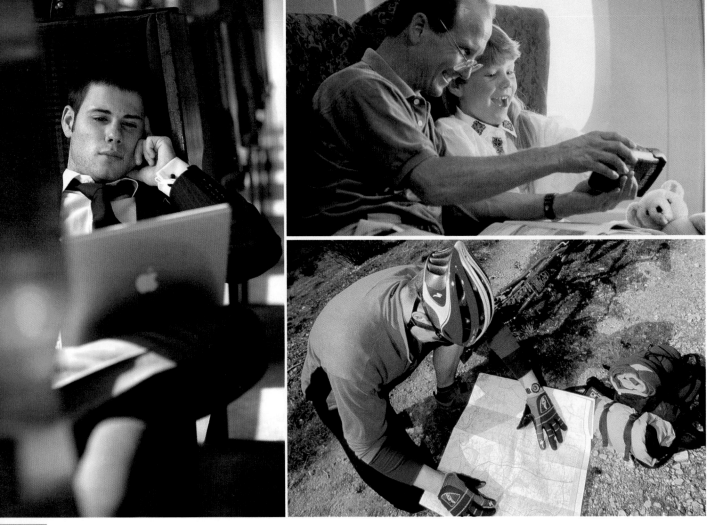

Unit 13 Speaking: discussion (Parts 3 and 4)

Exercise 1, p.158

Unit 14 Exam focus: Paper 5 Speaking (Parts 1–4), p.170

Candidate A photos

- Why might the people have chosen to read in this way?
- What difficulties might they have?

Unit 14 Exam focus: Paper 5 Speaking (Parts 1–4), p.170

Candidate B photos

- Why might the people have chosen to examine these things?
- How important might it be to examine the things carefully?

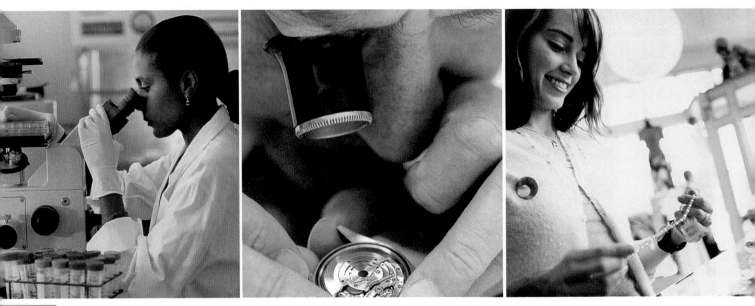

Unit 8 Speaking: comparing (Part 2)
Exercise 2, p.99

Unit 14 Exam focus: Paper 5 Speaking (Parts 1–4), p.170

Part 3

> • How do these pictures show the effect technology has had on life today?
> • Which picture best reflects the most significant change technology has brought about?

Unit 14 Exam focus: Paper 5 Speaking (Parts 1–4), p.170

Interlocutor

Part 1 (introduction)

Say: 'Good morning/afternoon. First of all we'd like to know something about you.'

Ask students the questions below in turn.
'Where are you from?'
'What do you do there?'
'How long have you been studying English?'
'What do you enjoy about studying English?'

Ask candidates in turn:
'What do you enjoy doing in your free time?'
'What kind of books do you enjoy reading?'
'What do you enjoy most about learning something new?'
'What kind of course would you like to take in the future?'
'What kind of holidays do you enjoy most?'
'What countries would you most like to visit?'

Part 2 (long turn)

Say: 'In this part of the test I'm going to give each of you three pictures. I'd like you to talk about your pictures on your own for about a minute, and also to answer a question briefly about your partner's pictures.'

Tell Candidate A: 'Here are your pictures.' **(Point to photos at the top of page 184.)** 'They show people reading in different situations. I'd like you to compare two of the pictures, and say why the people might have chosen to read in this way, and what difficulties they might have.'

Allow Candidate A to talk for a minute. Then stop him/her. Say 'Thank you'.

Ask Candidate B this question: 'Which of the situations do you think would be easiest to learn in?'

After about 20–30 seconds, say 'Thank you'.

Tell Candidate B: 'Here are your pictures.' **(Point to photos at the bottom of page 184.)** 'They show people examining different things. I'd like you to compare two of the pictures, and say why the people might have chosen to examine these things, and how important it might be to examine the things carefully.'

Allow Candidate B to talk for a minute. Then stop him/her. Say 'Thank you'.

Ask Candidate A this question: 'Which of the things do you think it is most important to examine carefully?'

After about 20–30 seconds, say 'Thank you'.

Part 3 (collaborative task)

Say: 'Now, I'd like you to talk about something together for about three minutes.
Here are some pictures **(point to photos on page 186)** showing different ways in which technology has changed the way we live today.
First, talk to each other about what these pictures show about the effect technology has had on life today. Then decide which picture best reflects the most significant change technology has brought about.'

After about three minutes, say 'Thank you' **and stop the candidates talking.**

Part 4 (discussion)

Ask Candidates A and B some of these questions in any order. Stop the discussion after about four minutes.

1 Is there any aspect of technology that irritates you?
2 What do you think has been the most positive impact of technology on the world today?
3 Some older people have difficulty using technology. Why do you think this is?
4 Some people say that computers save us time. Do you agree?
5 How would you like to see technology change in the future?

Communication activities and writing

Unit 1, Reading Exercise 6, p.9

hurl /hɜːl/ *v* **3 hurl yourself at/against etc sb/sth** *also* **hurl yourself down** to throw yourself at someone or something with a lot of force: *She wanted to hurl herself into his arms.*

hold back /həʊld bæk/ *phr v* **2 hold sth ➡ back** to stop yourself from feeling or showing a particular emotion: *She struggled to hold back her tears.* / *Anger flooded through her. She couldn't hold it back.*

stuff /stʌf/ *v*[T] **2** to fill something until it is full: *Volunteers were busy stuffing envelopes.* | **be stuffed with sth** *a pillow stuffed with feathers* | *boxes stuffed full of papers*

die hard /daɪhɑːd/ *n* [C] someone who opposes change and refuses to accept new ideas –**diehard** *adj: a few diehard fans*

twang /twæŋ/ *v*[I,T] if you twang something or if it twangs, it makes a quick ringing sound by being pulled and then suddenly let go: *She twanged the guitar strings.*

chill out /tʃɪl aʊt/ *v*[I] *informal* to relax completely instead of feeling angry, tired, or nervous: *'Hold it! Just chill for a second, won't you!'* | *I spent the afternoon chilling out in front of the TV.*

covers /kʌvəz/ **10 MUSIC** *also* **cover version** [C] a new recording of a song, piece of music, etc that was originally recorded by a different artist: *She's opted to do a cover version for her first single.*

venue /venjuː/ *n* [C] a place where an organized meeting, concert etc takes place: **sporting/conference/concert etc venue** | *The first thing to do is book a venue.* | *The band will play* (= perform at) *as many venues as possible.*

Unit 1, Writing Exercise 6, p.16

Read the following writing task. Underline the three things that you have to do in your letter. What is the best order to put them in?

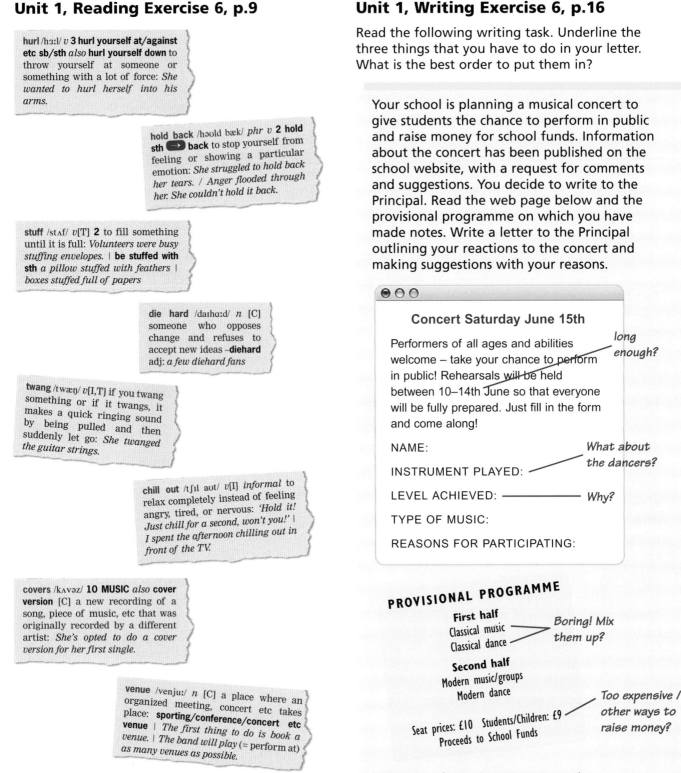

Your school is planning a musical concert to give students the chance to perform in public and raise money for school funds. Information about the concert has been published on the school website, with a request for comments and suggestions. You decide to write to the Principal. Read the web page below and the provisional programme on which you have made notes. Write a letter to the Principal outlining your reactions to the concert and making suggestions with your reasons.

Concert Saturday June 15th

Performers of all ages and abilities welcome – take your chance to perform in public! Rehearsals will be held between 10–14th June so that everyone will be fully prepared. Just fill in the form and come along!

long enough?

NAME:

INSTRUMENT PLAYED: *What about the dancers?*

LEVEL ACHIEVED: *Why?*

TYPE OF MUSIC:

REASONS FOR PARTICIPATING:

PROVISIONAL PROGRAMME

First half
Classical music
Classical dance
Boring! Mix them up?

Second half
Modern music/groups
Modern dance

Seat prices: £10 Students/Children: £9
Proceeds to School Funds
Too expensive / other ways to raise money?

Write your **letter** in 180–220 words.

Unit 6, Grammar 1 Exercise 2, p.70

Student A: Carlo

I live with Esther – she's my nan. It's my choice; I come from a large family and there just wasn't enough space in our house for me and my four brothers and two sisters. I was so busy with school work – I told my nan that I'd rather (1) *had / have / having* my own space, and as she only lives five minutes away she offered me a room in her house. Moving in with her is an ideal solution, though sometimes I wish she (2) *couldn't worry / hadn't worried / wouldn't worry* about me all the time! And if only she (3) *coped / copes / had coped* better with technology – it annoys me when she doesn't understand computers or DVDs – and I'd rather she (4) *didn't complain / doesn't complain / couldn't complain* about my music so much! But although there is a generation gap, on the whole Nan and I understand each other pretty well, and I never wish I (5) *hadn't moved in / didn't move in / wouldn't have moved in* with her.

Unit 11, Writing Exercise 4, p.139

The people producing your college magazine want to make it more interesting for everyone, and have asked students to submit an article for the next edition with the following title:
Happiness is a state of mind!

You decide to write an article, explaining what you think makes people happy and how they can achieve this.

Write your **article** in 220–260 words.

The editor of your college magazine is planning to include a special section in the next edition on people who are very happy with their life, and why. The article should be inspirational and motivating.

Write an article about a person you know who is happy, describing them and the characteristics or achievements of this person, and explain why they are happy and how this can motivate others.

Write your **article** in 220–260 words.

Unit 11, Speaking 2 Exercise 1, p.140

Student A

Tickling highlights how your brain pays more attention to surprising sensations. The physical touch on the skin is the same whether you are tickled or whether you tickle yourself, but your brain uses information from your motor system to make predicted sensations less noticeable. Feelings which are expected are suppressed. If the connection in your brain between your own movements and the sensations they cause disappears, then your brain cannot suppress the feeling. So if, for example, you use a feather, you can tickle yourself, because the feather doesn't move along your skin in a predictable way exactly in time with how you move your hand.

Unit 12, Reading 2 Exercise 1, p.146

Student A

Reading this book, it is difficult to believe that the author has not actually visited the sixteenth century. The heroine, Penelope, staying at a farm in Derbyshire, finds herself unexpectedly able to go backwards and forwards from the present to the sixteenth century during the reign of Queen Elizabeth I. It is here that she meets famous people from history as well as a distant ancestor, and the farm of the past and its inhabitants become more real to Penelope than her own time. She knows what the future holds for them all, but can do nothing to change history.

[*A Traveller in Time* by Alison Uttley]

Unit 6, Grammar 1 Exercise 2, p.70

Student B: Esther

The best thing about living with Carlo is that he keeps me in touch with teenage life – though the most difficult part is trying to keep up with him! Sometimes I wish he (1) *would slow down / had slowed down / slows down* a bit – at my age I get tired easily, although I wish I (2) *couldn't / didn't / wouldn't.* And I really wish he (3) *had turned / turned / would turn* his music down in the evenings! But then I think – suppose I (4) *had turned him away / would have turned him away / could turn him away* and not taken him in? I've really got to know him well, and I'd rather not (5) *had wasted / waste / will waste* the time I have with him with small complaints. It's high time all older people (6) *try / tried / could try* to understand the young – I wish I (7) *could tell / would tell / had told* everyone how easy it is for different generations to get on with each other.

Unit 11, Speaking 2 Exercise 1, p.140

Student B

You probably found that you couldn't tell what colour the card was, because you can't distinguish colour with your peripheral vision. The back of your eye – the retina – is coated with cells which detect light. These cells are divided into 'rods', which are sensitive to the amount of light, and 'cones' which are sensitive to the colour of the light. Most of the 'cones' are found in the middle of the retina, and the 'rods' at the edges, so only the centre of your vision is sensitive to colours. It means that if you catch sight of something out of the corner of your eye, it can't be something to do with colour changes. Most of the time this doesn't affect us, but it is important that red and green traffic lights appear and disappear in different places since the location change is what you detect with peripheral vision rather than the colour change.

Unit 12, Reading 2 Exercise 1, p.146

Student B

Dick Young has been lent a house in Cornwall by his friend Magnus Lane, a professor of bio-physics. He has agreed to act as guinea-pig for a new drug that Magnus has discovered. When he takes the prescribed dose he finds himself back in the fourteenth century, in this same Cornish countryside. During the following days he takes successive 'trips'. Each lasts only a short time, but he always returns to the same surroundings. What he doesn't know is whether the experiences are a result of the drug, a subconscious escape from dissatisfaction with his own life or whether he has really travelled back in time.

[*The House on the Strand* by Daphne du Maurier]

Unit 14, Writing, Exercise 3, p.175

Holiday of a lifetime, sample answer

Holiday of a lifetime

Perhaps my most exiting holiday was when I went on my motorbike with a group of friends to the south of Sinai. We were all working in the Cairo and this was going to be a two-weeks summer holiday. I was looking forward to it for months. The thought to get away from the noise and pollution in the city was very good.

We set of from Cairo on three bikes and drove down the west coast of Sinai. You feel very free when you are on a bike on the open road. There's nothing quiet like it really. The scenery was amazing. It was incradibly rocky and sometimes quite lonly. About halfway down the coast we stopped to see St. Catherine's monastery. You can stay overnight. In fact, we decided to walk up the near Mt. St. Catherine so that we could see the sun rise. We sat together in silence and savured the moment. It was very beautifull.

We continued our journey down to Sharm El Sheikh in the south. We stayed in cheap hotel and every day we were snorkelling or scuba diving. There's an incredible range of fish and coral and the colours are out of this world! We also made friends with some Australians who were travelling round the world. I still write to them.

Unit 14, Writing Exercise 2, p.172

a) Your college wants to add a section in its magazine on book reviews, and has asked students to write a review of a book they have really enjoyed. Write a **review**, giving reasons why you would recommend this book to other students. (220–260 words)

b) You have read a book in which an important decision has been made. Write an **essay** describing the decision and say why it was so important. (220–260 words)

Unit 1, Writing Exercise 4.2, p.16

Dear Sir,

I attended the film show last weekend with my young cousin, and I am writing to complain about several aspects of the evening.

Firstly, there were practical problems. The film started late, so I missed my bus home. The advertised running time was incorrect – it lasted over three hours, and although there was an interval as advertised, it was impossible to buy ice cream owing to the long queues and single seller. On top of that, I felt that the uncomfortable seats were too expensive.

However, these problems are less significant than the fact that the film was totally inappropriate for an audience largely made up of families with young children. Despite the fact that the review stated that the complex plot and extreme special effects made the film unsuitable for children, your advertisement said the opposite. In fact, it was billed as a comedy! We left before the end, as my cousin was extremely upset by some scenes, and has not slept properly since. I am sure that he is not alone.

I suggest that in future you choose your films more carefully, and state clearly what kind of film it is, thus avoiding such distressing situations. Much as I wish to support the school, I shall not attend future fund-raising events.

Yours faithfully,

Unit 2, Writing Exercise 4, p.28

You recently tried to buy an old camera on an Internet auction site, but had some problems. You want to tell a friend what happened. Write a letter to your friend, explaining what happened, what you did and giving your friend advice about buying things on auction sites.

Write your **letter** in 220–260 words.

Unit 5, Writing Exercise 3, p.64

This reference is for Joanna Price who is applying for the position of activities supervisor at the children's sports camp.

I have known Joanna for over ten years. She is a good friend of mine and we have been at school together for most of that time. She is a very sensible girl who is always kind and courteous. She is also extremely good fun and would be an excellent person to work with children. She has a younger brother and sister so she is accustomed to entertaining children.

She is very good at basketball and has been in the school team for three years. This demonstrates that she has good eye to hand co-ordination and would be proficient at any sport, even those she has not yet played. In addition, she goes running regularly so she is extremely fit. In the past she has played tennis and football at a high level, and consequently I am sure she could teach these sports. Last year she took a qualification to teach basketball so she has official coaching skills. Her interests are varied – as well as sport she loves music and she plays the guitar. She enjoys reading and is particularly keen on science fiction, which she reads all the time.

In the future she is hoping to become a sports teacher, and therefore this job would be very useful for her because she would gain valuable work experience. Her enthusiasm means that she would invest a lot of time and energy into making sure the children at the camp have effective sports training, but enjoy themselves at the same time.

Joanna would be an excellent person to do this job and I can highly recommend her for the position.

Unit 10, Writing Exercise 6, p.126

Your school is considering adopting an endangered animal. This would involve collecting money regularly and distributing information about the progress of the animal. Your class has been asked to select an animal to sponsor, and has sent out a questionnaire to all the students in the school asking for their suggestions with reasons. Write your report based on the questionnaires and your own ideas, suggesting different animals to sponsor with reasons, and suggesting ways of setting the project up.

Write your **report** in 180–220 words.

Polar bears – they're so cute! They'll die if the ice keeps melting.

African elephants – lots now but they are threatened by climate change

Bengal tiger – only a few hundred left!

waste of time – put the money towards IT in the school

Pointless adopting one animal – what good will that do? Let's save everyone!

Our money is a drop in the ocean – why not raise awareness with seminars and lecture – change behaviour?

Unit 12, Reading 2 Exercise 1, p.146

Student C

When a Victorian scientist invents a time machine and propels himself into the year 802,701 AD, he is initially delighted to find that suffering has been replaced by beauty, contentment and peace. Entranced at first by the Eloi, an elfin species descended from man, he soon realises that they are simply remnants of a once-great culture now weak and childishly afraid of the dark. They have every reason to be afraid: in deep tunnels beneath their paradise lurks another race descended from humanity, the sinister Morlocks. And when the scientist's time machine vanishes, it becomes clear he must search these tunnels if he is ever to return to his own era.

[*The Time Machine* by H. G. Wells (Web review)]

Unit 14, Writing Exercise 5, p.175

Examiner Comments

Content
The task has been completed even though it is slightly under-length.

Organisation and Cohesion
Sensible opening to the entry. However, it ends rather abruptly. Appropriate use of paragraphs.

Range
Some range has been demonstrated by the candidate, e.g. out of this world, savoured. However, the language is generally not very ambitious and there could have been more use of longer, complex sentences.

Register
Consistently and appropriately informal. The tone is lively and engages the interest of the reader.

Target Reader
Would consider shortlisting this entry for the competition.

Accuracy
There are some minor grammatical errors which do not prevent the reader understanding the writer's message but still spoil the impression on the target reader, e.g. the Cairo. Spelling is rather inaccurate, e.g. exiting

Grammar reference

Index

1 Articles

1.1 Indefinite article a/an

We use the indefinite article *a/an* for singular countable nouns:

- when we mention something for the first time
  *The concept of **a brand** is difficult to define.*
- when it doesn't matter which particular person or thing we are referring to
  *I bought this T-shirt in **a supermarket**.*

1.2 Definite article the

We use the definite article *the* for singular and plural countable nouns, and with uncountable nouns:

- when something has already been mentioned, so we already know which person or object is being referred to
  *My parents lived in a small house. **The** house was old …*
- when there is only one thing or person
  ***The actor** who played James Bond in 'Dr No' was Sean Connery.*
- when there is one thing, person, etc. that is especially important to the speaker
  *I've got an appointment at **the hospital**.*
- in generalisations with singular countable nouns
  ***The panda** is threatened with extinction.*

- for nationalities
  *Many of **the English** prefer coffee to tea.*
- with adjectives used as nouns
  *She goes to a special school for **the blind**.*
- for regions, mountain ranges, oceans, seas and countries (when these refer to a collection of states or areas)
  *England is part of **the British Isles**.*
- for hotels, restaurants, theatres and cinemas
  *We can't possibly afford to stay at **the Ritz**!*

1.3 Zero article

We use no article (the zero article):

- in generalisations with plural and uncountable nouns when we mean 'all'
  *I like **music**.*
- when we are referring to the general use of an institution rather than a particular place
  *He goes to **school** in Scotland.*
  *He's been taken to **hospital**.*
- for continents, countries and cities
  ***Perth** is in **Australia**.*
- for mountains and lakes
  ***Lake Vostok** is permanently frozen.*
- for most streets (except The High Street)
  *I live on **North Avenue**.*

2 Comparative and superlative structures

2.1 Basic forms

1 We use *more* or *most* before nouns, adverbs, two-syllable adjectives ending in *-ful*, *-less* and *-ing*, two-syllable adjectives where the second syllable is stressed, and longer adjectives.
  *I earn **more money** than she does.*
  *She works **more effectively** than anyone I know.*
  *She is the **most useful** member of the team.*
  *He is one of the **most misunderstood** artists of the twentieth century.*

2 We add *-er* and *-est* to one-syllable adjectives and two-syllable adjectives where the second syllable is unstressed.
  *It's **hotter** than it used to be.*
  *She's a lot **funnier** than her brother.*

3 To compare two things we can also use the structure *as + adjective/adverb + as*.
  *I don't go out **as often as** I'd like to.*

2.2 Intensifying comparative forms

To intensify comparative forms we can use the following expressions:

*I earn **considerably/a great deal/much/a lot** more now than I did ten years ago.*

*I see **loads/tons** more people than I used to. (informal)*

*I think the questions are getting **more and more** difficult.*

*The Plaza Hotel is **slightly/a bit/rather** more expensive, but it's worth it.*

*There haven't been **half as many/nothing like as many** complaints since Glyn became boss.*

3 Conditionals

3.1 Basic forms

1 We use (*if/when/unless* + present simple/*will*) + present simple to express general truths.
   When *you **heat** water to 100°C, it **boils/will boil**.*

2 We use (*if/when/unless* + present simple) + imperative to give a command.
   Stay *here **unless** I **tell** you to leave.*

3 We use (*if/when/unless* + present simple) + *will/might/may*/present continuous to express a condition referring to a possible present or future event.
   Unless *I **hear** from you, I**'ll** go on my own.*
   *He **might** be prepared to do the job **when** he**'s** finished his other work.*

4 We use (*if/unless* + past simple/past continuous) + *would/could/might/ought to* to express a hypothetical condition referring to the present or future.
   If *Anna **went** to college, she **could** study languages.*
   *I **wouldn't** take my laptop **unless** I **was planning** to do some work.*

5 We use (*if/unless* + past perfect) + *would/could/might/ought to have* to talk about a hypothetical condition in the past.
   *Even **if** I**'d got** the job, I probably **wouldn't have** enjoyed it much.*

3.2 Formal style

In more formal styles, *if* can be omitted and the auxiliary verb placed before the subject.

If I had been warned → ***Had I been warned*** *about the situation, I would have made other arrangements.*

If they had not been ordered to → ***Had they not been ordered to**, they would never have entered the building.*

3.3 if + should/happen to

We use *if* + *should/happen to* to suggest that something is rather unlikely to happen, or may just happen by chance. *Should* and *happen* can be used together.

If *you **(should) happen to** pass a pharmacy, could you get me some aspirin?*

3.4 supposing/imagine

We use *supposing* and *imagine* in place of *if*. The meaning is similar.

Supposing/Imagine *you won the lottery – what would you do with the money?*

3.5 if + was/were to

We use *if* + *was/were to* to make an event seem more hypothetical. This structure is not used with state verbs, e.g. *believe.*

If *they **were to** find a way of wiping out malaria, millions of lives would be saved.*

3.6 if + will/would

We use *if* + *will/would* to make requests more polite. In this case the auxiliary *will/would* means 'be willing to'.

If *you **will** just bear with us for a few moments, the Minister will answer your questions.*

If *you **would** be kind enough to send your account details, we will settle this matter immediately.*

4 Countable/uncountable nouns

1 Some words are always uncountable. They cannot be used with the indefinite article (*a/an*) and they do not have a plural form.
   *I need some **advice** about which course to choose.*
   *There's a lot of **information** available on the Internet.*
   *She's doing **research** into language learning.*
   *There isn't any **news** about the elections yet.*

2 Some words may be countable or uncountable, depending on their precise meaning.
   *There's **a space** between the cupboard and the wall.* (countable)
   *The astronauts will travel through **space**.* (uncountable)

5 Direct and reported speech

1 When the sequence of events is clear it is not necessary to backshift past tenses to past perfect.
   *I really **enjoyed** the party last Saturday.*
   *We heard you really **enjoyed** the party last Saturday.*

2 When the reporting verb is in the present, future or present perfect, and the situation is still true, the tenses don't usually change.
   *I **love** children.*
   *He **says** he **loves** children.*
   *I**'m** a vegetarian.*
   *She**'ll** probably **tell** you she**'s** a vegetarian.*
   *I**'m** terrified of heights.*
   *She **has** often **said** that she**'s** terrified of heights.*

3 When the reporting verbs are in a past tense the modal verbs *would, should, could, might, ought to* and *must* do not usually change their form.
You **should** visit the castle during your stay.
He **recommended** that I **should** visit the castle during my stay.

4 Reporting verbs that emphasise the importance of an action are often followed by *should* in British English, and by the subjunctive in American English.
They **recommended** that we **should** stay overnight in Madrid.
I **insisted** that he **accept** payment for the work he had done.

6 Emphasis

6.1 Cleft sentences with *what*

Important information can be emphasised by putting it at the end of a sentence. We put the less important information into a clause beginning with *what*, and open the sentence with this clause. We can then finish with the important information. The two parts of the sentence are joined with *is* or *was*, since we treat the *what* clause as singular.
I like Sam's sense of humour most of all.
What I like most of all about Sam **is** his sense of humour.
The lies she told really upset me.
What really upset me **was** the lies she told.

6.2 Emphasis with inversion

We can put certain restrictive words or phrases at the beginning of the sentence for emphasis. When we do this, there is inversion of the subject and auxiliary verb.
Under no circumstances should you let her go.
At no time would she consider any other possibility.
Not until the end **did I** realise the danger I'd been in.
Hardly had I put the phone down **when** it rang again.
No sooner had I put the phone down **than** it rang again.
Seldom have I read such an excellent piece of work.
Rarely will you see such a gifted performer.
Little did I know that he planned to resign that day.
Never before has the city looked so magnificent.
Only then **did I** realise how unhappy she had been.
Not only have you missed a week's classes, but you have also failed to hand in any work.

7 Hypothetical meaning

7.1 wish + *past simple*

We use *wish* + past simple (or *If only* + past simple) to express a wish about the present or the future.
I **wish/If only I had** my own computer.
I **wish/If only I was going** on the trip tomorrow.

7.2 would rather + *past simple*

We use *would rather* + past simple to express a preference about the present or future.
I'd rather you called back later, if you don't mind.
Would you rather I went to town tomorrow?

7.3 wish + *past perfect*

We use *wish* + past perfect to refer to things that we wish had been different in the past.
I wish I'd never met you!

7.4 I wish I could

We use *I wish I could* to talk about an ability we'd like to have, or a habit we'd like to be able to give up.
I wish I could drive.
I wish I could give up smoking.

7.5 wish + would

We use *wish* + *would* to talk about a habit we'd like someone else to give up.
I wish my grandfather would give up smoking.

7.6 It's (high) time

We use *It's time* or *It's high time* + past simple to describe something we think should be done in the present or future.
It's high time the government **did** something about the traffic in our cities.

7.7 suppose

We use *suppose* to describe something that may happen in the future or may have happened in the past. It means the same as *What if ...?*
Suppose you don't get a job – what will you do then?
Suppose he hadn't had a map – he'd never have found his way home.

8 Intensifiers/modifiers

1 The meaning of many adjectives can be intensified with adverbs such as *rather, very* or *exceedingly*.
It was **rather hot** in the room.
I only had a **very short** time to prepare for the test.
It was **exceedingly difficult** to cross the road.

2 Some adjectives already have an 'extreme' meaning. These adjectives can only be further intensified with adverbs such as *absolutely, completely* or *utterly*.
The plot of that film was **completely impossible**.
She was **utterly miserable** when the holiday ended.

9 *It* as preparatory subject/object

9.1 It *as preparatory subject*

It can be used as the subject of a sentence referring forwards to a word or phrase occurring later. This is a common structure in spoken English. It is often used:

- to precede an infinitive clause
  *It was really lovely **to see Philip again**.*
  *It makes me sad **to see her so frail and thin**.*
- to precede a *wh-* clause (with *that/who/what*, etc.)
  *It's unlikely **that he'll arrive on time**.*
  *It's terrible **how many people are unemployed**.*
- to give additional emphasis to the first piece of information in a sentence
  *It was **Sally** who gave me the present, not Ann.*

9.2 It *as preparatory object*

It can also be used as the object of a sentence, referring forwards to a word or phrase occurring later, in this pattern:
subject + verb + *it* + complement + infinitive/*wh*-clause.
*They thought **it** undesirable **to give him the prize**.*
*I found **it** puzzling **that she'd not said goodbye**.*

10 Modal verbs

Modal verbs can be used to express the following:

- possibility
  *That **could/might/may** be the answer.*
  *The thief **could/might/may** have had a knife.*
  *I **can't** have been more than two at the time.*
- logical deduction
  *That **must** be Tom on the phone.*
  *It **can't** be Susie's dress – she never wears pink.*
  *The applicant **must** have performed very well at the interview to get the job.*
- obligation/necessity
  *You **must** leave the building immediately.*
  *I**'ve got to** finish this report today.*
  *They **had to** record everything they did.*
- lack of obligation/necessity
  *You **don't have to** get a visa.*
  *We **didn't need to** pay to go in.*
  *We **needn't have** bothered to book seats.*
- prohibition
  *You **mustn't** leave your mobile phone switched on during lessons.*
- advice (weak obligation)
  *You **should** try to bring as little luggage as possible.*
  *You **ought not to** be playing music so late at night.*
  *They **should have/ought to have** taken out insurance.*
- permission
  ***Can** I borrow your dictionary?*
  ***May** I open the window?*
  *I asked if I **could** take some time off work.*

- ability
  *They **can** all speak several languages.*
  *I was afraid of the water because I **couldn't** swim.*

11 Participle clauses

1 A participle clause can be used after a noun instead of a relative clause.
- An *-ing* participle replaces an active verb.
  *Students **hoping** to go on the trip should register now.*
- An *-ed* participle replaces a passive verb.
  *Everyone **selected** for the team must see the coach today.*

2 A participle clause can be used to replace words like *because, since, so, as a result, when*.
  ***Tired** after the long journey, they went to bed early.*
  ***Having read** the book, I found the film easy to follow.*
  ***Having** finally **finished** our shopping, we went and had a coffee.*

12 Passives

1 We use the passive when the active form would require the use of an indefinite or vague pronoun or noun.
  ***Someone** will process your application soon.*
  *Your application **will be processed** soon.*

2 We often use the passive to make a statement sound less personal, or to avoid mentioning the agent.
  *Offenders **will be prosecuted**.*

3 We often use the passive with verbs such as *think, believe, know* and *say* to suggest that it is a general opinion.
  *She **is said** to be our greatest living writer.*

4 We sometimes use the passive to avoid an awkward change of subject in the middle of a sentence.
  She first saw the film when she was fifteen, and some of the scenes have haunted her ever since.
  *She first saw the film when she was fifteen, and **has been haunted** ever since by some of the scenes.*

5 If the subject is not the agent, we can use a passive infinitive.
  *There's nothing else **to be said** about it.*

13 Relative clauses

13.1 Defining relative clauses

Defining relative clauses say which person or thing (or kind of person or thing) we are talking about.
*I'd prefer to go to the session **which/that starts at 7.15**.*
*The matter **of which I am speaking now** is strictly confidential.*
*The man **she asked** couldn't tell her anything.*
*The apartment **where I lived** was very cheap.*

13.2 Non-defining relative clauses

Non-defining relative clauses tell us more about a person or thing that we have already identified.
On the 3rd of March, **which is a Saturday**, we're having a party.
The President, **for whom a press conference had been organised**, had to leave suddenly.
The treaty, **under the terms of which all prisoners are to be released**, was signed yesterday.

14 Substitution and ellipsis

We avoid repetition of words or expressions that have already been used by means of substitution and ellipsis.

14.1 Substitution

Substitution involves using other words such as *it, one, do, there, that, so, neither* and *not*.
I've been to Thailand several times but Alan has never been **there**.
Bill doesn't really like formal occasions and **neither do I**.
She picked up a packet of biscuits and opened **it**.
A: Would you like a cup of tea? B: I'd love **one**.
A: Are you going skiing this winter? B: We might **do**.
A: Can you come to a concert with Susie and me tonight?
B: **That** sounds great.
A: Is that all we have to do today? B: I hope **so**.
A: She won't go if Tom's there. B: I expect **not**.

14.2 Ellipsis

Ellipsis involves leaving out words to avoid repetition.
We do this:
- after *and, but* or *or* when the subject is the same
  She felt anxious **and** confused about the situation.
  He was excited **but** a little apprehensive about the job.
  I'll probably take them some flowers **or** maybe some chocolates.
- at the end of a verb phrase
  She wanted to visit her aunt in hospital but she **couldn't**.
  She promised to do her homework, and she **has**.
- with *to*
  I didn't want to go there, but my mother said I **had to**.
  He doesn't play much tennis now, though he **used to**.

15 Verb patterns

Verbs may be followed by a number of different structures:
- verb + *-ing*
  He knew that **he risked being** found out and sent to prison.
- verb + *to* infinitive
  He attempted to change his way of life.
- verb + object + *to* infinitive
  My sister always encouraged me to take chances.

- verb + object + bare infinitive (without *to*)
  My grandfather let me drive the tractor.
- verb + *-ing* or *to* infinitive – little change in meaning
  I began to learn French when I was six.
  I began learning French when I was six.
- verb + *-ing* or bare infinitive – little change in meaning
  I saw him get on the bus.
  I saw him getting on the bus.
- verb + *-ing* or *to* infinitive – change in meaning
  I tried to work more quickly, but I couldn't.
  I tried working more quickly, but I made lots of mistakes.
  I remembered telling her about the party – she'd been very interested.
  I remembered to tell her about the party, but she said she couldn't come.
- verb + *that* + clause
  He explained that the train had been delayed.
  She confirmed that I had passed the exam.
- verb + object + *that* + clause
  The guide told us that it was a very old building.
  The weather forecaster warned everyone that a storm was building up.
- verb + preposition + *-ing*
  He didn't admit to stealing the necklace.
- verb + object + preposition + *-ing*
  She congratulated me on doing so well.

16 Verb tenses

16.1 Talking about the past

1 The **past simple** is used to describe a state or event at a time in the past which is specified or understood.
   I started school in 1994.
   After that, **I** never **saw** Sally again.
2 The **present perfect simple** is used
   - to describe a state beginning in the past and leading up to the present
     I've been interested in astronomy ever since my uncle gave me a telescope.
   - to describe an event or events at an unspecified time in the past
     I've seen a lot of famous artists perform on stage.
3 The **past perfect simple** is used to make it clear that something happened before a given time or event in the past.
   I'd noticed him several times before we were actually introduced.

16.2 Continuous verb forms

In general, continuous verb forms may be used:

- to describe a repeated event
  She's always **trying** to help.
  He was tapping his fingers on the table.

- to describe a temporary situation
  I'm working as a receptionist at present.
  He had been staying at the Central Hotel for a few days.
  I'll be going to London next Tuesday.

- to stress the duration of a state or event
  By next May, **she'll have been living** in that house for ten years.
  I'd been sitting waiting for almost an hour by the time Josh arrived.

- to describe an incomplete action or event
  I was talking to the manager on the phone, but I got cut off.
  He had been studying in Rome for two years when his father phoned to say he was needed at home.

- to describe an activity where the results are apparent later on
  She'd been reading all day, and her head ached.
  I've been going to the gym regularly and I'm feeling a lot better.

16.3 Talking about the future

1 The **present continuous** is used to describe arrangements or plans that have already been made. (The future time reference is stated or known from the context.)
   I'm going on holiday next week.

2 The **present simple** is used to describe the future seen as fact, e.g. in timetables and formal arrangements.
   The exhibition **opens** next Tuesday.

3 going to is used:
- to make predictions based on present evidence
  I think **it's going to be** a lovely day.
- to express intentions
  I'm going to do the best I can.

4 The **future simple** is used:
- to make a general prediction
  They do not think the President **will be** there.
- to express a decision made at the moment of speaking
  OK then – **I'll come** with you.

5 The **future continuous** is used:
- to describe a definite plan
  I'll be leaving at six o'clock.
- to describe an event in progress around a time in the future
  This time tomorrow **I'll be lying** on the beach.

6 The **future perfect simple** is used to describe something that will or should be completed by a specified time in the future.
   They **will have arrived** in Moscow soon.
   They **should have finished** shooting the film by the end of next year.

7 Other expressions used to refer to the future:
- to be in for something: to suggest that something (often negative) will definitely happen
  I'm afraid **he's in for** a disappointment.
- to be due to: to indicate an event in the future that has already been scheduled
  The plane **is due to arrive** at 5.30 a.m., but it might be late.
- am/is/are to: used in formal contexts to indicate an event that has been officially scheduled and that is expected to take place
  You **are to report** to the managing director at 9.00 tomorrow morning.
  Participants **are to assemble** in the hall at 10.00 a.m.
- to be on the point of/to be about to: used to describe an event expected to happen very soon
  Ten years ago, doctors thought **they were on the point of wiping** out TB.
  I'm about to hand in my resignation.

16.4 Future in the past

1 The **past continuous** is used to talk about plans made at a specific time in the past.
   I was getting the eight o'clock train, so I had to hurry.

2 was going to is used to talk about intentions made in the past that were not fulfilled.
   Steve was going to pick up the dry-cleaning, but he forgot.

3 was thinking of is used for uncertain plans that may or may not be fulfilled.
   We were thinking of going to Morocco next week, but it depends if we can get a flight.

Writing reference (Paper 2)

Contents

Paper 2, Part 1

Task

You recently stayed at Happy Valley Campsite with a group of classmates on an end-of-course trip, but were disappointed with your stay.

Look at the brochure you received from Happy Valley Campsite before booking the trip and the notes you made while you were there. Then write a letter to the campsite director complaining about your stay and asking for compensation on behalf of your group, giving your reasons.

Write your **letter** in 180–220 words.

Model answer

DO use the person's name if you know it.

DO state the purpose of your letter clearly and concisely.

DO make links between paragraphs.

DO expand on the ideas in the input but make sure that you don't include things that are irrelevant.

If you have used the person's name at the beginning of your letter, DO end your letter like this.

DO begin by identifying and/or describing the situation you are writing about.

DO organise points from the input in a logical and coherent way.

DO make links between points within the paragraph.

DON'T use the same language as the input as this may cause you to use the wrong register.

DO say what you want the result of your letter to be in the final paragraph.

Dear Mr Thompson,

I am writing to complain about a holiday I spent at Happy Valley from 12th to 20th August with a group of student friends. We were unsatisfied with our stay for several reasons, and feel that we were misled by your brochure.

On the financial side, our first complaint is that we were charged the full fee despite the fact that we had originally been quoted a price with a student discount. Furthermore, and contrary to what is stated in your brochure, friends who had brought their own tents were not allowed to use them and had to pay to rent tents they did not need.

If this were not enough, we have complaints about the site itself. The trailers were cramped and had not been cleaned for some time. Although there was a mini-market, it was not at all 'convenient'; apart from being extremely expensive, it was closed for most of the day. Finally, I would hardly call one bar and one cinema in Grimscia 'fantastic nightlife' as your brochure claims.

I tried to speak to you during our stay, but this was impossible.

I feel that your brochure is misleading. I expect to receive financial compensation for our disappointment, otherwise I will take the matter further by contacting an organisation dealing with advertising standards.

I look forward to hearing from you.

Yours sincerely,

James Brown

James Brown

USEFUL LANGUAGE

STATING THE CIRCUMSTANCE

I am writing
- *to draw your attention to*
- *to complain about*
- *to express my concern about*
- *with regard to*

LISTING COMPLAINTS
- *My most serious complaint is ...*
- *Not only* (+ inversion, e.g. *Not only did your employee insult us*) *... but also*
- *Firstly, ... Secondly, ... Finally, ...*
- *If this were not enough ...*

DEMANDING ACTION TO BE TAKEN
- *Unless you ..., I have no option but to ...*
- *If I do not ..., I will have no choice but to ...*
- *Otherwise I will be forced to ...*

Paper 2, Part 2

Information sheet

DO think of a title for your information sheet that will arouse the reader's curiosity and interest.
DON'T provide illustrations.

Task

Your local tourist office has asked you to contribute to an information sheet for visitors to your country. The purpose of this information sheet is to inform visitors about the main public holidays that occur throughout the year.

Write your **information sheet** in 220–260 words.

Model answer

USEFUL LANGUAGE

TALKING ABOUT HISTORY
Founded in 1825, the city of ...
The Sports Centre was established in 1934 ...
1956 saw the creation of ...

TALKING ABOUT LOCATION
Nestling in the Saint Laurent Valley is the village of ...
A short drive along the coast road takes you to El Escobar ...
Directly opposite the Houses of Parliament, you will find ...

TALKING ABOUT FACILITIES OFFERED OR PRODUCTS AVAILABLE
The hotel offers superb ...
Marine sports facilities at Porto Rico cannot be bettered.
In addition to innovative products for financial management, our company also ...

LISTING POINTS OR FEATURES
New developments include:
• *a fully equipped laboratory* • *...*
The following courses will be available in the autumn:
• *interpreting* • *event management*

TALKING ABOUT FUTURE PLANS
We hope to expand this service further over the next few years.
Among several future projects are plans to create an online service.

The Land of the Long Weekend

We're famous for our public holidays, many of which are on a Monday or Friday. Here are some of the most important in each of the four seasons.
(Be warned: banks and most businesses are closed on days marked with an *!)

Summer
Christmas falls in the summer in the Southern Hemisphere, and we celebrate our national day in this season too.
• Christmas Day (25/12)*   • New Year's Day (1/1)*
• Boxing Day (26/12)*   • Australia Day (26/1)*

Autumn
When the leaves begin to fall, Australians think of Easter and of another national holiday, ANZAC day. The latter is a day on which Australians and New Zealanders remember their compatriots who lost their lives in the First World War. Members of the armed forces as well as ex-servicemen and women take part in a parade.
Good Friday*   Easter Monday*
ANZAC Day, April 25th (Australia and New Zealand)

Winter
Winters are mild in Australia so if you don't like very hot weather, this is a good time for visiting! The most important public holiday is 9th June* – Queen Elizabeth II's official birthday.

Spring
The most important public holiday is in Victoria on the second Tuesday in November, and is Melbourne Cup Day. The Melbourne Cup is a horse race, and locals go to watch it. People from all over Australia follow it closely on radio or television, especially if they have placed a bet!

So whenever you choose to come to Australia, you'll be able to join the Australians having fun on one of their many public holidays.

DO use section headings.

DO use bullet points if they are appropriate, but make sure that you also use a range of language.

DO think of an interesting way of introducing each section.

DON'T use language that is too simple if you choose to use bullet points; if you do, you will not demonstrate a wide range of structures and vocabulary and this may affect your mark in the exam.

DON'T forget to add a conclusion.

Informal letter

Task

You recently went on holiday abroad and stayed with a friend. Unfortunately, you misread the departure time on your return ticket and missed your flight. You were able to get another flight the same day but had no money left to pay for the ticket, so your friend paid for it. Write a **letter** to your friend explaining how you have arranged repayment and inviting him/her to stay with you when he/she visits your country.

Write your **letter** in 220–260 words.

Model answer

DO begin by telling your friend why you've decided to write.

DO divide your letter into paragraphs, each of which should cover a different element from the task input.

DO expand upon the task input by using your own ideas.

DON'T finish your letter with *Yours sincerely/faithfully.* DO use an appropriate INFORMAL phrase. There are various ways of closing letters to friends depending on how well you know them. For very close friends or relatives you can use *With (all my) love, Love* or *Lots of Love*; with friends use *All the best*; with people you still don't know very well use *(With) best wishes.*

DO close your letter by mentioning the next time you will see or speak to them.

Dear Clara,

I thought I'd better drop you a line straightaway to thank you for helping me out on Friday. I'm really sorry I had to bother you at such an unsociable hour and I know you can imagine how embarrassed I was about having to ask you to pay for my ticket!

I am now home safely, as you can see. I went into my bank this morning and arranged to transfer the price of the ticket from my account to yours, so the money should be with you any day now. I'm enclosing the receipt so you can see how much the ticket cost in dollars and check that the amount I've sent in pounds is correct. It should be, as I asked the bank cashier to double check the exchange rate.

Despite missing the plane like that, I had a wonderful time with you in San Francisco. I particularly enjoyed meeting your niece and going on the boat trip with her friends. I also loved the city, especially the bay area and hope I'll get to come back before too long!

I know you said you might visit London in the summer. I really hope you do manage to get the time off work, and that if you come, you will stay with me and my family. We have plenty of room and you'd be very welcome, so just let us know when you're coming. I'd love the chance to return your hospitality and to show you around London.

All the best ... I'll speak to you soon, and thanks again!

John

USEFUL LANGUAGE

BEGINNING THE LETTER

Thanks so much for your letter. It was really great to hear from you.
Sorry not to have written/been in touch for so long/such a long time. I've been really busy lately.
Thought I'd better/drop you a line/write to let you know ...

ENDING THE LETTER

I think that's all my news for the moment. Do write soon and let me know what you've been doing.
Once again, thanks very much for being so nice to Susie ...
Can't wait to see you **on the 24th/next week** in Cambridge ...
Don't forget to say 'hi' to ... from me.
Give my love to ...
Speak to you soon

APOLOGISING

I'm really/terribly/awfully sorry about what happened the other night.
Sorry I couldn't/didn't manage to see you last time I was in ...

INVITING

How about meeting up for a drink/coming over for a meal **some time**?
Why don't we try to get together some time soon?
I was wondering if you might like to get together with the rest of the old gang next time you're in town.

RESPONDING TO AN INVITATION

Thanks very much for inviting us to your party. We're really looking forward to it.
I was really excited when I got your invitation. Unfortunately, I've realised it's the same weekend as my cousin's wedding so *I won't be able to make it/it doesn't look as if I'm going to make it*.

MAKING A REQUEST

I was wondering if you happened to know anywhere we could stay.
If you've got a spare moment, do you think you could find out when the music festival is on this year?

REFERRING TO A PREVIOUS LETTER

Do you remember that sports centre **you mentioned in your last letter**?
You said in your letter that you were thinking of applying for a scholarship.
Last time you wrote you asked how Tina was getting on.
You know that course *I told you* I had applied for? *Well,* ...

Review

Task

The editor of your college English language magazine has asked you to write a review of two films you have seen recently saying why one of the films is likely to be of particular relevance and interest to students at the college and why you believe the other is not so useful.

Write your **review** in 220–260 words.

Model answer

Video of the Week

DO indicate the structure of your review in the first paragraph.

DO start your review with a humorous or catchy comment to attract your audience's attention.

The two videos I watched were 'Cure for Summertime Blues' and 'Days of Wonder'. The first was worth the time and money and has an important message; all I can say about the second is you'd be better off spending your cash on a take-away pizza!

'Cure for Summertime Blues' is a film about young people on holiday in Greece, and almost as soon as it started I found myself laughing till I cried and nodding in agreement with more or less every line of the script. I hadn't seen any of the actors before but I found their portrayal of teenagers from a London comprehensive completely convincing. The film has a clear message for young people: that caring about others and the planet means more than money or looks. The film was thought provoking as well as extremely entertaining.

DON'T forget to cover all the points mentioned in the task.

In reviews of more than one event, DO use the language of comparison and contrast.

Conversely, 'Days of Wonder' was a completely different kettle of fish. Despite a star-studded cast, a director with a string of film successes behind her and a screenplay based on the novel of the same name, 'Days of Wonder' just doesn't work. Changing the setting from seventeenth century Paris to contemporary Sydney, while leaving the script in the baroque style of the original novel, is particularly unsatisfactory. What's more, it's impossible to believe that a man would contemplate killing someone merely for speaking to his girlfriend. Such inconsistencies in the plot ruined the credibility of the film for me.

DO use vocabulary specific to whatever you are reviewing. DO try to make your review interesting for the reader by using a range of vocabulary, and a variety of structures.

DO give information about the cast, director or screenplay if you are writing about a film.

DON'T just describe the plot; offer your evaluation of it as well.

The purpose of a review is often to persuade the reader to see the film or read the book. DON'T tell your readers about the ending if it will ruin the film or book for them.

So, if you want to watch something that you'll enjoy and which has something important to say then 'Cure for Summertime Blues' is the one to choose.

DO end your review with a recommendation or final evaluation.

USEFUL LANGUAGE

BOOK (FICTION)

Types: thriller, mystery, whodunit, romance, science fiction, fantasy, historical

Elements: character, plot, dialogue, setting, atmosphere, author, novelist, writer

BOOK (NON-FICTION)

Types: coffee table book, cookery book, travel book, encyclopedia, dictionary, textbook, manual

Elements: chapter, section, index, glossary, illustration, author, editor

FILM

Types: (as for fiction) + adaptation, comedy, animation

Elements: screenplay, script, set, role, costume, design, photography, special effects, animation, soundtrack

People: cast, actor, director, producer, scriptwriter

PLAY

Types: (as for film) + farce, musical

Elements: act, scene, set, role, costume, lyrics, music, design, stage

People: (as for film) + playwright, composer

CONCERT

Types of group or musician: rock group/band/musician, (lead, bass, rhythm) guitarist, (lead/backing) singer, drummer, **folk** singer/guitarist, **country and western** singer, **jazz** band/quartet/trio/singer, **orchestra**, quintet/quartet/ensemble/soloist/violinist/cellist

Elements: song, lyrics, tune, piece, symphony, concerto, cantata, score, stage, theatre, hall, auditorium

People: songwriter, composer, conductor

EXHIBITION

Types: painting, sculpture, photography, furniture, design, handicrafts

Elements: gallery, catalogue, displays

TV PROGRAMME

Types: series, documentary, soap opera, drama, situation comedy, chat show, debate, current affairs programme

People: compère, presenter, host, director, producer, scriptwriter, cast, actor

PROVIDING BACKGROUND INFORMATION

'A Horse of a Different Colour' is Michael Gordon's **fourth novel/second film/first major role/second individual exhibition**.

'In the Beginning Was the Word' **came on at** *Odeon cinemas last week* **and I went along** *to see it.*

INTRODUCING A BRIEF ACCOUNT OF THE PLOT

Set in *eighteenth century London, the film* **tells the story of/recounts events in** *the lives of three sisters.*

In *the breathtaking landscape of northern Canada, the book* **examines the themes of** *solitude and intimacy.*

On the eve of *the First World War, the series* **introduces us to** *the Wilson household.*

COMMENTING CRITICALLY

I found *the plot* **rather conventional/predictable/contrived/completely bizarre/absurd/incomprehensible**.

The novelist **has succeeded in** *creating* **an extremely intricate/complex plot/entirely believable/life-like characters**.

The characters are completely believable/unconvincing and the dialogue is witty/stilted and natural/artificial.

The ballerina **was absolutely brilliant/was verging on the incompetent**.

A particular strength/weakness *of the production* **was** *the set design by Marcelo Camilleri.*

The exhibition catalogue **is economically priced/ridiculously over-priced**.

PROVIDING A RECOMMENDATION

I would strongly advise you *not to* **miss/waste your money on** *'Ain't Got a Clue'.*

I would definitely recommend seeing/visiting/reading/having a look at *'Melbourne: a Sentimental Journey'.*

For those who enjoy *contemporary music, Tropical String Quartet are* **not to be missed**.

Go and see *'Momix'.* **You'll be amazed**.

COMPARING AND CONTRASTING (STRENGTHS OR TWO EVENTS)

While/Whereas/Although/Despite the fact that/In spite of the fact that *characterisation was particularly strong, the plot gradually lost credibility.*

The cast is brilliant; *especially when you take into account* **how truly dreadful** *the script is.*

'I Remember What You Did Last Winter' **is a masterpiece**; *'Looking for Sam'* **is the opposite**.

Both films are likely *to appeal to younger audiences,* **but** *'Postmortem'* **will be especially appealing**.

Neither the novel nor the film *fully convinced me,* **though** *the character of Margo really* **comes alive on the screen**.

Report

Task

Your local council is conducting a review into sporting activities with the aim of encouraging more people to take part in sport. You agree to write a report describing the existing level of participation in sporting activities in your area including factors which discourage people from taking part in sport, and recommending ways of encouraging more people to take up a sport.

Write your **report** in 220–260 words.

Model answer

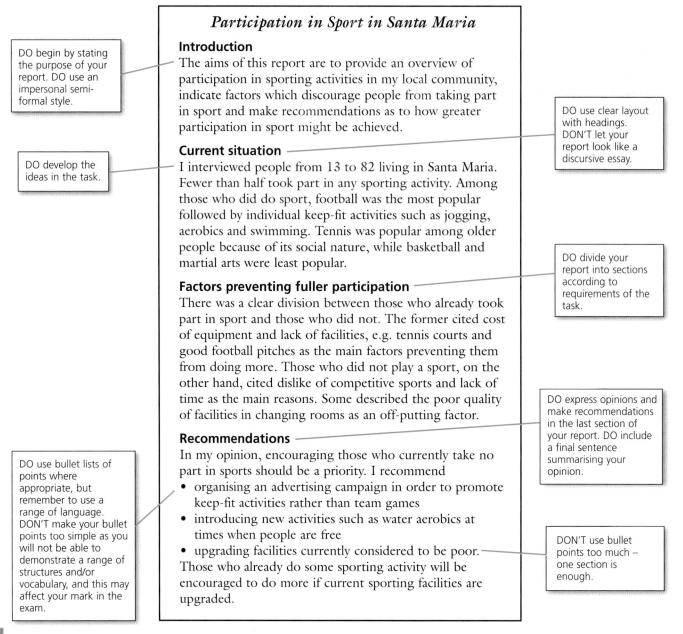

DO begin by stating the purpose of your report. DO use an impersonal semi-formal style.

DO develop the ideas in the task.

DO use bullet lists of points where appropriate, but remember to use a range of language. DON'T make your bullet points too simple as you will not be able to demonstrate a range of structures and/or vocabulary, and this may affect your mark in the exam.

DO use clear layout with headings. DON'T let your report look like a discursive essay.

DO divide your report into sections according to requirements of the task.

DO express opinions and make recommendations in the last section of your report. DO include a final sentence summarising your opinion.

DON'T use bullet points too much – one section is enough.

Participation in Sport in Santa Maria

Introduction

The aims of this report are to provide an overview of participation in sporting activities in my local community, indicate factors which discourage people from taking part in sport and make recommendations as to how greater participation in sport might be achieved.

Current situation

I interviewed people from 13 to 82 living in Santa Maria. Fewer than half took part in any sporting activity. Among those who did do sport, football was the most popular followed by individual keep-fit activities such as jogging, aerobics and swimming. Tennis was popular among older people because of its social nature, while basketball and martial arts were least popular.

Factors preventing fuller participation

There was a clear division between those who already took part in sport and those who did not. The former cited cost of equipment and lack of facilities, e.g. tennis courts and good football pitches as the main factors preventing them from doing more. Those who did not play a sport, on the other hand, cited dislike of competitive sports and lack of time as the main reasons. Some described the poor quality of facilities in changing rooms as an off-putting factor.

Recommendations

In my opinion, encouraging those who currently take no part in sports should be a priority. I recommend

- organising an advertising campaign in order to promote keep-fit activities rather than team games
- introducing new activities such as water aerobics at times when people are free
- upgrading facilities currently considered to be poor.

Those who already do some sporting activity will be encouraged to do more if current sporting facilities are upgraded.

Report v Proposal

The layout and format of a proposal can be very similar to a report. However, where a report is usually based on an event or situation that has happened or already exists, a proposal tends to be based on a future situation or plan and is more forward looking. The recommendations section is the most important part of a proposal.

USEFUL LANGUAGE (FOR A REPORT)

STATING THE PURPOSE OF THE REPORT

The aim/purpose of this report is/was to describe/evaluate/present ...
In this report, I will describe/evaluate/present ...
This report provides a description/evaluation/presentation ...

DESCRIBING HOW YOU GOT YOUR INFORMATION

I spoke to/interviewed several members of staff ...
Members of the local police force answered a questionnaire ...
I visited three hotels: the Maritima; the Plage Royale and the Shackelton ...
I conducted a survey among college graduates ...
Car owners were invited to attend a focus group ...

REPORTING YOUR RESULTS

Most people **said/expressed the opinion that** ...
According to Dr Ann Wilkinson, the funding is ...
A high/small/significant proportion of those surveyed/respondents said that ...
25% of the students ...
A small number felt that the situation had deteriorated.

PRESENTING A LIST

The points in favour/against introducing genetically modified foods can be summarised as follows:
1 ...
2 ...
The following reasons were given for lack of participation in local festivals: firstly ..., secondly ...
Arguments put forward in favour of/against the introduction of a local television channel were:
1 ...
2 ...
There are a number of ways in which facilities for the parents of small children could be improved:
1 ...
2 ...

MAKING RECOMMENDATIONS

In the light of the results of the survey/questionnaire the introduction of a small fee would seem to be the best choice/option/solution.
I would recommend, therefore, the purchase of five more computers and laser printers.
My recommendations are as follows:

USEFUL LANGUAGE (FOR A PROPOSAL)

STATING THE PURPOSE OF THE PROPOSAL

In this proposal, I will describe/evaluate/present/ assess ...
This proposal is for ...

BACKGROUND INFORMATION

Feedback from student questionnaires suggests ...
Following a survey among college graduates ...
Interested parties were invited to attend ...
There were several issues arising from the last event, which was not a success ...

MAKING RECOMMENDATIONS AND SUGGESTIONS

A focus group **should be** set up by ...
There should be an investigation into ...
I recommend that a new centre be established ...

FINAL RECOMMENDATION

In the light of the results of the survey/questionnaire the introduction of a small fee would seem to be the best choice/option/solution.
If these recommendations are followed, then the situation will be greatly improved.
If these suggestions are implemented, there will be a marked improvement in the situation.

Article

Task

You read the following announcement in an international travel magazine.

Tourism – is it a good or a bad thing for the place where you live?
- Do you think that there is too much or too little tourism where you live?
- What benefits do tourists bring?
- What would be the disadvantages if there were more tourism?

Write us an article and we will publish the most interesting in our next edition.

Write your **article** in 220–260 words.

Model answer

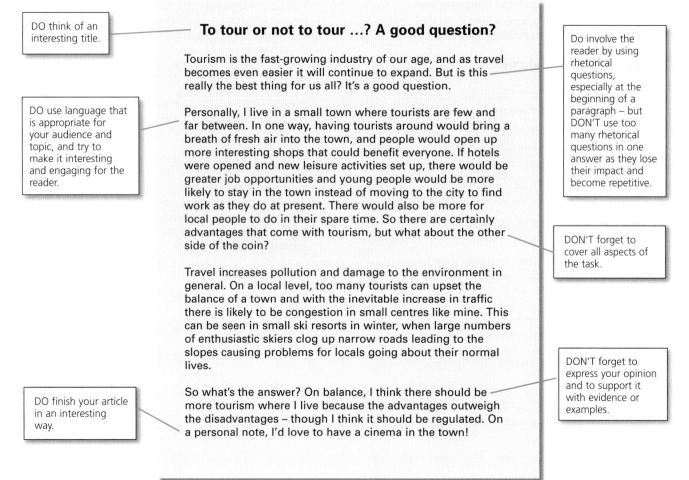

DO think of an interesting title.

Do involve the reader by using rhetorical questions, especially at the beginning of a paragraph – but DON'T use too many rhetorical questions in one answer as they lose their impact and become repetitive.

DO use language that is appropriate for your audience and topic, and try to make it interesting and engaging for the reader.

DON'T forget to cover all aspects of the task.

DON'T forget to express your opinion and to support it with evidence or examples.

DO finish your article in an interesting way.

To tour or not to tour …? A good question?

Tourism is the fast-growing industry of our age, and as travel becomes even easier it will continue to expand. But is this really the best thing for us all? It's a good question.

Personally, I live in a small town where tourists are few and far between. In one way, having tourists around would bring a breath of fresh air into the town, and people would open up more interesting shops that could benefit everyone. If hotels were opened and new leisure activities set up, there would be greater job opportunities and young people would be more likely to stay in the town instead of moving to the city to find work as they do at present. There would also be more for local people to do in their spare time. So there are certainly advantages that come with tourism, but what about the other side of the coin?

Travel increases pollution and damage to the environment in general. On a local level, too many tourists can upset the balance of a town and with the inevitable increase in traffic there is likely to be congestion in small centres like mine. This can be seen in small ski resorts in winter, when large numbers of enthusiastic skiers clog up narrow roads leading to the slopes causing problems for locals going about their normal lives.

So what's the answer? On balance, I think there should be more tourism where I live because the advantages outweigh the disadvantages – though I think it should be regulated. On a personal note, I'd love to have a cinema in the town!

USEFUL LANGUAGE

RHETORICAL QUESTIONS

We're all supposed to hate advertising, but do we? I don't think we do at all.
What's Lodz got to offer the tourist? Everything from magnificent architecture to one of the loveliest parks in Poland.
So what are we really talking about?
So is this really true?

ADDRESSING THE READER DIRECTLY

I'm sure you will agree with me when I say that ...
We all hate it when someone keeps *us* waiting.
Why not give it a try? You've got nothing to lose.
Is this really the answer for *all of us?*

INFORMAL LANGUAGE

Let's look at the problem from two different points of view.
So, the government should clear up this mess as soon as possible.
I think that another problem with banning traffic from the city centre is deliveries to shops.
It seems to me that what's important here is ...

FINISHING WITH A PUNCHLINE

On a personal note, I'd like to say that ...
How fantastic would that be?
After all, in the end it may be the only thing to do!

If an article is also a competition entry:
remember that the aim of the article is to win the competition, so your finishing sentence should reinforce this. It may be something like:
So all in all, that is why Pedro should win the nomination!

Essay

Task

You have had a class discussion on why it is important to preserve the past. Now your teacher has asked you to write an essay giving your opinions on the following statement:

We should spend more money on preserving our past – it is too important to lose.

Write your **essay** in 220–260 words.

USEFUL LANGUAGE

INTRODUCING THE TOPIC

Some people claim that museums are a waste of money.
It is often said that children should be taught more history in school.
What is often stated is that history should be an important part of the curriculum.

LINKING IDEAS

While it is true that spending some money is a good thing, *it may not always be right to spend too much*.
Not only is it right to spend money, *but also* to invest in the future.
Conversely, it may not be the right thing to do.
On the contrary, there is a groundswell of opinion against the plan.

GIVING OPINIONS

I can honestly say that I agree with the plan.
Personally, I feel that spending money on preserving the past is a complete waste.
From my perspective it seems to be a good idea.

CONCLUDING

On balance, I feel that more money should be spent on preserving history.
Taking everything into consideration there is a clear case for cutting the budget on the arts.

DON'T start with your own opinion or giving your conclusion – make sure that your essay leads to the logical conclusion.

DO use connectors to link your ideas together.

DO have a balanced approach.

DON'T forget to support your opinions with evidence or examples.

DO involve the reader by using rhetorical questions.

Do remember to use a semi-formal register, and to present your ideas in an objective way.

DO give your own opinion at the end.

Some people feel that there is no point in spending any money at all to preserve the past, while others think that not enough money is spent because it is vital to preserve our full heritage. Why do they feel this?

There are many reasons why the past is important. For one thing, we can learn from mistakes that people made in history, so that we don't make them again. For another thing, if we understand where we have come from, then we might understand where we are going! A final point is that it is important to preserve artefacts from the past so that future generations can understand how life used to be. Money is currently spent on teaching history and on building museums and preserving historical sites, but is it enough?

It is expensive to preserve the past – building museums, excavating sites, promoting exhibitions – all these take both time and money. Some people feel that we should look forwards, not back, and that the money would be better spent on such useful amenities as hospitals. Others accept that although some money should be spent, we should not spend too much.

In my opinion it is necessary to have a perspective on the present, and this can only be achieved by studying and preserving the past. There are more things in life than simply being practical, and if we spend more money on preserving the past, then we are investing in future generations. For this reason, I agree with the statement that we should spend more money on preserving our past – it is too important to lose.

Improving your marks on Paper 2

Each of the two pieces of writing produced by a candidate for Paper 2 is given an impression mark as follows:

Band 5   For a Band 5 to be awarded, the candidate's writing has a very positive effect on the target reader. The content is relevant* and the topic is fully developed. Information and ideas are skilfully organised through a range of cohesive devices, which are used to good effect. A wide range of complex structures and vocabulary is used effectively. Errors are minimal, and inaccuracies which do occur have no impact on communication. Register and format are consistently appropriate to the purpose of the task and the audience..

Band 4   For a Band 4 to be awarded, the candidate's writing has a positive effect on the target reader. The content is relevant* and the topic is developed. Information and ideas are clearly organised through the use of a variety of cohesive devices. A good range of complex structures and vocabulary is used. Some errors may occur with vocabulary and when complex language is attempted, but these do not cause difficulty for the reader. Register and format are usually appropriate to the purpose of the task and the audience.

Band 3   For a Band 3 to be awarded, the candidate's writing has a satisfactory effect on the target reader. The content is relevant* with some development of the topic. Information and ideas are generally organised logically, though cohesive devices may not always be used appropriately. A satisfactory range of structures and vocabulary is used, though word choice may lack precision. Errors which do occur do not cause difficulty for the reader. Register and format are reasonably appropriate to the purpose of the task and the audience.

Band 2   For a Band 2 to be awarded, the candidate's writing has a negative effect on the target reader. The content is not always relevant. Information and ideas are inadequately organised and sometimes incoherent, with inaccurate use of cohesive devices. The range of structures and vocabulary is limited and/or repetitive, and errors may be basic or cause difficulty for the reader. Register and format are sometimes inappropriate to the purpose of the task and the audience.

Band 1   For a Band 1 to be awarded, the candidate's writing has a very negative effect on the target reader. The content is often irrelevant. Information and ideas are poorly organised, often incoherent, and there is minimal use of cohesive devices. The range of structures and vocabulary is severely limited, and errors frequently cause considerable difficulty for the reader. Register and format are inappropriate to the purpose of the task and the audience.

Band 0   For a Band zero to be awarded, there is either too little language for assessment or the candidate's writing is totally irrelevant or illegible.

* Candidates who do not address all the content points will be penalised for dealing inadequately with the requirements of the task.
Candidates who fully satisfy the Band 3 descriptor will demonstrate an adequate performance in writing at CAE level.

This general impression mark scheme is used in conjunction with a task-specific mark scheme, which focuses on criteria specific to each particular task (e.g. report, article, formal letter). These criteria include **content**, **relevance**, **range of structure and vocabulary** and **register**.

Look at the task below and the answer a student has written. The student's work has been annotated by their teacher. Look again at the CAE marking criteria on page 211. Into which band would you put this answer?

Task

The tourist authority wants to encourage tourists and locals to spend more time walking around the capital city in your region or country, and has decided to prepare an information sheet which will include suggestions for walks that people can take. The information sheet will suggest three walks taking in important buildings and monuments, parks and open spaces and a part of the city that is particularly interesting for cultural or historical reasons. You have been asked to prepare this section of the sheet.

Write your contribution to the **information sheet** in 220–260 words.

Not a very interesting title and taken straight from the question. What about the tourists? It's not their capital city after all.

Another rather dull heading taken straight from the question.

Think of another more interesting way of saying this.

This sounds as if you don't like the park very much yourself. Try and make it sound more attractive. You could suggest that it is a good place to go for people who want to relax after shopping or taking the other walk.

Make this more interesting. Describe the walk itself and introduce each of the buildings in order.

SPEND MORE TIME WALKING AROUND YOUR CAPITAL CITY!

There are lot of walks around your city you can take and get to know better. Here are three nice ones:

Important buildings and monuments
San Cristobal has many important buildings and monuments. There is the cathedral of the Immaculate Conception which were built in the seventeen century. There are also very nice houses that once belong to rich marchants in the area near to the market. You should also see the Bishop's Palace and the History Museum.

Parks and open spaces
This is a short walk because there are not so many parks and open spaces. You have to go out to the country or to the mountains for this. If your are stuck in San Cristobal the only green space is the Humboldt Park. This is not a large park and you can walk around it in about twenty minutes or half an hour. There is a pretty flower show in the park in April so it is better if you go then.

A part of the city that is interesting for cultural reasons
The area around the State theatre is very interesting, Apart from the theatre there is an important art gallery with a collection of peintings by famous artists. You can also find some small private galleries around here. Next door to the theatre is a very grand building. This is the State Library. You can't borrow any of the books though.

I hope you enjoy this walks.

Try to make the idea of walking sound more inviting.

Think about who you are writing for and why. People will presumably want to take these walks so it would be better to describe the buildings and monuments in the order in which they will see them during the walk. You could begin like this: 'Start out from the magnificent cathedral and walk straight on until …'.

This needs a heading that will make people want to take the walk. Do not just copy phrases from the question.

Is this relevant?

Can you come up with a way of finishing that will have more of an impact on your audience?

Now check your assessment of this answer with the
teacher's comments below.

Teacher's comments and advice on improvement

Obviously you know your city very well and you've
got plenty to say. You've also thought carefully about
the layout of your material. Nevertheless, this would
be graded as Band 2 if it were an exam answer
because you don't really expand on any of the ideas
in the input task and you have taken a lot of
language directly from it. Another problem is that a
great deal of the language you use is very simple
(adjectives such as *nice*, *important* and *beautiful*;
sentence structures with *There is/are …*). I don't think
that anyone reading this would feel like taking the
walks, do you? I've made some suggestions on how
your answer could be improved, but you need to edit
your work thoroughly for grammar and spelling
errors using the Editing checklist (see page 214).
Work on it and then hand it in again.

Now look at the student's second attempt at the same
task. This is now a Band 5 answer. Compare the two, and
see what the student has done to improve it.

Getting to know San Cristobal … on foot!

The best way to discover any city is on foot. We've come up with
three exciting walks to show just how varied our city is.

Walk 1: Architectural marvels
Start at the awe-inspiring cathedral of the Immaculate Conception, built
in the seventeenth century. Walk down Santiago Street with its luxurious
villas, once homes of rich merchants trading in silks and spices. Perhaps
the most magnificent of these are the Bishop's Palace and the Villa
San Pedro which now houses the History Museum. At the end of the
street you'll find the market with its wide variety of exotic fruits
and flowers. Walk through, buying your picnic lunch on the way.

Walk 2: A breath of fresh air
Head off towards Humboldt Park and enjoy a pleasant stroll among
shaded paths. If you're lucky enough to be there in April, you'll also
be able to enjoy the annual flower show. Whatever the time of year the
park is a wonderful spot for a picnic, so sit down on a bench facing
the glorious central fountain and enjoy your lunch.

Walk 3: The art of the city
This walk takes you from the State Theatre and its imposing neighbour
the State Library, through quaint winding streets to the Municipal
Gallery. The Gallery houses an impressive collection of works by local
artists, but many other small galleries in the area also have plenty to
offer.

Stop for a coffee in one of the many attractive cafés. You'll probably
need to put your feet up, but we know you will have thoroughly
enjoyed getting to know San Cristobal on foot!

Editing checklist

When you have finished the first draft of a piece of work check that you have:

- done everything you were asked to do in the task input
- used language appropriate for your target reader consistently in your answer
- used appropriate layout for the task (headings, paragraphs, etc.)
- used a range of structures and vocabulary, even if you have chosen to use bullet points in part of your answer
- used different language from the language of the input to avoid register problems
- made links between paragraphs and between sentences in paragraphs
- checked the accuracy of your grammar, spelling and punctuation
  - Have a mental list of the kinds of errors you tend to make and pay particular attention to looking for these errors.
  - Read your work at least three times and look for a different aspect of the answer each time, e.g. the first time check for clarity of message and general organisation, the second time check for grammar and punctuation, and the third time for spelling.

COMMON MISTAKES

GRAMMAR

Agreement: nouns and pronouns

My brother works at home. ~~She~~ **He** has a computer and ~~her~~ **his** boss sends work through the Internet for ~~her~~ **him** to do.

Agreement: subject and verb

People often find~~s~~ it difficult to adjust to change.
Sarah and Jeff's three teenage children who had just got home from school ~~was~~ **were** surprised to find their grandfather in the kitchen.

Verb tense

First I ~~had~~ washed the dishes and then I swept the floor.
I ~~am~~ **have been** living in London for six months now.

Word order

Do you **often** go ~~often~~ to the cinema?

Questions

I wonder what ~~are~~ Bill and Alan **are** doing now?
Who ~~did come~~ **came** to the party?

Irregular verbs

Nanette has ~~teached~~ **taught** herself to play the guitar.

Verb form

I have ~~being~~ **been** meaning to write to you for weeks.
If I ~~would have~~ **had** realised the phone was out of order, I wouldn't have been so worried.
He suggested we ~~going~~ **go** to a Mexican restaurant.
~~To smoke~~ **Smoking** is not allowed in any part of the airport.

Articles

I think that without ~~the~~ love we could not survive.
Design of the living room was blend of modern and classical styles. ✗
The design of the living room was **a** blend of modern and classical styles. ✓

PUNCTUATION

Commas

My cousin who is coming to dinner tonight lives in New Zealand. ✗
My cousin, who is coming to dinner tonight, lives in New Zealand. ✓

Question marks

I've been meaning to ask you where you buy your coffee? ✗
I've been meaning to ask you where you buy your coffee. ✓
How often does the average student use the Internet. Our survey shows that it is more often than you might think. ✗
How often does the average student use the Internet? Our survey shows that it is more often than you might think. ✓

Apostrophes

The streets appearance had changed. ✗
The street**'s** appearance had changed. ✓
The visitor's carpark was full so we had to park in the street. ✗
The visitor**s'** carpark was full so we had to park in the street. ✓

Quotation marks

Soon 55% of households will be connected to the Internet, said Mark Wilcox. ✗
'Soon 55% of households will be connected to the Internet,' said Mark Wilcox. ✓

Hyphens

My sixteen year old niece is studying fashion at school. ✗
My **sixteen-year-old** niece is studying fashion at school. ✓

SPELLING

Omission of silent letters

sychology ✗ **p**sychology ✓

Suffixes and prefixes

responsable ✗ respons**ible** ✓
desadvantage ✗ **dis**advantage ✓

Homophones

here/hear there/their where/wear piece/peace

Letter doubling

neccesary ✗ ne**c**essary ✓
occurence ✗ occur**r**ence ✓

Letter order

recieve ✗ rec**ei**ve ✓
rethorical ✗ r**h**etorical ✓

Pearson Education Limited
Edinburgh Gate
Harlow
Essex CM20 2JE
England
and Associated Companies throughout the world.

www.longman.com

© Pearson Education Limited 2008

First edition published 2008

978-1-405-87680-3 CAE Gold Coursebook, CD ROM Pack

Set in Frutiger 45 Light 10/12pt
Printed by Graficas Estella

ACKNOWLEDGEMENTS

Publisher Acknowledgements

The publishers and authors would like to thank the following people and institutions for their feedback and comments during the development of the material: Miriam Ozores (Argentina); Enni Bakola-Kofina (Greece); Sharon Gleave (Italy); Marek Doskocz (Poland); Rachel Walsh (Spain); Elaine Boyd, Andrew Cowley, Eric Ellicock, Judith Wilson (UK)

Author Acknowledgements

The authors would like to thank the Publisher Jacqui Robinson for her constant patience and understanding, and the editor Clare Nielsen-Marsh for her incisive editorial work. They would also like to thank the Picture Researcher Sally Cole for her perseverance in finding just the right images, and Judith Wilson for all her helpful comments and advice during the project.

We are grateful to the following for permission to adapt or reproduce extracts from copyright material:

Amazon.co.uk for 'review of "Never-ending story"' published 2 May 2004 © 2007 Amazon.com. All rights reserved; BBC Magazines Bristol Ltd for 'How you can help science' and 'The greatest ever journey', both by Robert Matthews, published in *BBC Focus* in April 2003 and February 1999, 'The eco-footprint test' by Sally Palmer published in *BBC Focus* in January 2006, 'Truth behind a smile' published in *BBC Focus* in April 2000 and 'Elephant artist' published in *BBC Focus* in January 1999, and for 'The nature of song' by David Rothenberg, published in March 2004 in *BBC Wildlife*; BT Yahoo! News for 'Costly tickets for the world's costliest painting' (accessed 18 July 2006) and 'Who do you think you are?'; Condé Nast Publications Ltd for 'Are you a binge thinker?' by Virginia Ironside, published in *Easy Living* © The Condé Nast Publications Ltd; *Cosmo Girl!* for 'Beat your parents in every argument' by George Utley © National Magazine Company; CMP Information Ltd for 'Back to the Futuro' by Catherine Croft, published in *Building Design* on 6 June 2003; *Choice* Magazine for 'The front stalls guide to performance poetry' by Mike Parker published in September 2002; Loudmouth Publishing for 'Wish you had a bit more cash?' by Charlotte Sankey and Avril Groom, published in *Cambridge Agenda* in October 2003; Eastern Daily Press for 'Thrills and skills' by Jo Malone, published in the *Norfolk Magazine* in August 2003; *The Economist* for 'Icarus online' by Howard Banks and 'More than words can say' by Luke Collins, published in *Intelligent Life* © The Economist Newspapers Ltd, London 2006; Entrepreneur.com for 'What makes a good written ad' © 2007 Entrepreneur.com, all rights reserved; Express Newspapers for 'Mouldy old dough' by Phillip Blackmore, and 'The power of saying sorry' by Rose Rouse, published in the *Sunday Express Magazine* on 30 June 2002 and 10 May 2004, ' Four strangers will spend a week of their lives in a shop window' by Michelle Stanistreet, published in the *Sunday Express* on 19 May 2002, and 'In a class of their own' by Janet Haslam, published in the *Daily Express* on 24 September 2002; *Financial Times* for 'Clicking through a mag' by Caroline Lucey published on 8 January 2005; Future Publishing for 'Turn in … log on … get heard', published in *Computer Music Special* 2006; Guardian News Service for 'Do I have to give up my annual ski trip?' by Lucy Seigle, published on 7 January 2007, 'How to concentrate' by Guy Browning, published on 23 September 2006, 'The New Gods' by Madeleine Bunting, published on 9 July 2001 © Copyright Guardian News & Media Ltd 2007; Independent News and Media Ltd for 'Funny Business' by Andrew Gumbel, and 'Record-breaking flashmobbers come dancing' by Helen McCormack published in the *Independent* on 28 April 2007 and 2 December 2006 © The Independent; Hodder Headline for the extract from 'The Island' by Victoria Hislop; Ink Publications for 'West and wild' by Lisa Goodman published in easyJet *Inflight* magazine in September 2001, and 'Bag manners' by Eloise Napier published in *CNBC European Business* in April 2005; MB Media Ltd for the publicity leaflet from the London Guitar Show 2006; *New Scientist* magazine for extract adapted from 'First Words' by Helen Phillips; NI Syndication for 'Where's my mind?' by Anita Chaudhuri published in the *Sunday Times* on 16 April 2006, 'Multi-tasking young spurn old media' by Amanda Andrews published in *The Times Business* on 11 August 2006, 'Computers make for chatty children' by Mark Henderson published in *The Times* on 21 February 2006, 'On the scent of success' by Karen McVeigh, published in *The Times* on 20 December 2005, 'The artist as a very young man' by Russell Jenkins, published in *The Times* on 29 December 2005, 'Self-starters have spark' by Daniel Allen, published in *The Times* on 13 October 2005, 'Designer brands are for monkeys' by Mary Anne Sieghart published in *The Times* on 28 April 2004, 'Big mistake: with family more isn't always merrier' by Monica Porter published in *The Times* on 30 April 2004, 'Take on a role that has all the fun of the fair' by Deborah Stone, published in *The Times* on 10 March 2003, 'Who will be the first man on Mars?' by Patrick Moore published in *The Times* on 5 January 2001; *OK!* Magazine for 'Temper, temper'; The Open University for 'What's science all about?' accessed 21 February 2007; Penguin Books for extract from *A House Unlocked* by Penelope Lively; Ripley Entertainment Inc. for 'Ripley's believe it or not museum'; Solo Syndication Ltd for 'I'm so very sorry' by Linn Branson, published in the *Evening Standard* on 10 March 2003, 'A day in the life of a henna artist' by Joyce Lynn, published in the *Evening Standard*, 'Prize for boss who told staff: spend less time at work' by Rob McNeil, published in the *Evening Standard* on 23 May 2002, 'Slave labour gave us our big break' by Amy Williams, published in the *Evening Standard* on 20 June 2005, 'A Londoner's diary' by Alain de Botton, published in the *Evening Standard* on 1 August 2003, 'A day in the life of a memory banker' by Gregg Watts, published in the *Evening Standard* on 24 March 2003, 'Digging up London's past' by Stephen Hoare, 'How far can talent go?' by Molly Gunn and 'They're looking for the perfect pitch' by Christopher Middleton, published in the *Evening Standard* on 3 February 2003; 'What's in a name?' by Angela Epstein published in the *Daily Mail* on 19 February 2003, 'The effect of gender' by Frances Hardy published in the *Daily Mail* on 9 June 2001; 'Extinct tigers that could growl again' by Wendy Vukosa, 'Let your mobiles live again' by Mark Harris and 'Chips with every ping' by Andrew Williams published in the *Metro* on 29 May 2002, 8 January 2007 and 24 January 2007; Telegraph Media Group for 'Living with grandparents' by Iwan Watson, published in the *Daily Telegraph* on 10 June 2000, 'Send in the clones' by Jim White and 'Ghost stories' by John Preston, published in *Sunday Telegraph Seven* on 6 August 2006 and 3 September 2006, 'Modern manners: mobile phones on holiday' by Christopher Middleton, published in *Telegraph Weekend* on 24 June 2006, 'It's important to save, but don't forget to live' by Paul R. Brown, published in *Sunday Telegraph*, NYT supplement, on 16 April 2006, 'The fastest girl on ice' by William Church published in the *Sunday Telegraph Review* on 27 January 2002; *Washington Lawyer* for 'Safe shopping online' by David Simms, published in November 2003; Susan Aldridge for 'Revenge is sweet', first published in *BBC Focus* Magazine in May 2004; John Crouch for 'Feminist praises old-time values'; Natalie Graham for 'Swimming against the tide', and 'It pays to doll yourself up', first published in the *Financial Times Weekend* on 8 January 2005 and 16 September 2006; Amar Grover for 'A safari to save the big cats', first published in the *Financial Times Weekend* on 2 September 2006; Nicole Swengley for 'Cut the excess consumer fat' and Lesley Gillilan for 'A case of collection madness', first published in the *Financial Times Weekend* on 8 January 2005; Professor Timothy Chappell for 'Frontiers of knowledge', first published in the *Financial Times* magazine on 10 January 2004; Beatrice Newbery for 'Now here's a smart move', first published in the *Financial Times Weekend* in April 2004; *Pride* Magazine for 'The ultimate guide to money management' by Akwasi Duodu; *TNT* magazine for 'Lava louts' by Gen Swart; Scottish *Field Magazine* for 'On the moo-ve' by Alexandra Rutherford, published in May 2006; David Straker for 'Counterfactual thinking' from www.changingminds.org (accessed 11 July 2007); Sally Jones for 'Music while you homework', first published in *The Sunday Times* on 24 March 2004; Tom Wilkie for 'Review of "The Red Canary"', first published in the *Times Educational Supplement* on 15 August 2003; Annalisa Barbieri for 'Forget being the biggest' first published in *The Guardian* on 21 May 2002, Anita Jain for 'India's youth moves out', first published in the *Financial Times Weekend* on 10 September 2005; Tom Stafford for 'Why can't you tickle yourself?', first published in *BBC Focus* in May 2006; Clair Woodward for 'Idol pursuits', first published in *Night and Day* on 21 April 2002; Tom Kevill Davies for 'The hungry cyclist', http://thehungrycyclist.com; John Crace for 'Inside the news resources: advertising', first published in *Guardian Education* on 8 February 2000; Jo Carlowe for 'The persuaders: "How easily are you persuaded by advertising?" and "How easily are you persuaded by salespeople?"', first published in *BBC Focus* magazine in February 20004; Preethi Nair for 'I faked my identity to get my dream job' and Beth Gibbon for 'I want what she's got', first published in *B Magazine* in September 2004; Lucy Brighty for 'How to write the perfect CV', first published in *B Magazine* in October 2002; Joanna Pinnock for 'A bug's life', first published in the *Cambridgeshire Journal* in February 2005; Paul Grogan for 'How to behave properly abroad', first published in *Global Adventure* in August 2002; Pamela Coleman for 'My best teacher', first published in the *Times Educational Supplement*; MSNBC Interactive News LLC for 'Celebrities make giving part of the job', published on 5 May 2006; Hearst Corporation for 'The science of Star Trek' by Janet Wells, published in the *San Francisco Chronicle* on 13 November 2000; Alexa Moses and Elicia Murray for 'Good game but is it art?', first published in the *Sydney Morning Herald* on 2 September 2006; Wikipedia for 'Ads are everywhere' and 'Martin Halstead', permission granted under terms of GNU Free Documentation Licence.

The publisher would like to thank the following for their kind permission to reproduce their photographs:

(Key: b-bottom; c-centre; l-left; r-right; t-top)

Action Plus Sports Images: Neil Tingle 55; **Alamy Images:** Ace Stock Ltd 184tr; Andrew Hasson 75; blphoto 37t; Bubbles Photolibrary 43tc; Charlie Newham 137; Chuck Franklin 183tr; David Crossland 104bc; David Levenson 149br; David R. Frazier Photolibrary, Inc. 183cr; David Taylor 159; Eddie Linssen 186tr; Enigma 146; f1 online 138; Frank Chmura 68–69; Gary Roebuck 166; Golden Gate Images 116t; Jeff Greenberg 179br; Huw Jones 182l; Ian Shaw 180tl; Ilan Amihai 18c; Ilene MacDonald 179tc; Janine Wiedel Photolibrary 178tc; Mark J. Barrett 179bl; Mervyn Rees 104tr; Motoring Picture Library 180bc; Photofusion Picture Library 51, 183bl; Profimedia International s.r.o. 179c; Rob Walls 10–11; SCPhotos 72t; Seb Rogers 182br; Sherab 72b; Simon Bracken 112; Steve Bloom Images 124; The Photolibrary Wales 134; Wonderlandstock 180tr; **Archant Norfolk:** Archant Norfolk 57bl, 57tl, 57tr; **Bridgeman Art Library Ltd:** 1665–6 (oil on canvas), Vermeer, Jan (1632–75) / Mauritshuis, The Hague, The Netherlands, 181tl; **Corbis:** Andrew Brookes 148; Andy Willsher 9; Artiga Photo 130tc; Bettmann Archive 181cl; Corbis 111br (C), 179tl; David Samuel Robbins 104b; Frederic Astier 184bc; Gabe Palmer 85; Gideon Mendel 186bl; Jerome Prebois 98–99; Jim Craigmyle 183c; JLP/Jose Luis Pelaez 84l; Joe McBride 179bc; John Henley 178tl; Jon Feingersh 32; Juanjo Martin 104cl; Laureen March 38b; Manjunath Kiran 81; Martin Harvey 119; MGM 186cr; Norbert Schaefer 77b; Ole Graf 111l (A); Patrik Giardino 41; Photomorgana 19tl; Ragnar Schmuck 180bl; Roger Ressmeyer 104t; Sergio Pitamitz 18tl; Tom Grill 29; William Sallaz 63; Yves Gellie 107br; **Getty Images:** A.B 21; Alan Thornton 54; Andy Andrews 184tl; Brad Wilson 130bc; Bruce Ayres 182tr; Charles Gullung 184br; Chris Moore 18tr; Chris Windsor 30–31; Darrin Klimek 178tr; David Lees 43tr; David McNew 82–83; Denis Felix 179tr; Erik Dreyer 136l; Erik Dryer 177; Erik Von Weber 185br; Flying Colours 43br, 185bl; Frank Herholdt 183tl; Henrik Sorensen 104c; Hulton Archive 77t; J Kim 60; Jeff Haynes 80; Jose Luis Pelaez 136tr; Joseph Drivas 149tl; Lisa Spindler Photography Inc. 180br; Mark Harmel 184bl; Martin Poole 162; Martine Mouchy 20r; Michael Brauner 169; Mike Powell 178bl; P.E. Reed 25; Peter Cade 20l; PicturePress 176; Rayes 183br;

Richard Ross 130t; Rick Graves 57br; Ryan McVay 6–7; Schultheiss Selection GmbH & CoK 107tl; Steve Krongard 186tl; Steve Teague 181tc; Stuart O'Sullivan 141; Thomas Coex 136br; Tony Hutchings 62; Yellow Dog Productions 185t; Zia Soleil 180tc; Zubin Shroff 130b; **Ronald Grant Archive:** 230th Century Fox/RGA 181br; Roy Export Company/RGA 33; Cover of 'House Unlocked" by kind permission of **Grove Atlantic** 143; **Masterfile UK Ltd:** Albert Normandin 19bl; Boden/Ledingham 23; Dave Robertson 149tr; John Lee 37bl; Masterfile 185c; Michael Goldman 184tc; Rick Gomez 19r; **PA Photos:** South Yorkshire Police 121; **Panos Pictures:** David Rose 186br; **Photolibrary.com:** Photolibrary 23r, 37tl, 84r, 111tr (B), 113, 116b, 149bl, 149cr, 178br, 181bl, 186cl; **preethi@preethinair.com:** Preethi Nair 95, 95l; **Reuters:** Kieran Doherty 183cl; **Rex Features:** Everett Collection 150; Jonathan Hordle 12; Lehtikuva OY 142; **Ross Parry:** Ross Parry 87; **Science Photo Library Ltd:** GUSTOIMAGES 43l; Mehau Kulyk 42, 133; Science Photo Library 48, 140; **Stuart Nielsen-Marsh:** Nielsen Photographic 170; **Tom Kevill Davies:** Tom kevill Davies 109, 109r; **TopFoto:** Kilby Jak 181tr; Book cover of 'Somebody,Someday' published with permission of **The Random House Group Ltd:** 154.

All other images © Pearson Education

Picture Research by: Sally Cole

Every effort has been made to trace the copyright holders and we apologise in advance for any unintentional omissions. We would be pleased to insert the appropriate acknowledgement in any subsequent edition of this publication.

Illustrated by: Jonty Clark and Clive Goddard

Designed by: Oxford Designers & Illustrators, Oxford

Project Managed by: Jacqui Robinson